The Literate Executive

Laurie Rozakis, Ph.D.

McGraw-Hill

New York   San Francisco   Washington, D.C.   Auckland   Bogotá
Caracas   Lisbon   London   Madrid   Mexico City   Milan
Montreal   New Delhi   San Juan   Singapore
Sydney   Tokyo   Toronto

McGraw-Hill

*A Division of The **McGraw·Hill** Companies*

1 2 3 4 5 6 7 8 9 0 DOC / DOC 9 0 9 8 7 6 5 4 3 2 1 0 9

ISBN 0-07-135288-0

Printed and bound by R.R. Donnelley & Sons Company.

This publication is designed to provide accurate and authoritative information in regard to the subject matter covered. It is sold with the understanding that the publisher is not engaged in rendering legal, accounting, or other professional service.If legal advice or other expert assistance is required, the services of a competent professional person should be sought.

> *—From a Declaration of Principles jointly adopted by a Committee of the American Bar Association and a Committee of Publishers and Associations.*

McGraw-Hill books are available at special quantity discounts to use as premiums and sales promotions, or for use in corporate training programs. For more information, please write to the Director of Special Sales, McGraw-Hill, 11 West 19th Street, New York, NY 10011. Or contact your local bookstore.

This book is printed on recycled, acid-free paper containing a minimum of 50% recycled de-inked fiber.

Contents

Part 1

GOOD WRITING IS GOOD BUSINESS

Chapter 1

Communication Counts

Picture this: You're about to present a project that you've been working on for months. You know it's a great idea; you've even run the plan by a half a dozen colleagues and incorporated their suggestions. Perhaps you've even hired a consultant to gather more feedback. Everyone agrees that you're on to something hot here. Then why are you so afraid that your idea won't fly with the people who make the decisions?

If you're like most business executives, at least part of your fear comes from your concern that your writing won't be clear or correct. After all, you probably haven't taken a writing class since college, and then it was likely the bare-bones basics, English 101 and 102. Maybe you were a good writer in high school and managed to talk your way out of basic writing in college. In that case, the last writing class you took was … well, let's not go *there*.

Why Expressing Yourself Effectively Matters

Unfortunately, your fear might be justified. Studies have shown that how well you express yourself in writing really does matter—a lot. Here's why:

1. Writing Well = $$$

Did you know that 350 million people speak and write English as their native language? An additional 350 million people speak and write English as their second language. More than half the world's books are published in English; 80 percent of the world's computer text is in English.

These statistics reveal that English is *the* global language. It's the language of world diplomacy, business, finance, science, and technology. As a result, having a firm command of the rules of business English and knowing how to express yourself in writing can make a difference in the bottom line—for you as well as your company.

2. Writing Well = More Effective Communication

How often have you thought of the perfect way to say something important—right after the conversation was over? That's another reason writing is so important in business situations. Putting your ideas in writing makes it easier for you to communicate your points in the most effective ways. This is especially crucial in delicate situations, when you definitely don't want to be fumbling for words or using the wrong ones. Unlike speech, writing can be revised. This gives you additional chances to get it right, thus avoiding potentially expensive and embarrassing business blunders.

3. Writing = Good Business

"But I spend more time talking and listening than I do writing!" you claim. You might be completely correct—but no company depends exclusively on oral communication. Unlike speaking, writing enables you to think more carefully before you communicate, convey complex information in more detail, make things convenient for the reader, save time, and save money.

4. Writing Well = A Necessity

According to a recent survey, most people in business and government write at least ten letters and memos a week. In some cases, managers and other executives are called on to write 20 to 30 pages a day. Did you know that 80 percent of the partners in the major accounting firms write memos every day? The further you advance in your career, the more you write. According to the most recent statistics, 99 percent of all executives write *at least* one letter or memo a day. You can run, but you can't hide.

5. Writing Well = Unavoidable

You may be fortunate enough to have someone else type your writing, and this keyboarder might correct errors in mechanics, spelling, and formatting. But even the best keyboard specialists cannot cover for basic problems in a document's organization, logic, sentence structure, and paragraphing. If they could, *they'd* have the corner office.

In high-tech companies, technical writers may draft many of the documents that go to bid, but even in these companies, computer programmers and engineers still write their own proposals, reports, and letters.

What about form letters, those nifty prewritten fill-in-the-blank letters designed to fit standard situations? There is nothing wrong with a good form letter, but an ill-fitting form letter can do far more harm than good.

Furthermore, even the best form letters cover only commonplace situations. The closer you get to the top of the heap, the more often you'll face situations that aren't routine, situations that demand creative solutions. If you develop the skills you need to meet these demands, you're far more likely to advance in your career.

6. Writing Well = A Legal Issue

One of the most important reasons why written communication is preferable to oral communication is that putting information in writing enables you to document your communication. In today's litigious business world, leaving a "paper trail" is recommended in all transactions and is vital in some. In fact, it may even be required by law, especially in matters of job terminations. If you have established a pattern of written communication, you will be less open to litigation. If a lawsuit does develop, you'll have the documentation you need to prove your side of the case.

Did you know that when a lawsuit is filed against a company, the attorneys for the plaintiffs have the right to subpoena documents written by the company's employees? Such documents may be used as evidence that an employee was fired without sufficient notice. Businesses that have treated their employees with willful negligence or irresponsibility deserve to be taken to task. But it's also possible that a careless or unskilled writer could plunge a company into a completely undeserved legal morass. Let it not be *you*.

7. Writing Well = Job Security

In his article, "No Accounting for Poor Writers," author Gordon S. May reported that the inability to write was a key reason why accountants were fired (*Wall Street Journal*). No one is ever secure in a job, but the better your writing skills, the greater your chance of avoiding the ax when it falls. Your technical skills probably got you the job; your ability to write well may help you keep it.

8. Writing Well = Professional Advancement

The ability to write well can help you get promoted. By the year 2000, more than 40 percent of all new jobs will require high-level skills in reasoning, mathematics, and written communication (*Workforce 2000*). When several candidates for the same promotion have comparable technical skills, the ability to write well can tip the scales in your favor. Sometimes a candidate's writing skill is the *only* factor that separates him or her from another candidate.

Executive Writing

Managers produce a wide variety of documents. Read the list and see how many *you* have to write on the job:

employee evaluations	purchasing plans
bid proposals for vendors	spec sheets
rejection letters	want ads
reference guides	proposals
specifications	marketing plans

job descriptions	advertising copy
data sheets	business plans
newsletters	journal articles
stock offerings	user's manuals
letters of credit	letters of introduction
memorandums of understanding	thank-you letters
sales guides	press releases
brochures	memos
product overviews	product announcements

All these documents—and everything you write on the job—share one or more of the three basic purposes of business writing: to *inform*, to *persuade*, or to *build goodwill*. Here's what each task entails.

❖   *Writing that informs* explains something, gives facts, imparts information.

❖   *Writing that persuades* moves the reader to action or belief. With this type of writing, you want your reader to be motivated to act in a certain way, such as to buy a product or accept a bid.

❖   *Writing that builds goodwill* creates a positive image of you or the company you represent. With this type of writing, you seek to create the feelings in your reader that will make him or her want to do business with you.

Most business writing has more than one of these purposes. For example, when you write a letter to a client in response to a question, you are informing, but you are also building goodwill for the company. You do this by suggesting that you are intelligent, sensitive, and concerned with the client's needs. You "make nice."

Here are some sample writing tasks executives are often called on to perform. Next to each task is its purpose or purposes.

Writing	Purpose(s)
Annual report	Inform stockholders of financial status Persuade people to buy or retain stock Build goodwill with stockholders
Bid quote	Inform customer of price Build goodwill, for price is fair Persuade people to accept the bid
Claims adjustment	Inform customer of terms of settlement Build goodwill with customer

E-mail message of congratulations	Build goodwill with colleague
Job description	Inform applicants of job requirements Persuade candidates to apply Build goodwill by showing you're fair
Monthly report	Inform about profits and problems Build goodwill with reader
Performance appraisal	Inform employee of assessment Persuade employee to improve
Policy bulletin	Inform colleagues of instructions Build goodwill with company
Procedure memo	Inform colleagues of company policies Build goodwill with colleagues
10-K report	Inform Securities and Exchange Commission of financial status

Business Writing Is Big Business

Effective business writing is expensive. Although some executives can write a good letter in less than 15 minutes, it usually takes them more than an hour to *plan* the letter—and sometimes far more time than that. As a result, it usually costs somewhere between $75 and $100 per letter.

Further, it's rare that an executive writes an important document alone. Usually, a key document is written with others or shown to others before it is finalized. On average, a key document may be read by *ten* people before it is completed. Of course, each time a manager reads and comments on a document, the document's cost rises.

The longer the document, the greater the cost. Major reports and outside bids can involve huge teams of executives and technical writers and cost $500,000 to $1 million, on average. These are big numbers and big bucks.

But effective business writing is worth every minute it takes and every penny it costs. According to a survey conducted by the International Association of Business Communicators, communication yielded a 235 percent return on investment. Try getting *that* from your mutual fund.

The Costs of Poor Business Writing

Poor writing can harm companies in three main ways: lost time, lost effort, and ill will. Let's look at each one in turn.

❖ *Lost time.* Only 3 percent of our reading time is spent moving our eyes across the page; the rest of the time is spent trying to understand what we're reading. Garbled, incorrect writing takes longer to read and understand than clear prose. As a result, bad writing wastes a tremendous amount of time. If a document is clear, at least people can spend their time arguing whether or not they should adopt it, rather than wasting time trying to understand it.

Poor writing also wastes time because it has to be rewritten. Employees have to conference to decide how to revise a document; the memo may have to be supplemented with phone calls, E-mail messages, and faxes. If the writer isn't in the office when someone calls for clarification, even more time is wasted. All this adds up. Further, bad writing often results in long, drawn-out meetings to resolve the issues the document created in the first place. Because no one is really sure what the document means, busy executives are forced to spend tedious hours trying to straighten out the misunderstandings. If people disagree about the issue, the meetings can drag on even longer. This is not fun.

❖ *Lost effort.* Ineffective messages don't achieve their desired aims. First of all, readers won't understand what the writing means and so may not do what is being asked. As a result, the company will have to send out other communications—letters, E-mail messages, faxes, and so on—to achieve the original aim. In the worst-case situation, the reader will simply discard the document because it's just not worth the effort to try to decode it. This leads into the final effect of poor business writing: ill will.

❖ *Ill will.* Bad writing can cause bad feelings. Vague or insulting language can destroy the goodwill the company has worked so hard to build. Stiff or sexist language, poor word choice, or misused words all have the same effect. A poorly written document creates the impression that the executive didn't care or didn't know any better. Both are bad news for the company—and for you.

Hallmarks of Good Business Writing

Good business writing meets five basic standards: it's *clear, complete, correct, efficient,* and *effective.* Here's what I mean:

❖ *It's clear.* The reader gets the meaning you, the writer, intended. There's no ambiguity or guesswork; everyone understands what the document means.

❖ *It's complete.* An effective business document includes all the information the reader needs to evaluate the message and act on it.

❖ *It's correct.* An effective business document is free from errors in grammar, usage, and mechanics. There are no spelling, capitalization, or sentence errors, either. The format suits the content as well.

❖ *It's efficient.* A good business document has a style and organization designed to save the reader time. The layout is clear and crisp, so the message is easy to track. There is nothing in the design to confuse or distract the reader.

❖ *It's effective.* Because the document is clear, complete, correct, and efficient, it conveys a positive image of the writer and his or her company, organization, or group. Because it treats the reader with consideration, it creates good feelings, too.

Talk the Talk and Walk the Walk

In Chapter 2, you'll learn how to begin composing effective business documents. To prepare, learn the lingo of good writing:

❖ *Grammar. Grammar* is a branch of linguistics that deals with the form and structure of words. It's an attempt to make explicit and conscious what the skilled writer and speaker of English does intuitively and unconsciously.

❖ *Usage. Usage* is the customary way we use language in speech and writing. Usage includes:

adjectives	active and passive voice
adverbs	coordination
correct word choice	double negatives
misplaced modifiers	parallel structure
pronoun choice	subordination
subject and verb agreement	redundancy
verb conjugation	verb use

Each of these elements is explained in detail later in this guidebook.

Because we use language for different purposes, there are various levels of usage. In all your business documents, you will be using *Standard Written English,* the level used in business communication written by educated professionals. This level of usage is based on conventional punctuation, business vocabulary, and lack of contractions.

❖ *Mechanics.* Mechanics are the nuts and bolts of clear writing, including *punctuation, numbers, quotation marks, capitalization, abbreviations,* and *font choices.* Mechanics allow writers to show the grouping and relationship of words. They signal pace and intonation. Best of all, they help you say what you mean clearly and so avoid misunderstanding.

❖ *Style*. A writer's *style* is his or her distinctive way of writing. Style is made up of elements such as word choice, sentence length and structure, punctuation, figures of speech, and tone. Writers may change their style for different kinds of writing and to suit different audiences. A *business style* is formal, authoritative, and knowledgeable.

Write Angles

You want to write well, so let's tilt the scales in your favor. Try the following easy but effective methods. They've worked well for many busy executives—people just like you.

1. First of all, recognize that you *can* succeed. Many people who weren't very good at writing have learned more than enough to get where they want to be.

2. Realize that you're not going to become an outstanding writer instantly. It will take you some time to master the information you need.

3. Set your mind to learn. Make a commitment to do it.

4. Try not to avoid writing situations. You'll only get better with practice. Look for opportunities to write on the job.

5. Find someone who will read your writing and give you an honest critique. You're best off getting someone outside the job.

6. If you need a great deal of help, consider taking an on-line writing class. It has the advantage of being private and can offer you more opportunities to write in nonthreatening situations.

7. Keep a journal of your work habits, strengths, and accomplishments. Not only is it good writing practice, but it's also handy to have at review time. When you talk to your superior about promotions and raises, you can refer to this journal for specific examples of your accomplishments.

8. Just do it! Don't put off writing that proposal because you think your writing isn't good enough yet.

Summary

❖ The ability to write well can increase your salary and your value to the company.

❖ Good written communication skills also help you communicate effectively, think more carefully before you communicate, convey complex information in more detail, make things convenient for the reader, and save time.

❖ Business writing is important when legal issues arise on the job.

❖ Increasingly, the ability to write well is a necessity in business. It can also help increase your job security and help get you promoted.

❖ All business writing is designed to *inform*, to *persuade*, or to *build good-will*.

❖ Effective business writing is expensive but well worth the cost. Poor writing causes lost time, lost effort, and ill will.

❖ Good business writing is *clear, complete, correct, efficient,* and *effective*.

❖ *Grammar* deals with the form and structure of words. *Usage* is how we use language in speech and writing. *Mechanics* are punctuation, numbers, quotation marks, capitalization, abbreviations, and font choices. A writer's *style* is his or her distinctive way of writing.

Chapter 2

The Writing Process

Writing is a process, and like any process, it can be learned with some instruction, practice, and concentration. In this chapter, you'll learn the writing process. This will make it far easier for you to create the documents you need on the job. And it won't hurt a bit ... I promise.

Overview of the Writing Process

Start by recognizing that writing is a *process* as much as a *product*. This allows you to write most efficiently by focusing on one task at a time, rather than trying to juggle many different aspects of writing simultaneously.

Most researchers agree that the writing process includes six different steps: *planning, researching, shaping, drafting, revising,* and *proofreading.* In brief, the steps can be described as follows:

1. *Planning.* This step includes all the thinking you do about the writing task. Here, you consider the problem, define your reason for writing, and analyze your audience. In addition, you select a plan of organization and set a schedule for completing the project. (Warning: This is the white-knuckle ride for most people. Here's where we get performance anxiety, writer's block, and stress puppies.)

2. *Researching.* In this step, you gather all the information you need to write. On one hand, this can be as simple as getting a copy of the memo, E-mail message, or letter you have to answer. On the other hand, researching can be as involved as finding statistics on the Internet, generating your own data through surveys, or speaking with colleagues or clients for input.

3. *Shaping.* At this stage, you find the best way to organize your material. You sift through all the data you have and decide what you're most likely to use and what you'll probably set aside.

4. *Drafting.* Now you write your first copy by constructing sentences and paragraphs. Although it might seem that you spend most of your time drafting, studies have shown that only about one-third of your time is actually spent at this stage. Nonetheless, people can still work up a serious sweat here, leading to first-class procrastination.

5. *Revising.* At this stage, you look back at your rough draft and rethink your ideas. You add, cut, move, and rewrite. In some cases, you may rework your draft completely; in other instances, you may only need to correct errors in spelling, grammar, punctuation, and capitalization.

    After you've revised your draft, you'll most likely want to solicit feedback from others. You'll ask your readers to see if your draft is complete, convincing, and concise. Does it accomplish your aim? Does it convey the message you need to convey? Also check that the writing is the correct length and format.

6. *Proofreading.* Finally, check the draft for typographical errors.

Although I've arranged the steps in a specific order, be aware that the writing process is rarely this linear. Here are some guidelines to consider as you work through these steps:

❖ *You don't have to do all the steps in order.* Some executives gather data after they write a rough draft. This helps them see exactly what material they need to make the point clearly. Or you may find yourself needing additional data after you have written several drafts, based on the feedback you get from readers.

❖ *You may skip some steps.* Depending on your audience and purpose, you may find yourself compressing some steps and even skipping some. You may also have to adjust the process depending on outside constraints, such as lack of time and research support.

❖ *You may double back and repeat a step.* Some writers plan and draft the entire document at the same time; others, in contrast, plan and draft one section at a time. The latter method is especially common with long documents such as bid proposals. Many writers evaluate and revise as they write, rather than waiting to finish drafting.

Take the writing process as an analysis of how most successful business writers compose, not as a hard-and-fast blueprint. It's carved in sand, not granite.

While not everyone follows the writing process in this precise order, all good business writers *do* share several characteristics. Adopting their methods can make your writing easier and more successful.

Eight Habits of Successful Business Writers

1.   Recognize that writing may look effortless, but it requires a great deal of concentration, time, and effort. Good writers may exhibit grace under pressure, but the pressure is still there.

2.   Understand that your first draft won't be perfect. Even when time is tight, you'll have to revise and proofread.

3.   Write as often as you can. Writing is like any skill; the more you do it, the better you'll get.

4.   Divide big writing jobs into smaller pieces. You'll be less likely to get discouraged by the task confronting you.

5.   Have a clear set of goals for each writing task. Know why you're writing and who is going to read your document. Keeping your audience and purpose in mind makes it easier to accomplish your aims.

6.   Set up a schedule and stick to it. It's tempting to put off writing, as with any task we find arduous or challenging. Don't.

7.   Allow time to elapse between the drafting and revising stages. If you let your draft "cool off," you'll be more likely to see flaws in logic, organization, word choice, and support.

8.   Be flexible. I'm going to teach you several different approaches, including ways to get started and to overcome "writer's block." Try not to get locked into any one approach.

Now that you've got the overview, it's time to apply the writing process to planning and shaping your own business writing. Let's look at each step in detail.

Planning

All planning begins with thinking about four key elements: *topic, purpose, audience,* and *special circumstances.*

❖   *Topic.* Your *topic* is what you will write about. Always be sure before you write that you clearly understand the subject. Don't hesitate to get any unfamiliar terms defined before you start to write.

The topic and content of your document might sometimes be completely dictated by the situation. At other times, in contrast, it is up to you to determine what to include. In these instances, you have to select a topic and decide how to limit it.

❖   *Purpose.* Your *purpose* is your reason for writing. In Chapter 1, you learned the three main purposes for any business document: to *inform*, to *persuade*, or to *build goodwill*.

❖   *Audience.* Your audience is made up of your readers, such as your colleagues or clients.

❖   *Special circumstances.* Today, the average executive works 12 hours a day just to stay in place. Getting ahead requires even more time and effort. In today's competitive corporate marketplace, there's rarely enough time to meet the deadline, much less pore over your writing. In addition, you're likely faced with budgetary constraints, which limit the amount of help you can get for researching and writing. You've got to consider all these special circumstances as you plan your writing task.

That said, how can you generate ideas? Getting started can be the most difficult part of writing. Here are some ways to jump-start *your* engine:

1.   *Brainstorming.* With this method, you come up with as many ideas as possible without initially judging them as valid or invalid. To brainstorm, let your mind relax and drift. Then write down whatever comes to mind. It takes some practice to brainstorm successfully, but it's a great way to encourage divergent thinking and to help type A executives (Who, *you?*) get something good down on paper.

      Brainstorming works equally well either when you have to come up with your own topic or when you already have a topic and want to consider what elements to include.

2.   *Listing.* List all the ideas you have on your topic. You can use words or phrases. As with brainstorming, listing works best when you let your mind free-associate on automatic pilot. List at least ten ideas before you start scrutinizing them. Try to work in one concentrated burst of energy. You can always add as many ideas as you like later on, but your mind will kick in faster if you set aside about ten minutes to jot down ideas without judging them.

3.   *Webbing.* Also known as "clustering" and "mapping," this is a more visual means of planning your writing. A web looks different from a list of words, and so it helps some writers branch off in exciting new directions.

      To start a web, draw a circle in the middle of a sheet of paper. Then draw lines radiating out from the circle. If you wish, you can label each line with a major subdivision of your topic. At the end of each line, draw a circle and fill it in with a subtopic.

      Here is a sample web for a job description an executive is writing for a new job position, a production assistant.

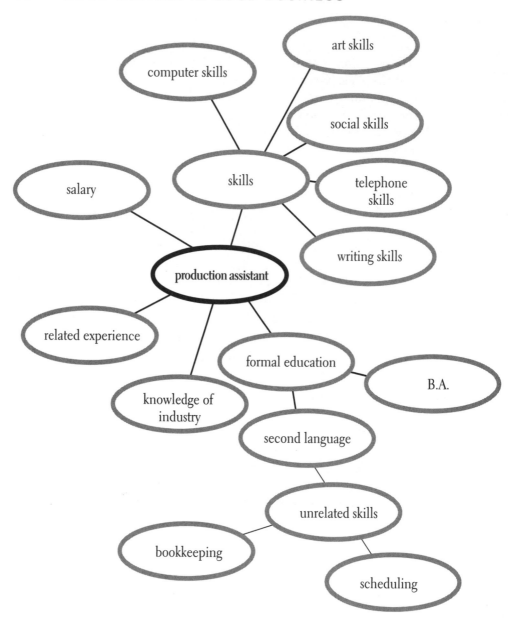

4. *Charting.* Charting is another visual method you can use to generate ideas. While there are no restrictions on the charts you can design, the most common ones usually involve columns. For example, here's a sample chart for a memo about purchasing a color copier or having the copies made by an independent contractor.

purchasing copier	using an outside contractor
instant turnaround, always available	takes more time to get copied
cost per copy lower when done in house	people think twice before making copies = lower cost
you own the machine	better access to upgrades in technology
pay for all copies;	no waste; pay only for what used
potential for waste	
lower quality copies	higher quality copies
needs maintenance; jams	no maintenance
potential for abuse no automatic feed; need staff person to make copies	no potential for staff abuse
downtime for mechanical problems	no delays

5. *Freewriting.* When you freewrite, you write without stopping for five to ten minutes. At the end of the time, read what you've written, select the best points, and set the passage aside. Then write for another five to ten minutes. Now read this draft and identify the most potentially useful points that it contains. Take the material you identified from both drafts and use it as the basis for your research and draft.

6.   *The Five W's and H.* The six letters stand for *Who? What? When? Where? Why?* and *How?* Asking these questions as you plan forces you to approach a topic from several different vantage points.

Researching

"All the news that fits, we print," might be the unofficial motto of a free press. One of the great strengths of a free press is its ability to print anything that doesn't libel its subject. As far as researchers are concerned, however, that very freedom presents its own problems. Just because a source appears in print, in the media, or on-line doesn't mean that it is valid. As a result, you must carefully evaluate every source you find before you use it. You must read critically and carefully.

As you gather your sources, evaluate them carefully. Recognize that every source is biased, because every source has a point of view. Bias is not necessarily bad, as long as you recognize it as such and take it into account as you evaluate and use the source. For example, your company's annual report may have a very different slant from an exposé on your company that is published in a trade journal. The former will be positive; the latter may be far less laudatory.

Problems arise when the bias isn't recognized or acknowledged. Check to see if a source is biased. A writer or speaker can lie outright, or be more subtle, inventing false data or "facts." In addition, dishonest writers often twist what their opponents have said. To misrepresent this way, they use oversimplification.

How can you protect yourself from being misled by this type of bias? Here are some issues to consider as you evaluate a text for misrepresentation:

❖   Is someone quoted out of context?

❖   Are facts or statistics cited in a vacuum?

❖   Does the quotation reflect the overall content of the source or does it merely reflect a minor detail?

❖   Has key information been omitted?

A Special Note on Evaluating Electronic Sources

Be especially leery of sources that you find on the Internet. They can be difficult to authenticate and validate. Unlike most print resources such as magazines and journals that go through a filtering process (e.g., editing, peer review), information on the Web is mostly unfiltered.

Check the Web document for its three main elements: *head, body,* and *footer.* Within each of these pieces, you should be able to determine the following vital elements for evaluating information:

❖   When was the information created or last updated? How old is this information?

❖   Who wrote the piece?

❖   Does the author list his or her occupation, years of experience, position, or education?

❖   Where does the on-line source come from? You can often find clues to the origin of an on-line source in its address, called the *URL* (Uniform Resource Locator). Look at the suffix to help identify the source. Here are the common URL suffixes you'll encounter:

Suffix	Meaning
com	commercial (business or company)
edu	education (academic site)
gov	government
int	international organization
mil	military organization
net	Internet administration
org	other organizations, including nonprofit, nonacademic, and nongovernmental groups
sci	special knowledge news group

In summary, all sources are *not* equally valid. Be sure to evaluate every source carefully and completely before you decide whether to use it in your document. Weak or inaccurate sources can seriously damage your credibility.

Shaping

In effective writing, all the ideas are presented in an organized, logical manner. Shaping your writing involves *grouping similar ideas, eliminating nonessential ideas, selecting a tone,* and *arranging ideas in a logical order.*

❖   *Group ideas.* When you *group* ideas, you make connections and find patterns. Sort ideas into two piles: *general* and *specific.* Then place all the specific ideas under the general ones. Thinking about levels of abstraction also helps you realize that powerful writing starts with general statements backed up by specific details.

❖   *Eliminate nonessential ideas.* If an idea doesn't fit, set it aside. Thanks to the wonders of computers, you can safely stash it in another file and return to it later if you change your mind.

❖   *Select a tone.* The *tone* of a document conveys the writer's attitude toward his or her subject matter. Generally speaking, the tone of a document can be *formal* or *informal.*

In business writing that will be going *outside* the company or to your superiors, you'll want a formal tone. Documents going *internally* to people on your level or below can be more informal. Therefore, consider your audience and purpose carefully as you select your tone. Because tone in business writing is crucial, it is covered in greater detail in Chapters 3 and 4.

❖ *Arrange ideas in a logical order.* At this stage in the writing process, you have to decide what you want your audience to read first, second, third, and so on. If your ideas aren't in a logical order, your readers won't understand your purpose or message. Deciding on a structure also makes it easier to write.

You can order your ideas in several different ways. Most business documents are arranged in *chronological order (order of time), order of importance (most important to least important),* or *spatial order* (left to right, right to left, and so on). These options are covered in detail with each specific document, in Part 3.

Many busy executives find *outlining* a useful way to order their ideas at the shaping stage of the writing process. Outlines provide a great way to break big writing tasks—like this book—into manageable chunks. On the next page is a general outline format you can use for your writing. Photocopy this page and fill it in as needed when you shape various documents.

Drafting

Different business writers compose in different ways, each guided by his or her style, purpose, and audience. Your personality type may affect your writing method. Extroverts tend to do little planning, preferring to work out their ideas as they write. Introverts, in contrast, tend to work out their ideas fully before they put pen to paper or finger to keyboard.

If you work from your notes, use them as a scaffold for your first draft. Work through all your material in the order you've established. If you're using an outline, revise it as you work to take into account changes you make in organization. Try to write at a steady pace until you reach a natural breaking point, such as the end of a section or main idea.

If you decide to set aside all the notes you made when you planned and shaped your ideas, try to forge connections among ideas. Remember, you're not under any obligation to use all or even part of the first draft. This realization can free you to explore new directions.

Title: _____

I.   First main idea _____
   A. Supporting point _____
      1. Reason or example _____
         a. Detail _____
         b. Detail _____
      2. Reason or example _____
         a. Detail _____
         b. Detail _____
   B. Supporting point _____
      1. Reason or example _____
         a. Detail _____
         b. Detail _____
      2. Reason or example _____
         a. Detail _____
         b. Detail _____

II. Second main idea _____
   A. Supporting point _____
      1. Reason or example _____
         a. Detail _____
         b. Detail _____
      2. Reason or example _____
         a. Detail _____
         b. Detail _____
   B. Supporting point _____
      1. Reason or example _____
         a. Detail _____
         b. Detail _____
      2. Reason or example _____
         a. Detail _____
         b. Detail _____

Revising

Effective writers improve their drafts by making changes to suit their purpose and audience. When you revise, you *cut* material, *replace* material, *add* material, and *rearrange* what's already there. Consider changing words, sentences, paragraphs —even the entire document. Don't be surprised if a revised draft looks radically different from a first draft.

Before you revise, first read your draft once all the way through. This is especially important if the document incorporates blocks of text from other writers. In this case, you'll need to pay close attention to make sure all the different parts fit together smoothly.

Then decide whether you want to revise this draft or start again. If you revise, go step by step. Concentrate on one issue at a time. For example, first read for tone, then for organization, and next for details.

Consider creating a checklist to help you use your time most efficiently. A sample checklist is provided to get you started, but I strongly recommend that you create individual checklists to fit the needs of each specific document you write.

Revision Checklist

_____   Is your purpose clear?

_____   Is your writing organized in a logical way?

_____   Did you suit your language and topic to your audience?

_____   Have you cut all material that's off the topic?

_____   Are your sentences concise and correct?

_____   Is your writing fluid and graceful?

_____   Is your writing free from sexist or biased language?

_____   Have you corrected all errors in grammar, usage, spelling, punctuation, and capitalization?

Feedback

An excellent way to improve a document is to get feedback. This method is so effective, in fact, that in many companies it is required, especially for documents written for external distribution. To get the most from this method of revising, try these suggestions:

❖   Select readers whose opinions you value. Be careful, of course, not to reveal confidential material to people who do not have the appropriate security clearance.

❖   Tell your readers exactly what you want them to look for in your document. For example, if you're circulating a first draft, you'll most likely want comments about organization and tone. By the second draft, however, you'll probably be looking for feedback on style rather than content.

❖ Try not to be defensive. If the feedback is negative, set the document aside for a few days so you can look at it more objectively. Don't shoot the messenger.

Proofreading

When you proofread your writing, look for errors in spelling, punctuation, grammar, and usage. Studies show than most writers make the same errors over and over. For example, you might have trouble spelling certain annoying words or remembering to check for errors in capitalization. To make the most of your time, then, be sure to check for these errors. This is especially important if you have to do a fast proofreading. But even if time is short, *never* skip this stage in the writing process.

To proofread effectively, slow your reading speed so that you see each individual letter. Proofreading your own work is hard because writers tend to see what *should* be there rather than what *is* there. Here are some techniques that professional proofreaders use. See which techniques work best for you as you write different business documents under different situations.

❖ Read your document aloud while another person follows along on a typed copy. Say the punctuation marks and spell out all names. It's tedious, but effective.

❖ Read the document twice. The first time, read it slowly for meaning and to see that nothing has been left out. Then read it again. If you find an error, correct it and then reread that line. You tend to become less vigilant once you find a few errors. Double- and triple-check numbers, names, and first and last paragraphs.

❖ Because it's always easier to proofread something you haven't written, you may wish to exchange documents with a colleague and proofread each other's work.

The larger the type, the easier it is for any reader to assume that what's printed is correct. Be extra careful with titles and headings; that's where some of the worst errors occur.

Dealing with Writer's Block and Procrastination

It is natural to avoid situations that cause distress or fear, like fanged creatures, deep water, and business writing. Many writers get blocked when they have to move from planning to actual writing. Once writers get started writing, it is usually not difficult.

Here are some ideas to help you deal with the very real problems of writer's block and procrastination.

1. Brainstorm, freewrite, web, or use any other prewriting method to generate ideas.

2. Share your ideas with a friend. It is often easier to speak to a real audience than to imagine an artificial one.

3. If a parameter such as line length or word count is holding you back, ignore it for the first draft. You can always go back and reshape your writing to fit a specific format.

4. Write the part that's the easiest to write. You can fill in the rest later. There's no rule that says you have to start at the very beginning. Start in the middle or start with the conclusion, as long as you start.

5. Try using a different method of transcription. If you're keyboarding, for example, try writing longhand. If you're writing longhand, try a tape recorder.

6. Draw a picture or a diagram to show what you mean. Use the visual to help you spark ideas and order your thoughts.

7. Jot down your thoughts about writing. If the thoughts are negative, try to substitute positive ideas. For example, if you're thinking, "I just can't do this," try writing, "I can write. I can write very well."

8. Identify the problem that keeps you from writing. Deal with the problem, and then go back to writing.

9. Force yourself to write for the specific amount of time you've set aside, even if you don't think you're producing anything usable.

10. Keep your goals realistic. Decide to write a paragraph or a page at a time, not an entire letter or memo in one sitting.

Summary

❖ Writing is a process and, like any process, it can be learned with instruction, practice, and concentration.

❖ The writing process includes *planning, researching, shaping, drafting, revising,* and *proofreading.*

❖ Write as often as you can; divide large writing jobs into smaller pieces; have a clear set of goals for each writing task; set up a schedule and stick to it.

❖ There are effective techniques for dealing with writer's block and procrastination.

Chapter 3

Getting Your Point Across in Print

Knowing who you are addressing is basic to the success of all communication. When you write any document, you need to adapt your message to fit your audience as closely as possible. This is especially important in business writing, because you are representing not only yourself but the corporation as well. In this chapter, you'll learn how to adapt your message to your readers.

Analyzing Your Audience

The most important tools in audience analysis are common sense and *empathy*, or the ability to put yourself in someone else's place. Your writing will be most successful if you target your audience as closely as possible. Use what you already know about people and what you find out about the organization to predict likely responses to your message. This isn't as easy as it sounds, but what is?

For example, before a major department store took a survey of its customers, managers were asked to describe the typical customers.

The CEO answered, "About age 60, upper-income, well-respected in the community."

The vice presidents replied, "About age 40, with grown children. Upper-middle-class, moving up economically."

The middle managers said, "In their thirties, earning about $50,000 a year, people with lots of drive and ambition."

The actual survey revealed that the store's customers were in their mid-20s, had been married only a little while, and earned about $20,000 a year. What can we conclude from this survey? Executives looked at their customers but saw only themselves. Most likely, your audience is *not* just like you, especially when you're writing within a corporation.

Identifying the Company Culture

As abused as the idea of corporate culture has become, it is a fact of life. Every company has an open culture as well as layers of hidden subcultures, social networks, and alliances.

Overall, a company's *culture* is comprised of the company's history, traditions, values, and style. A company's culture is usually formed from top to bottom, but sometimes workers on the lower rungs can have a significant impact too. Each organization has its own style, a combination of management's behavior and fantasies, middle management's interpretations, and the average worker's understanding of what's really valued.

Understanding your corporate culture requires keen analysis of how it does business internally and externally. For example, brash new Whiz-Bang Web Sites, Inc. is likely to encourage individual initiative, state-of-the-art, cutting-edge innovation, and fire in the belly. If you work for this firm, you can probably write directly to the CEO and address him or her as a colleague. Further, your written communication will likely be electronic, via E-mail. The company's culture encourages such informality.

But in a large, traditional company that stresses experience, reliability, and service, you'll be expected to follow the chain of command with any spoken or written communication. The corporate culture in this firm dictates that employees send memos through channels and adopt a deferential tone. E-mail might not be used at all.

Some companies expect long messages; others, brief memos. Some firms make their executives conference at great length before committing anything to writing; others prefer that their managers work out the details on their own and then present the results in a memo. What does this mean for you? Here's the inside skinny: Messages that match the corporation's culture have a far greater chance of succeeding than those that don't.

The Company's Culture and Your Writing

A company's culture is conveyed both directly and indirectly. Here are some ways it gets transmitted:

1. Whom does the company hire—and whom do they fire? Constructing an informal employee profile can help you figure out what type of values (and by extension, type of writing) the company prefers.

2. What is said at employee orientation sessions? Also "read" the subtext: What is implied? This can help you suit your writing style to the prevailing culture.

3. What rules and guidelines are included in the employee handbook? How stringently are the rules enforced? In what ways? Knowing the rules can help you understand what type of writing you'll be doing and what elements of writing the company values.

4. What are people taught in training programs? Also be alert to the emphasis the company places on training itself. If training is a priority,

the company is likely high-powered and focused on grabbing market share. This suggests that your writing should be more lively and aggressive.

5. What is the company's avowed mission? All things being equal, for-profit companies have a very different culture from nonprofit groups. The writing tends to be more aggressive in for-profits.

6. What is the company's marketing position? How does your writing style match that mission?

7. What types of advertisement does the company use? The answer should have a tremendous impact on your writing style.

8. Listen to office rumors. For example, see if the gossip focuses more on people who succeed or on those who fail. If the rumor mill hums with the news that someone was passed over for promotion, you'll know this company places tremendous importance on independent achievement rather than consensus-style management. This suggests you can send individual communications up the ladder rather than engaging in group writing.

9. Listen to stories. Who are the company heroes? What did they do that helped them win kudos? Who are the company villains? What did they do to incur corporate wrath? This information can give you valuable hints as to the chain of command and how your writing will be vetted. It can also help you identify your audiences.

10. How formal or informal is the language that is used in the office? The level of spoken diction is directly keyed to the level of written discourse.

11. Pay attention to the method of communication used in the company. Do people interface through technology—E-mail and phone—or do they prefer meeting face to face? The answer to this questions suggests how much writing you will have to do and how strongly you'll be judged on your written communication.

12. You can pick up ideas about the company's culture by reading their literature—annual reports, brochures, and manuals. Note how they describe the company. What personality profile emerges?

13. Check the tone of company newsletters. Are they cheery little articles about employees' personal achievements, or succinct reports on executives' achievements as visionary planners? The former indicates a more relaxed, even folksy atmosphere; the latter, a high-pressured culture. Again, the tone of the company greatly influences the tone of your writing.

14. Ask your boss to critique your memos—and pay attention to the comments. If the boss circles typos, that's a clue to what's valued in the company. They are clearly into getting it *all* right, down to the last detail.

15. Does the organization value diversity or homogeneity? Does it value independence and creativity or being a team player and following orders? Organizations that value diversity often encourage executives to take the initiative, while those that favor conformity lean toward conservative discourse and group writing. We'll discuss this in more depth in Part 2, Chapter 8.

Understanding the style of the company you work for and the way style filters through the ranks is often key to successful business writing. Now let's focus on individual members of the audience.

Identifying the Five Main Audiences

You know that in order to be an effective writer, you must identify your audience. But the person to whom you are writing is not necessarily the only audience—or the most important one.

In nearly all business writing, you have to consider five different audiences: the *primary audience, secondary audience, initial audience, gatekeeper,* and *watchdog audience.* Let's analyze each one:

❖ *Primary audience*: These readers will decide whether to act on your message or accept your suggestions. You must always reach this audience in order to achieve your aim.

❖ *Secondary audience*: These readers may be asked to offer their suggestions on your ideas, or they may be the ones to carry out what you suggest in your communication. It's also crucial to realize that secondary audiences can include attorneys who may use your written documents years later as evidence in a lawsuit. Your writing provides evidence of the corporate culture, climate, and practices.

❖ *Initial audience*: These readers send your message on. In some instances, the initial audience may be the person who asked you to create the document in the first place.

❖ *Gatekeeper*: This reader has the power to prevent your message from reaching its intended audience. As a result, the gatekeeper decides whether your message even makes it to the primary audience. In some instances, the supervisor who assigns the writing task is the gatekeeper; in other cases, the gatekeeper is even higher in the company. A gatekeeper can be in another company as well.

❖ *Watchdog audience*: This reader scrutinizes the interaction between you and the primary audience. The watchdog audience may predicate future actions on the results of this situation. As a result, the watchdog audience has political, social, and economic power to affect your career.

As you can see, one person can belong to two or more audiences. Here's a sample situation that illustrates the overlapping roles of audience members:

Richard is a vice president for a market research company. His boss, the senior vice president, asks him to write a marketing proposal for a new line of clothing the agency's most important client is considering. Richard's boss, who must first approve the plan, is both the *initial audience* and the *gatekeeper*. Richard's *primary audience* will be a committee for the client's company, who will decide whether or not to accept the proposal. The *secondary audience* includes the creative staff of the client's company, who will be asked for their comments on the plan.

Persuasive Business Writing and Audience

Recall that all business writing shares one or more of the three basic purposes of writing: to *inform*, to *persuade*, or to *build goodwill*. Further, researchers have divided audiences into eight different types: *perceiving types, judging types, introverts, extroverts, sensing types, intuitive types, thinking types*, and *feeling types*. Understanding the way your audience approaches your writing can help you better meet their needs, the company's needs, and your own needs.

You can use the following scale to anticipate your audience's likely response to your proposals. This scale works best when you are evaluating persuasive documents, those most likely to encounter resistance.

Audience	Characteristics	Writing Strategy
Perceiving Types	Weigh all options; postpone decisions.	Show you have weighed all sides; ask for a decision date.
Judging Types	Make quick conclusions; like to move on.	Present your ideas quickly in a well-organized memo.
Introverts	Inner-directed.	Write the document and give your audience ample time to respond.
Extroverts	Outward-motivated.	Present your ideas before drafting the document.
Sensing Types	Judge facts, but rely their own feelings.	Present facts step by step; be very precise.
Intuitive Types	Creative, impatient with many details.	Start with an over-view; stress creative aspects.
Thinking Types	Rely on logic, not emotion.	Use logic, not emotion; stress fairness.
Feeling Types	Strive for harmony.	Stress emotional as well as economic aspects.

Group Think

When you're writing on the job, you'll often have to analyze your audience as members of a group rather than as individuals. In some cases, it won't be too difficult to understand your readers' attitudes; in other cases, however, you'll have to look more closely to figure out how to best approach your audience. Here are some factors to consider:

1. *Gender and male to female ratio.* A number of researchers believe that gender differences in communication styles are responsible for the miscommunication that sometimes occurs between men and women. As a result, it will sometimes be crucial to find out what percentage of your readers will be female and what percentage will be male.

    Also consider whether male and female readers might view your topic differently. In part, this is because men and women will very likely have different interests, experiences, and knowledge about certain topics. This clearly affects your choice of topic and method of development.

2. *Level of knowledge.* It's easy to overestimate the knowledge that your readers have. People outside your own area of expertise may not really know what it is you do. Even people who have once worked with you may have forgotten specific details now that their work is different.

    When you are presenting new information, try to open your document with familiar facts, make a special effort to be clear, link new information to familiar information, and use visuals to illustrate difficult concepts.

3. *Demographics.* Along with gender and level of knowledge, pollsters can measure other qualities that affect your audience and their perception of your writing. These include age, race, religion, and income. Sometimes the demographic information will be irrelevant to your document; at other times, it will matter a great deal. Analyze your audience and purpose in depth to decide whether you need this information.

Made to Fit

No matter how well you know your audience, you'll still have to decide on the best way to appeal to them. As you write, keep your audience firmly in mind. Also consider your audience as you revise all your documents.

Consider the following issues as you evaluate your audience. These considerations serve as a useful starting point, but you may wish to tailor the items to your specific writing task and such variables as current events and the political climate.

1. *Who will be reading my document?* Identify *all* readers, primary as well as secondary.

2. *How much do my readers know about my topic at this point? What else must they know about the subject for my message to be successful?* There's a delicate balance between providing enough information and providing too much information. Carefully consider what to include—and what to omit.

3. *What is the basis of the information they have?* The source of their information matters because it tells you their level of expertise. Possible sources of information include observation, reading, and personal experience.

4. *Have I considered how my readers will approach my message?* Are they neutral, hostile, enthusiastic, or somewhere in between? Readers who have already made up their minds are not likely to be open to change. Clearly, this makes your task more difficult.

5. *What first impression does my document create with my readers? Do I show from the very first sentence that my message is important to my audience?* In writing as in life, first impressions count. Readers whose initial response to your message is positive are far more likely to take the action you request than readers who react badly to the document from the start.

   Form equals function: A document's design conveys its importance. Be careful that your document creates the impression you wish. For example, readers feel tricked (and justifiably so) if a document looks important but is insignificant; conversely, a document that is important can be inadvertently discarded because it looks trivial. Chapter 000 is devoted to this issue.

6. *Have I used the tone most likely to elicit a favorable response from my readers?* Documents that create goodwill from the start are more successful than those that don't. Sounds obvious, but you'd be surprised how many people begin business communications with an insult or a line that is open to a negative interpretation. Readers usually toss these messages without reading any further than the first paragraph. Wouldn't you?

7. *Have I used the style of writing my audience prefers?* Effective writers adapt their style to suit their readers' preferences. For example, your audience might prefer a casual style with contractions and informal language, or a more formal style with elevated diction.

8. *Have I used the structure most likely to appeal to my audience?* Some readers favor a direct approach; others, a more circuitous organization. Your writing will be most successful if you use the approach your readers expect. This is so important that both Chapters 000 and 000 focus on it.

9. *Have I considered how my audience will use my document?* For example, will it be used as general reference, as a detailed guideline, or as the basis for a lawsuit?

10. *Am I starting from a position of strength or weakness?* Does my organization have a history of conflict or cooperation with the group I am addressing? Do *I* have a history of conflict or cooperation with this person or department?

    If you have a good relationship with your audience, you're starting with a natural advantage. Unfortunately, if someone doesn't think favorably of you or your organization, they'll be more likely to find fault with what you have to say.

11. *My reader may be opposed to my message; have I opened the document by establishing a bond?* You can do this by pointing out common ground or areas of agreement from the very start of your document. I'll show you how to do this in Chapters 4 and 7.

12. *Have I checked my diction to make sure it matches what my audience expects?* If you know your audience is likely to be hostile, take special care not to use any language that could be construed as rude. An unfriendly audience is quick to find offense, even when none is intended.

13. *Will my message be clear to my readers?* This is especially important when you're dealing with a negative audience. They are far more likely than a positive audience to misread messages.

14. *Have I limited the amount of bad news I'm delivering to my readers, based on their level of tolerance?* If you must deliver bad news, give only the news that is absolutely necessary. If part of your message can be delivered later, do so. You'll create ill will by offering more bad news than you need to.

15. *If the document contains a request, have I made it as easy to follow as possible, based on what I know of my audience?* Successful business writers often include a subject line to make it even easier for the reader to understand what action needs to be taken.

16. *If action is required, have I set a realistic deadline, based on my readers' timetable?* The key word here is *realistic*. Carefully consider your audience's needs as well as your own.

17. *Have I developed my points fully and arranged my points logically?* A well-organized document has a far greater chance of success than a poorly organized one. If your reader must figure out what you're saying, your document is apt to be tossed in a flash.

18. *Is the message as concise as possible?* Brief messages are far more likely to get positive responses than long messages.

19. *Have I used titles and headers to indicate key information?* Not only do titles help readers isolate important ideas, but they also serve to break up

long blocks of information. This makes your document easier to read. You'll find more on this subject in Chapter 9.

20. *Do I allow my audience to avoid potential embarrassment?* Always try to leave your reader an escape hatch by suggesting that changing circumstances call for new ideas and approaches. Never back a reader into a corner. In addition, consider pointing out that your solution is the best resolution currently available, even though it isn't perfect. Saving face is an especially challenging issue when dealing with multicultural readers who often approach an issue from different vantage points. See Chapter 8 for more information on this topic.

Here's a brief version of these guidelines to use as a checklist every time you draft a business document:

Audience Analysis Checklist

1. Who is my audience?
2. What is their level of knowledge about this topic? What information must I provide?
3. How does my audience feel about this topic, situation, and my organization?
4. What obstacles (if any) must I overcome for my message to be successful?
5. What style of writing does my audience anticipate and prefer?
6. Is my message clear and concise?
7. Have I considered the amount of bad news I'm delivering?
8. Have I developed my points fully and arranged my points logically?
9. Have I used titles and headers to indicate key information?
10. Do I allow my audience to avoid potential embarrassment?

Summary

❖ When you write any document, you need to adapt your message to fit your audience as closely as possible.

❖ The most important tools in audience analysis are common sense and empathy.

❖ Start by analyzing your company's corporate culture, its history, traditions, values, and style.

❖ Consider the primary audience, secondary audience, initial audience, gatekeeper, and watchdog audience.

❖ Consider whether you're addressing perceiving types, judging types, introverts, extroverts, sensing types, intuitive types, thinking types, or feeling types.

❖ When writing for large audiences, you may also want to analyze the gender and male to female ratio, their level of knowledge, and demographic considerations.

❖ Tailor your message to your audience by using a checklist of significant considerations.

Chapter 4

Building Goodwill through Writing

The writing you do on the job represents your employers (those nice folks who give you a paycheck), so it's vital to build goodwill as well as convey a message. You can do this by using a *you-attitude* and *emphasizing the positive.* What about delivering bad news? I'll teach you how to build goodwill even when the message is negative.

The Power of Words

Read these two letters. Which one do you think will be more effective in maintaining and increasing business? Why?

Letter #1

April 4, 1999

Mr. Robert Harris, President
American Widget Corporation
2 Marie Court
Elmont, New York 11003

Dear Mr. Harris:

Our records indicate that your account is in arrears. The last two payments we received from the American Widget Corporation were 90 days late each. This situation is very upsetting to us and obviously cannot continue.

It is important that we keep our accounts receivable current to make less work for our credit department. We cannot be expected to extend any further credit; after all, you've only been our customer for five years. As a result, your credit is forthwith canceled. We know that you are no doubt upset about this, but you brought it on yourself by not planning ahead.

We understand that you have had some problems lately with the downturn in business. Unfortunately, that's not our problem. It is vital to maintain good credit.

Sincerely,

Diana Cason

Diana Cason, Executive Director
Credit Department

Letter #2

April 4, 1999

Mr. Robert Harris, President
American Widget Corporation
2 Marie Court
Elmont, New York 11003

Dear Mr. Harris:

Over the past five years, we have appreciated your account with us and considered it one of our most valued ones.

With the recent downturn in business, however, we have noticed that your practice of remitting payment every month has ceased. The last two payments we received from the American Widget Corporation were 90 days late each.

It is important that we keep our accounts receivable current; therefore, it is with regret that we ask you to make future purchases on a cash basis only.

We would like to offer you a 10 percent discount on all your future cash purchases in appreciation of your years of patronage. We value your business, Mr. Harris.

Sincerely,

Diana Cason

Diana Cason, Executive Director
Credit Department

Both letters contain just about the same information, but the second letter is far more effective than the first one because it creates goodwill. It does so by ...

❖ Thanking the customer for prompt payment in the past. A negative opening might prevent the recipient from reading further; at the very least, it will create ill will.

❖ Bringing up the problem tactfully.

❖ Avoiding the negative aspect of the situation.

❖ Suggesting a viable solution.

- ❖ Offering special help.
- ❖ Keeping the tone polite and businesslike.
- ❖ Not sharing the writer's own feelings.
- ❖ Not presuming to know how the recipient feels about the situation.
- ❖ Using neutral expressions and impersonal constructions to avoid assigning blame.
- ❖ Protecting the reader's ego.

Overall, the second letter uses the *you-attitude* to see and present the issue from the recipient's point of view. Here's how to do it when *you* write on the job.

The You-Attitude

It is natural to consider a situation from our own standpoint, but in business writing, it is vital to consider how the problem appears to the reader as well. This is called using a *you-attitude*. It is a style of writing in which the writer looks at things from the reader's point of view. It stresses what the reader wants to know, respects the reader's intelligence, and protects the reader's feelings.

Use the following guidelines to build goodwill with the you-attitude in your own writing:

1. Always keep your audience firmly in mind. Try to look at the situation through their eyes.

2. At the same time, never assume that you know how the reader feels. You don't. Ditto for the way a reader will react. People are full of surprises.

3. Since you're focusing on your reader, leave your own feelings out of it. Bringing in your own reactions automatically shifts the emphasis from the reader to the writer.

4. Consider the effect your words will have. Always keep your language neutral and professional to avoid offending your reader. Avoid using the word *you*, which tends to assign blame.

5. If you have bad news to deliver, preface it with a polite comment. Otherwise, the reader might not read any further.

6. Don't avoid the topic. Even if it's unpleasant, refer to the situation or the reader's request. Few things frustrate a reader more than empty rhetoric.

Let's consider some of these guidelines in greater detail, starting with always keeping the emphasis on the audience.

1. *Focus on your audience.* Readers want to know how the situation will help them. They want to focus on their benefits, which means that this is not

the time to announce your own accomplishments or bemoan your own troubles. Look at these two examples that show how the same information can be presented from a you-attitude and a me-attitude. The second example is much more effective than the first one because it focuses on the reader rather than the writer.

Me-Attitude: I have negotiated an agreement with Sun & Fun Resorts that gives you one night free for every three nights you stay.

You-Attitude: As a valued customer, **you** are now entitled to *one* night free for every three nights you stay and Sun & Fun Resorts.

Of course, there will be times when you will have to explain what you and the organization you represent are doing. How can you make sure that you're not focusing too much on the company's needs? Check the number of *I*'s you have used. Try this rule of thumb: use one *I* for every four *you*'s. The word *we* is fine as long as the reader is part of the *we*. If the reader isn't, count the *we*'s as *I*'s.

2. *Don't presume to know the reader's feelings.* Clients and colleagues are likely to take offense if you assume that you can judge their emotions or reactions. This can be especially embarrassing if you're incorrect in your assessments. To be safe, simply avoid alluding to the reader's feelings, as the second example illustrates:

Me-Attitude: You will be delighted to hear that Office Supplies Unlimited now offers free delivery within a five-mile radius!

You-Attitude: Office Supplies International now delivers free within a five-mile radius!

3. *Don't share your feelings.* Your feelings shouldn't enter into written business communication. Business writing is not an occasion to share your pain or let it all hang out. How you feel about this specific situation and your job in general is not relevant to the reader's concerns. All the reader wants to know is how the situation affects him or her. Here are two examples that illustrate how to focus on the reader, not yourself.

Me-Attitude: I am happy to offer you financing on your purchases at only 5% per year.

You-Attitude: You can now finance any purchases at only 5% per year.

However, it *is* appropriate to share your feelings in a personal letter to a business associate or special client. This includes letters of congratulation and condolence, for example. This topic is covered in detail in Part 3.

4.   *Protect the reader's ego.* In many negative situations, the word *you* tends to assign blame—even when none is intended. Instead, try using a general noun in place of the specific *you*, as the example illustrates:

Me-Attitude: You must file an expense report within one week of returning from a business trip.

You-Attitude: All managers must file an expense report within one week of returning from a business trip.

You can also use an impersonal construction, omitting the person altogether. This is not the most grammatically pure construction, but it is preferable in business writing, where effective communication outweighs grammatical purity. Talk only about things, as the examples show:

Me-Attitude: You did not include the cost of a print overrun or a night differential in your estimate.

You-Attitude: *This estimate* did not include the cost of a print overrun or a night differential.

5.   *Preface bad news with a greeting or good news.* If a document starts with bad news, your reader is not likely to read to the end. Starting with good news shows your concern for your reader's goodwill. The second example creates goodwill, while the first one is off-putting:

Me-Attitude: Sav-More Electric will be closed for six months so you will have to get your supplies elsewhere.

You-Attitude: We are pleased to extend the following special offer to show our appreciation for your patience during our upcoming reorganization, designed to serve you better.

6.   *Make your point.* Vague phrases such as "your situation" or "your problem" convince readers that they are getting a form letter. That's because they usually are. Instead of whipping out the same stale letter, start from scratch. Describe the exact order, as this helps your readers understand that you're really concerned about the situation from their point of view. Notice that the second example here creates goodwill because it uses the you-attitude.

Me-Attitude: *Your order* will be mailed this week.

You-Attitude: *The genuine vinyl ergonomically correct WonderChair you ordered on May 21* will be mailed this week.

Emphasize the Positive

Read the following two e-mail messages. Which one would you rather receive? Why?

E-Mail #1

Subj:	Adjustment Letter
Date:	3/19/99 9:57:01 AM Eastern Standard Time
From:	TSchmidt@Survive.com

To: SFitz@Networld.com

Dear Ms. Fitzpatrick,

Regarding your request, we can't sell individual reams of paper. The minimum order is a box of 24 reams.

Tim Schmidt

_____Headers_____

Return-Path: <newstand@dir.con.co uk> ...

E-Mail #2

Subj:	Adjustment Letter
Date:	3/19/99 9:57:01 AM Eastern Standard Time
From:	TSchmidt@Survive.com

To: SFitz@Networld.com

Dear Ms. Fitzpatrick,

Regarding your request, to keep down shipping and handling costs and help you save on transportation charges, we sell paper only in boxes of 24 reams.

Tim Schmidt

_____Headers_____

Return-Path: <newstand@dir.con.co uk> ...

Both messages have the same information, but the second one frames the information in a positive light. By providing the reason—"to keep down shipping and handling costs and help you save on transportation charges"—the writer suggests that the drawbacks are offset by advantages. In this instance, the drawback is having to take 24 reams of paper at a time, when you may only want a few. The advantages are logical and persuasive, however.

You should never lie to a colleague, customer, or client by deliberately withholding bad news. But bad news is bad enough under normal circumstances without making it sound any worse than it is. Stressing the downside may just make things seem even more bleak than they are. Because people are apt to blame the messenger for bad news, this negativity is likely to rub off on you. Here are some additional ways you can emphasize the positive:

1.   Don't use negative words or words with negative connotations.
2.   Omit unimportant bad news.
3.   Place bad news in the middle of the document so it doesn't jump off the page.

Let's examine each way of stressing the positive in greater detail.

1.   *Avoid negative words.* Try to avoid using words that create a pessimistic mood. All the words in the following list carry negative connotations or overtones. If you must use a negative word, use the one that is least negative in the context of your document.

afraid	anxious	avoid	bad
careless	damage	delay	delinquent
deny	difficult	disapprove	dishonest
dissatisfied	eliminate	error	fail
fault	fear	hesitate	ignore
ignorant	impossible	incompetent	insincere
incomplete	injury	lacking	loss
mistake	misfortune	missing	neglect
never	no	not	problem
reject	terrible	trivial	trouble
weakness	worry	wrong	unfair
unpleasant	unreasonable	unreliable	unsure

Here's how it works:

Negative Slant: We have failed to complete the report by the deadline.

-or-

We did not complete the report by the deadline.

Positive Slant: We will complete the report by Tuesday.

2.   *Omit minor bad news.* When the reader doesn't need the bad news, leave it out of a document completely. You can also omit bad news if it isn't important. For example:

Negative Slant: This ream of paper costs $2.95. Our competitor charges $.25 less.

Positive Slant: This ream of paper costs $2.95.

3. *Place bad news in the middle.* Readers focus on the opening and closing of any document. As a result, they're apt to skim over information placed in the body paragraphs, making bad news less obvious. You can also make unpleasant information fade into the background by presenting it in a concise manner: State the point and move on. Remember that stressing any point (especially with visuals such as bullets) makes it stand out, so don't use bullets for bad news.

Be sure the bad news can be noticed, however. If it's not, the reader may miss the message altogether. In that case, you'll have to write *another* message, delivering the bad news still again.

When the News Is All Bad ...

A veteran congressman was asked what he had learned in the rough-and-tumble of the political arena. "Well," he said, "I found it wasn't so much whether you won or lost, but how you placed the blame."

Rejections, refusals, and blame are facts of life, especially in business. As an effective executive, you must know how to frame negative messages that still create goodwill with colleagues, clients, and customers.

Even when you're not able to make a reader happy about the bad news you have to deliver, your job is to make the readers feel that ...

❖ Their concerns are valid and have been taken seriously.

❖ Your decision was fair and reasonable.

❖ They would make the same decision, if the situation were reversed.

Delivering Bad News

Here's how to structure a bad-news letter to cushion the blow and create goodwill:

1. Don't open with the bad news. Instead, start with a neutral statement.

2. Give your reasons *before* you give the bad news. This prepares your readers for the bad news and helps them understand that you made the best possible decision under the circumstances.

3. Deliver the bad news in a straightforward, clear manner.

4. If possible, present a compromise. Giving your readers a choice creates goodwill by suggesting you care about them and want to meet their needs.

5. End on a positive note.

Let's examine each part of the document in more detail, starting with the opening.

1. *Start with a neutral opening.* The opening of a bad-news document is often called a "buffer," because it serves as a bulwark against the bad news to come. Use the buffer to prepare the reader for the bad news to follow and provide some background on the situation. For example:

    > *In January, we invited you to participate in the Teleconference Executive Writing Program at no charge to you.*

    If you can't think of an appropriate opening, omit the section completely from your document. You're always better off having no opening than using one that doesn't serve your purpose—or even worse, that creates ill will.

    Remember that the first rule of effective business communication involves considering your audience. With this in mind, leave out the neutral opening if your reader prefers more direct communication. You may also want to leave out the opening if you think your reader will decide it's not important and discard the entire message without reading it. Finally, omit the buffer if your reader is unusually aggressive and just won't take "no" for an answer. In that case, come right out with the bad news to convince your reader that no really means *no*.

2. *Provide reasons.* Now provide one or more reasons why things have changed. The reasons must be strong, or your argument will collapse. If you don't have a good reason, leave it out. A weak or insignificant reason is worse than none at all because it makes you and the company look foolish. Further, don't blame anyone else for the situation (even if it *is* their fault) or try to pass the buck.

    Here's an effective reason that is a simple statement of fact:

    > *Yesterday, we received your letter stating that you will not be able to attend six classes due to your work schedule.*

3. *Deliver the bad news.* Now, deliver the bad news. Use businesslike language, selecting simple and appropriate words with neutral connotations. Here's a sample:

    > *Since the class meets only ten times and must be held at the scheduled time due to the nature of teleconferencing, we must withdraw our offer to you at this time.*

4. *Present a compromise.* If possible, offer the reader a way out. This helps the reader save face and creates goodwill. It also lets you end on a positive note and show that your organization is dedicated to helping the customer gain satisfaction. For instance:

    > *Another session of the Executive Teleconferencing class will be given next January. Please consider applying for that session.*

5.   *Use a positive ending.* Always end on a positive note. You might offer your thanks, for example, as in this example:

Thank you for applying for the January-June session of the Executive Teleconferencing class. We appreciate your interest in this exciting new program.

Summary

❖   Create goodwill in business writing by using a you-attitude and emphasizing the positive.

❖   With the you-attitude, the writer looks at things from the reader's point of view to stress what the reader wants to know, to show respect for the reader's intelligence, and to protect the reader's feelings.

❖   Emphasize the positive by providing reasons for an action, avoiding negative words, omitting unimportant bad news, and placing bad news in the middle of the document.

❖   Deliver bad news in writing by opening with a neutral statement, giving reasons before you give the bad news, delivering the bad news in a straightforward way, presenting a compromise, and ending on a positive note.

Chapter 5

Writing in a Group

Writing in a recent issue of *Time* magazine, Microsoft CEO Bill Gates explained his twelve Rules for Success in the twenty-first century. Rule 4, Using Digital Tools to Create Virtual Teams, points the way to future business writing. "A collaborative culture," Gates argues, "reinforced by information flow, makes it possible for smart people all over a company to be in touch with each other." Managers should aim to "enhance the way people work together, share ideas, sometimes wrangle and build on one another's ideas—and then act in concert for a common purpose."

It's plain that teamwork is vital to the success of any organization, and working together equals a lot of writing together. Gates predicts that more and more managers will be writing with people they have never even met, people who are based around the globe. The facts are inescapable: Not only will you be writing more, but you'll be writing more in teams. That's what you'll learn to do in this chapter. Let's plunge right in by exploring how we communicate to see what we can do to communicate more effectively.

How We Communicate

Communication is a social process of making meaning in writing or speech. As such, communication is *not* a series of separate, isolated acts. Rather, it's a process whereby a speaker sends a message and a receiver decodes it. Unfortunately, between the sending and the receiving is a lot of wiggle room for misunderstanding, misinterpretation, and mistakes.

Communication would be easy if people asked and answered questions in predictable ways. It would be even easier if every exchange were scripted in advance and we just read from the pages. But this is not the case.

Communication is also influenced by what we want to perceive. In many cases, we assume that other people feel the same way that we do. As you have no doubt discovered the hard way, this is also not always the case. We tend to tune out messages that are unpleasant, threatening, or disturbing—especially on the job. Instead, we understand messages that reinforce our sense of well-being or tell us what we want to hear.

Our interpretation of words in a specific situation and the way we respond to them depend on our experiences, values, and emotions. Our culture, heritage, and background are also factors. Further, many words carry loaded overtones, or *connotations*, different from their dictionary meanings or *denotations*. The following chart illustrates what I mean. Each word pair has the same denotation but a very different connotation.

Word	Denotation	Connotation
resolute	persistent	positive: determined
stubborn	persistent	negative: obstinate
famous	well-known	positive: celebrated
notorious	well-known	negative: disreputable
thrifty	inexpensive	positive: frugal
cheap	inexpensive	negative: tight-fisted

Communication isn't easy, but it *is* a process that can be taught and learned. Training and practice can make an enormous difference in your ability to make your meaning understood, and in your ability to understand what others are saying.

Listening is a crucial element in the communication process. Read on to find out just how important it is, especially in group writing situations.

Listen and Learn

One summer day, famed newscaster Walter Cronkite steered his boat into the port of Center Harbor, Maine. Cronkite, known the world over, was amused to see a group of people on the shore waving their arms to greet him. Since they were some distance away, however, he could barely hear their shouts of "Hello Walter, Hello Walter."

As Cronkite got closer to shore, however, the group swelled to a crowd, still yelling, "Hello Walter, Hello Walter." Delighted at the warm greeting, Cronkite took a bow and doffed his sailor's hat at the crowd.

Just before he reached the dock, however, Cronkite's boat suddenly ran aground. The crowd was hushed. The famous reporter suddenly realized that the crowd had been shouting, "Low water, low water."

As this story illustrates, what someone is saying may not be what you are hearing. The inverse is also true: What you are saying may not be what they are hearing. What can we conclude? Listening is not as easy as it sounds.

Listening and Group Communication

Speaking is a two-way process, involving both making contact with people and receiving feedback from them. To communicate effectively, it is not enough to be a good speaker; you also have to be a good listener. There are three main kinds of listening: *empathic listening, informational listening,* and *evaluative listening.* Let's look at each one in turn.

Empathic Listening

This type of listening provides the speaker with emotional support to help him or her come to a decision, solve a problem, or resolve a situation. Empathic listening focuses more on emotions than on reason or judgment. As an empathetic listener, you …

❖ Restate the issues.

❖ Ask questions.

❖ Critically analyze the issues.

Your intention here is not to make a decision for the speaker, however. Rather, it is to support the speaker in his or her own independent decision-making process.

You do this by providing speakers with the chance to express their ideas and feelings. For example, if you and a small group of colleagues are writing about a problem you encountered with a product, you might want to ask questions to bring certain facts to light. By supplying these facts, you give your version of events as you allow your colleagues to express their fears about future problems with the product. You can allay those fears as you provide emotional support.

Informational Listening

An informational listener gathers as many facts as possible, focusing on accuracy of perception. This is the type of listening you do when members of a group ask you questions and offer comments. It's the type of listening you need to use when you're first asked to speak, to make sure that you understand the task and the audience. Informational listening demands that you …

❖ Focus on specific details.

❖ Distinguish between different pieces of information.

❖ Organize the information into a meaningful whole.

Evaluative Listening

In evaluative listening, you weigh what has been said to decide whether you agree with it or not. Start group writing situations with informational listening to make sure you have the facts before you generate words and ideas. When you're fairly sure that you understand the issues, you can then evaluate them and make decisions based on the facts, evidence, and speaker's credibility. This type of listening is most helpful when you're in decision-making situations and confrontational positions.

Listening Traps

Listening on the job is far more difficult than listening in a classroom setting. In part, that's because classroom lectures are usually well-organized, with clear topics and divisions of information. The information given in a business meeting, in contrast, is rarely well-organized. Key nuggets of information are often hidden in piles of useless blather. When it comes to doing business, feelings matter as much as facts do.

That's why it is vital to identify and overcome bad listening habits. *Pseudolistening, self-centered listening,* and *selective listening* are three of the most common bad listening habits. Here's what they mean and how to overcome them:

❖ *Pseudolistening* occurs when you only go through the motions of listening. You look like you're listening, but your mind is miles away. Correct this by really focusing on what the speaker is saying.

❖ *Self-centered listening* occurs when you mentally rehearse your answer while the other person is still speaking. It's focusing on your own response rather than on the speaker's words. Correct this listening fault by letting the other person speak before you begin to frame your answer.

❖ *Selective listening* happens when you listen only to those parts of a message that directly concern you. For instance, during a group writing situation you may let your mind drift away until you hear your name, your department's name, or some specific information that's directly relevant to your concerns. You'll be a more effective communicator if you listen to the entire message.

Listening Skills

Here are ten ways that listening and communication get blocked when writers work together. Along with each situation, you'll find a sample solution. As you read each problem and resolution, notice how many of them are created by looking at the situation from only one side. In those cases, the solution can often be as simple as considering the problem from the other person's point of view—the essence of effective team communication.

1. *Ordering:* When you give orders, you shut off the flow of communication. Comments such as, "I don't care how you do it—just have the report finished today," block effective cooperative work. Instead, rephrase the information you received, as in, "I hear that there's a problem with getting this report finished today."

2. *Threatening:* Pulling rank serves only to intimidate. Threats include comments like, "If you can't get this report written, I'll find someone who

can." Try asking for further clarification, as in, "Would the task be easier if you had additional help?"

3. *Preaching:* Lecturing workers belittles them. For example, saying, "You should know better than to turn in work like this," humiliates a colleague or subordinate. A more effective approach involves mirroring the person's response, as in, "This must be very upsetting to you."

4. *Interrogating:* Giving a worker the third degree rarely elicits the information you need. For instance, saying, "Even a child could understand this job. Are you *that* stupid?" is a good move when it comes to getting writing done in a team. A better communication technique is sharing your own feelings. For instance, say, "I'm worried about getting this bid completed on time."

5. *Name-calling:* This is a favorite technique with insecure administrators as well as the rank and file. A typical comment goes like this: "That remark just shows what an idiot you are." Sharing your feelings gets a more constructive response. Notice that the following comment focuses on "I" rather than "you": "I get upset when I'm put under pressure. It makes me feel I have too much to do in too little time. How can we all pull together to finish this job?"

6. *Shaming:* You've encountered this situation before. Someone says something like, "Look at this garbage you wrote. It's filled with spelling errors and typos. Parts of it don't even make any sense." Instead of humiliating colleagues, a more effective communication technique involves offering to work together to resolve the problem. Switch from you-centered to we-centered statements: "We need to rework this document. What's the most effective way to get this done in the time we have?"

7. *Buttering-up:* Excessive and insincere praise is used to put a person on the spot in a typical comment like, "You're so clever. I know someone of your extraordinary caliber can save us one more time." Nothing like putting on a little pressure, eh? A more productive communication method involves zeroing in on the situation. Try, "Which parts of this project do you feel most comfortable writing? When can you get the job completed?"

8. *Psychoanalyzing:* This method assumes that the person's motivation is plain. It usually backfires because it makes the person defensive, even if the comment is on target. A typical comment runs, "You really have a problem supervising others, don't you?" Try rephrasing the other person's comments to see if you heard what they were saying. For instance, you might say, "Are you saying that we have too many people writing this project?"

9. *Minimizing the problem:* Not all problems are created equal; some are far more serious than others. Making light of a major dilemma won't make it go away; usually, the inverse is true. That's why the following comments and others like it don't cut the mustard when it comes to communication: "You think *you've* got a lot to write? I have to do all the employee evaluations by the end of the month. Now, *that's* a real problem." Mirror the person's feelings to achieve more constructive communication. Here's a model response: "This must be an overwhelming situation for you."

10. *Seizing control:* When you have power and are used to exercising it, it's tempting to take over the whole situation. After all, that's why you're in charge. But seizing control not only prevents your employees from achieving their potential, but also loads too much on your plate. Micromanaging makes real communication very difficult to achieve; who wants to say what needs to be said when the boss is always looking over your shoulder? Here's an example of seizing control: "Why don't you just assign the opening statement to Luis, the middle to Tyrone, and the closing to Myra? Then you can have Alana edit the whole document and S.J. proofread it." Instead, offer to work together with the employee or team to iron out the problem. You might say, "Is there anything I can do to help this project move along more easily?"

Notice that in some instances, the communication quagmire is created by misuse of language. More effective communication can often be achieved by using *we* rather than *you*, thereby showing a commitment to working as a team rather than assigning blame.

Using Active and Passive Voice

You can also switch from the *active voice* to the *passive voice* to work together more effectively with other writers. This is such an important group writing technique that I'll cover it here and reinforce it in Chapter 6 as well.

Verbs can show whether the subject performs the action or receives the action. This is called *voice*. English has two voices: *active* and *passive*.

A verb is *active* when the subject performs the action, as in these examples:

❖   You made a mistake.

❖   You did not get the bid in on time.

A verb is *passive* when its action is performed upon the subject, as in these examples:

❖   A mistake has been made.

❖   The bid was not completed on time.

In most writing, the active voice is preferable because it is less wordy than the passive voice. As a result, the active voice creates a more concise style. But the passive voice is preferable over the active voice when you don't want to assign blame, which is especially important in collaborative writing.

For example, rather than playing the blame game and using the active voice to say, "You made a lot of spelling mistakes on this document," try the passive voice: "A lot of spelling mistakes were made on this document." By saving someone's feelings, you've achieved far more effective communication, especially crucial when you're forced to write a document as a group.

Being an Active Listener

As you're working together, be an *active listener*. With this technique, receivers show they have heard and understood the message by giving feedback. Active listening can reduce the conflict that results from miscommunication, although it can't eliminate problems that arise from differing goals. Here's how to do it:

❖   Start by genuinely accepting the other person's ideas and feelings.

❖   Show that you understand by smiling, nodding, or verbally acknowledging the message.

❖   Ask for additional information when you need it.

Here are some other ways to make sure you listen for the information you need when you're writing in a group:

1.   Come into a group with questions you want answered. Know the facts you need to get. This will help you listen for the answers you need.

2.   Listen to everything, but focus on getting answers to your questions.

3.   Consider why a speaker is making a specific point. What in the person's background and experiences makes such a comment necessary?

4.   When a meeting or conversation is over, check your understanding with the other people. Make sure you all heard the same thing. You can do this by restating the speaker's comments in your own words.

5.   After the meeting, write down the key points. Focus on deadlines and evaluations. Then distribute a memo or E-mail message to make sure everyone is on the same page.

Collaborative Writing

Although writing is often thought of as an individual effort, with writers working in isolation from the rest of the world, most writing actually involves social interaction. This is especially true when it comes to business writing, as you learned in the beginning of this chapter. In fact, two writing process scholars recently surveyed 700 professionals in seven fields. They discovered that 87 percent of the executives wrote jointly some of the time. About 58 percent of those surveyed found joint writing productive. The fact that 42 percent of the executives did not find group writing worth the time or trouble suggests that collaborative writing isn't everyone's cup of tea. However, when it comes to writing business documents in groups, there's no escape.

Collaborative writing involves several people working together to create a document. The participants may be working in the same place or in different places, at the same time or at different times.

You'll most likely be asked to write in a team in situations like these:

* ❖ The writing task is too big for one employee.
* ❖ The deadline is too tight to allow one person to complete all the writing on time.
* ❖ No one has all the knowledge needed to do the writing.
* ❖ It is important to reach consensus and present a group viewpoint.
* ❖ The stakes are so high that the company wants the best efforts of as many people as possible, for a government bid or major advertising campaign, for example.

Executives write well in groups when they have the following characteristics:

* ❖ flexibility
* ❖ respect for others
* ❖ dependability
* ❖ confidence
* ❖ ability to accept criticism
* ❖ ability to deal with conflict

Allocating the Task

Collaborative writing groups can take several different forms, depending on the type of task, the time constraints, the importance of the task, and the company's culture. Here are some ways the work can be divided:

* ❖ The group can work together to plan the document and then divide the work. Each members does his or her research, writes a draft, and revises it. Then the entire group evaluates the parts and combines them into a whole. This is the most common method used in business, especially when the document is large and important and it is crucial that every participant feels his or her input has been weighed equally.

❖ An executive can run the group and allocate all the tasks, including planning, shaping, writing, editing, and proofreading. This is a commonly used method in traditional organizations whose executives like to keep close control.

❖ The group gathers the information and conferences about the topic, then one member writes the entire draft for the group to review. This method tends to give the document a consistent tone that is difficult to achieve otherwise unless you're working with highly skilled writers. As a final step, the whole group revises the document. Many committee reports are written this way.

❖ One member of the group assigns the writing tasks, each member performs his or her individual part, and another person combines these segments and revises the whole document. While this method gives the document a single vision and uniformity of tone, it may cause the person who combines the sections and revises the entire draft to feel overburdened. It's also important here to keep a close watch on deadlines so the last person has sufficient time to work.

❖ The group works together to plan and write the draft, then one or more members revises the draft without consulting the writers. This method is often used with huge writing projects when time is short.

❖ One person plans and writes the draft. Then one or more people revise the draft without consulting the first writer. This method may not work well when consensus is desired.

❖ One member of the group dictates the information while another person transcribes the dictation and revises the text.

Collaborative writing is most successful when the group is able to select the method to use. When you're deciding on a method, consider these factors:

1. *Your audience*: Who will be reading the document?
2. *Your purpose*: Why is the document being written?
3. *Your team members*: What are their strengths and weaknesses? Recognize that different people have different work styles and different writing styles. So-called interpersonal types work well in groups, while intrapersonal people are most productive when they're allowed to work independently.
4. *Special considerations*: These include time constraints, budget, and the need for consensus.
5. *Company culture*: Which method of organization best suits the company's prevailing structure?

Words to the Wise

❖   Make the time to build group cohesion and loyalty. Most group writers feel that establishing and supporting group relationships is at least as important as the content of the work itself. Group members will work harder and better if they're united and feel invested in the project.

❖   Be a responsible group member. Even though meetings can be a real bore, try to attend every one. Carry out your assigned tasks and be co-operative.

❖   Collaborative writing sessions tend to be most effective when they are brief, but this isn't always possible. If you're running the meeting, you can set the style and go for brevity. Otherwise, go with the flow.

❖   Recognize the need for flexibility and support. Be willing to bend and help others.

❖   Don't assume that everyone knows what you mean or how you feel. Follow the rules of effective communication outlined earlier in this chapter. Recognize that there are times when reinforcing a point can be useful. At other times, though, running off at the mouth just makes the situation more difficult. There are even times when it's best not to say anything at all. Keeping quiet can prevent people from saying things that they might later regret, especially in group writing situations. The most effective communicators know when to speak—and when not to.

❖   Always build in extra time. A few extra days can make the difference between a merely acceptable document and a superb one, as well as between failure and success.

❖   Try to have one person proofread the entire document for errors in spelling, grammar, mechanics, and usage. If possible, this should be someone who didn't participate in the group composition process. A fresh pair of eyes can pick up errors that everyone else might have overlooked.

❖   A computerized spell-checker is no substitute for a real, live proofreader.

Summary

❖   Communication is a social process of making meaning in writing or speech.

❖   Speaking is a two-way process, making contact with people and receiving feedback from them. To communicate effectively, it's not enough to be a good speaker; you also have to be a good listener.

❖   There are three main kinds of listening: empathic listening, informational listening, and evaluative listening.

❖ Overcome ineffective listening habits, including pseudolistening, self-centered listening, and selective listening.

❖ When you write in groups, avoid ordering, threatening, preaching, interrogating, name-calling, shaming, buttering-up, psychoanalyzing, minimizing the problem, and seizing control.

❖ Use the passive voice when you don't want to assign blame.

❖ Be an active listener.

❖ Collaborative writing involves several people working together to produce a document. When you allocate tasks, consider your audience, purpose, team members, special considerations, and the company culture.

Part 2
BUSINESS STYLE

Chapter 6

Business Style

"I did very well in English class, earning A's and B's on my compositions," you might say. "So why am I having so much trouble writing business documents?" The answer lies in the difference between *literary* and *business* writing.

Schools teach literary writing: how to express yourself to a general audience. You were taught how to analyze and respond to a novel, short story, or poem. Perhaps you were even taught how to write a short story or a poem. In school, you were taught how to express or entertain readers with written language.

Business writing, in contrast, never aims to entertain and very rarely to express. Rather, memos, letters, E-mail messages, reports, and faxes are designed to transact business, create goodwill, or get a job done. In this chapter, you'll learn how to develop a clear and concise business writing style.

What Is *Style* in Writing?

A writer's *style* is his or her distinctive way of writing. Style is the result of a series of choices that writers make, including voice, emphasis, word choice, transitions, sentence length and structure, and punctuation.

Business executives advance in their careers in part because of their ability to write clearly and effectively. For example:

- ❖ Lawyers need to make their briefs logical.
- ❖ Accountants must write clear cover letters for audits.
- ❖ Managers often write employee evaluations.
- ❖ Insurance brokers write letters soliciting business.
- ❖ Computer specialists write proposals.
- ❖ Marketing personnel write sales reports.
- ❖ Engineers write reports, E-mail messages, and faxes.
- ❖ Stock and bond traders write letters and prospectuses.

What busy executive doesn't want to write resumés, cover letters, memos, faxes, and business letters that get the desired results in the least amount of time? It's plain that an effective writing style is a powerful asset in business.

Style and Substance

It would be easy if there were one "right" style that everyone in business and government could use. However, this isn't the case. Different places and different times call for different writing styles. Successful writers adapt their language to the audience and circumstances because they know which words are appropriate in a specific situation. When you select a writing style, the three main considerations are:

❖ subject

❖ purpose

❖ audience

A stock prospectus for a public offering, for example, requires a different style from a letter of congratulations to a colleague. The stock prospectus is formal and creates a distance between the writer and audience. The letter, in contrast, is informal and seeks to forge a bond between writer and reader. While the two styles are unquestionably different, each document must be equally well written.

In addition, style in business writing, like English itself, is not frozen in time. It has altered over the years to meet the changing needs of its users, and it continues to do so. As a result, you must adjust your writing style as you advance in your career. In some technology companies, for example, writing styles are becoming increasingly informal, largely as a result of the rise of E-mail. In more traditional companies, however, the preferred writing style remains formal and detached.

Three Levels of Style

The following chart compares and contrasts three different levels of writing style: daily speech, business writing, and college writing.

Daily Speech	Business Writing	College Writing
informal style	conversational style	formal style
may have grammar errors	no grammar errors	no grammar errors
friendly tone	friendly or formal tone	formal tone
slang may be used	words depend on audience	abstract and scholarly words
sentence fragments	complete sentences	long sentences
contractions	some contractions	no or few contractions
first-person pronouns (*I, we*)	first- and second-person pronouns	use of *one*, not *I*
no visual impact	visual impact matters	visual impact doesn't matter

Examples of Business Writing Style

Below are samples of the most common writing styles used in business documents. We know that one size *doesn't* fit all when it comes to business style, so the following examples include a range of successful styles.

The first document is taken from a business report, the second from a cover letter in response to a job ad, the third from a flyer, the fourth from an E-mail message, and the fifth from an informal letter of thanks. The audience and direction of the communication (up, down, across, internal, or external) are listed on the left.

Audience	Sample Style
Same level, sales staff	A Diamond Guard is an instrument used to authenticate diamonds. The Diamond Guard consists of three parts: 1) a pointer, 2) indicator lights, and 3) the body.
Upward: human resources staff	I have been responsible for overseeing the purchasing and printing of over $1million annually of marketing, advertising, and promotional materials.
External: shareholders	Strong cash flows and positive investor psychology suggest the market will continue in its present upswing. Of course, the U.S. is not immune to global difficulties, which will continue. However, our economy is protected by steady domestic expansion, a shift in export trade, and a solid U.S. banking system.
Outside: technical consultant to executive staff	Companies that install digital nervous systems capture and capitalize on customer input to differentiate themselves from the competition. Because transmitting bad news from customers to the design groups is a continual challenge, I recommend the following approach: 1. Focus on your most unhappy customers. 2. Use technology to gather feedback from them. 3. E-mail the responses to appropriate staff members.
Upward: individual	I have just spoken with my cousin Alan and he told me that the marketing position at executive GraphicTron is open again and that you intend to contact me for the job. As I'm sure Alan has told you by this time, my job search was successful and I'm now the marketing manager for IGV, Ltd. I wanted to thank you for your help and for thinking of me again. The job at GraphicTron sounds exciting and I would enjoy being involved in the marketing of such a great product. I plan to build a long career at IGV, but let's stay in touch about any future possibilities at GraphicTron.

Selecting a Writing Style

What style should *you* use in your job? Effective writers in every field, including business, adapt their styles to suit their audience and purpose for writing, but all effective business writing shares the following qualities:

1.   It is clear and easy to read.
2.   It is concise.
3.   It is coherent.

Let's look at each of these stylistic elements in greater detail.

Write Clearly

There are three main ways you can make your writing clear: use the active voice, use emphasis, and use strong verbs. These three techniques will help you achieve an effective writing style in all your business communication. Let's start with the active voice, introduced in Chapter 5.

Write Clearly by Using the Active Voice

Use the *active voice* to make your writing clearer. As you learned in Chapter 5, verbs can show whether the subject performs the action or receives the action. This is called *voice*. English has two voices: *active* and *passive*. A verb is *active* when the subject performs the action. A verb is *passive* when its action is performed upon the subject. The active voice is clearer and more concise than the passive voice. For example:

Active Voice	Passive Voice
The client ordered 200 units.	Two hundred units were ordered by the client.
I propose this solution.	This solution is proposed by me.
The marketing department will review the proposal.	The proposal will be reviewed by the marketing department.

To identify passive constructions, find the verb and determine whether it is doing the action or being acted on. Then decide whether you want to use the active voice to be clear and vigorous or the passive voice to avoid assigning blame.

❖   To change a verb from the active to the passive voice, make the direct object the subject.

Active voice: The chief engineer approved the draft.

Passive voice: The draft was approved by the chief engineer.

❖ To change a verb from the passive to active voice, make the agent ("by—") the new subject.

> *Passive voice:*   A decision will be made by the committee later today.

> *Active voice:*   The committee will decide later today.

❖ Passive voice sentences may not have subjects. In that case, you'll have to supply one.

> *Passive voice:*   The document was lost.

> *Active voice:*   Sidney lost the document.

Although the active voice is clearer and more concise than the passive voice, a number of documents are written in the passive voice. For instance, scientific writing often contains the passive voice; the authors are therefore given less importance and the facts are made to speak for themselves. Even in nonscientific writing, however, not all passives can or should be avoided. Suit your voice to your subject and audience.

Write Clearly by Using Emphasis

The latest studies suggest that readers best remember a message delivered at the very beginning or the very end of a sentence. If the material you are presenting is especially important, you will want to position it at these key points.

In addition, select the subject of each sentence based on what you want to emphasize. Because readers focus on the subject of your sentence, make it the most important aspect of each thought.

The following sentences all contain the same information, but notice how the meaning changes based on the choice of subject:

❖ *Our research* showed that 15 percent of employees' time is spent answering E-mail. (*Research* is the subject.)

❖ *Employees* spend 15 percent of their time answering E-mail. (*Employees* is the subject.)

❖ *Answering E-mail* occupies 15 percent of employees' time. (*Answering mail* is the subject.)

❖ *Fifteen-percent* of employees' time is spent answering E-mail. (*Fifteen percent*, the amount of time, is the subject.)

Which one should you use? Start by deciding which part of the sentence to emphasize. Then craft your sentence to place that information first.

Write Clearly by Using Strong Verbs

Strong verbs make your sentences clearer and easier to read, so use verbs rather than nouns to communicate your ideas. This makes your writing more forceful and less wordy. You can accomplish this by replacing forms of *to be* with action verbs, as in the following examples:

Weak: The overall benefit of reserving space now **is** a 20 percent discount.

Clearer: Reserving space now **saves** you 20 percent.

Weak: The advantages of preparing your taxes early **are** less time and worry.

Clearer: Preparing your taxes early **reduces** time and worry.

Write Concisely

A *redundant style* is crammed with unnecessary words that fog your meaning. Wordy writing forces your readers to clear away clutter before they can understand your message. Here's an example:

Wordy: In fact, the factory, which was situated in the local area, was, in a very real sense, the heart of the neighborhood.

Better: The factory is the heart of the neighborhood.

Write simply and directly. Omit unnecessary details or ideas that you have already stated. Use a lot of important detail, but no unnecessary words. You want your writing to be *concise*. Business writing demands a style that is succinct, because the documents you draft at work must communicate their meaning quickly. No one wants to waste time trying to find the point.

There are four easy ways to eliminate a redundant style: delete redundant words and phrases, delete stock phrases, revise sentences that begin with expletives, and combine sentences that repeat information. Let's look at these techniques one at a time.

Delete Redundant Words and Phrases

Why say it twice? Once will do, especially since unnecessary repetition annoys busy readers. The following chart includes some common redundant phrases and concise alternatives. I found all these redundant phrases in business documents.

Redundancy	Revision
1. honest truth	truth
2. past experience	experience
3. revert back	revert
4. foreign imports	imports
5. partial stop, complete stop	stop

6. free gift	gift
7. live and breathe	live
8. null and void	null (or void)
9. most unique	unique
10. cease and desist	cease (or desist)
11. at 8:00 AM in the morning	at 8:00 AM
12. sum total and end results	sum total
13. proceed ahead	proceed
14. successfully escaped	escaped
15. forward progress	progress
16. set a new record	set a record
17. kills bugs dead	kills bugs
18. repeat again	repeat
19. extra gratuity	gratuity
20. continue to remain	remain
21. small in size	small
22. few in number	few
23. new innovation	innovation
24. combine together	combine
25. final end	end

Delete Stock Phrases

Stock phrases are also redundant because they obscure meaning. When you read a stock phrase such as "due to the fact that" or "as per your request," you automatically feel distanced from the writer. There may indeed be instances when you wish to create distance between yourself and your audience, but in most cases, your business writing will try to achieve just the opposite—a connection with the reader.

Below is a list of stock phrases and suggested replacements. Select from the column that will best achieve your purpose.

Stock Phrases	Suggested Replacements
after careful analysis, we decided	we decided
as a consequence of	because of
at the present time	now
at this point in time	now
because of the fact that	because

come to a mutually satisfactory solution	agree
due to the fact that	because
for the purpose of	for
I have reason to believe	I believe
I am writing to inform you	[delete]
I would like to take this opportunity	I will take ...
if it is agreed upon	if you agree
in light of the fact that	because
in consideration of your immediate reply	when you reply
in keeping with	[delete]
in the very near future	soon [or date]
in order to utilize	to use
it is evident that	[delete]
in view of the fact that	because
it has been noted	[delete]
in the event that	if
it has come to my attention	[delete]
more than happy	happy
needless to say	[delete]
on your behalf	for you
pleased be informed	[delete]
until such time as	until
utmost importance	important
we are in receipt of your letter	[delete]
vital importance	important
weather event	snow (etc.)

Revise Sentences That Start with Expletives

Expletives are constructions that fill holes when writers invert subject-verb word order. Here are the most common expletive constructions:

- ❖   It is
- ❖   There is
- ❖   There are
- ❖   There were

These constructions only delay the point of the sentence. Whenever possible, replace the expletive with an action verb, as in the revised sentence:

Wordy: It is necessary for all employees to select a health care plan.

Better: Employees can choose from three health care plans.

Combine Sentences That Repeat Information

You can also combine certain sentences to make your writing more concise. Start by looking for sentences that contain the same information or relate to the same ideas and so logically belong together. Then combine the related sentences. Finally, cut any words that take up space like an unwanted house guest. Here are some examples:

Wordy: *The Testament* was a best seller. It was written by John Grisham. *The Testament* was a novel.

Better: *The Testament*, by John Grisham, was a best-selling novel.

You can also eliminate unnecessary words by reworking extraneous relative pronouns and adjective clauses. For instance:

Wordy: The high cost of multimedia presentations is due to the combined cost of the studio shoot and expensive media compression. The costs of graphic design and technical support are also high.

Better: Studio shoots, media compression, graphic design, and technical support all contribute to the high cost of multimedia presentations.

Write Coherently

All effective writing is *coherent:* The ideas are logically related to each other. Coherence is especially important in business writing, when your readers are often impatient to get to the point. If your readers can't follow your ideas, they are likely to discard or misunderstand your message. Wouldn't *you?*

To check your drafts for coherence, see if the ideas fit together so your readers can follow your train of thought. If your ideas aren't logically connected, you may need to add some *transitions.* A transition can be a whole paragraph of text or simply a *transitional expression,* a word or phrase that shows how the ideas are connected. For example:

Lack of coherence: Many entrepreneurs-to-be underestimate the power of a known brand to generate sales. A little-known franchise is often much more challenging and less rewarding to operate than a large brand-name one.

Coherent: Many entrepreneurs-to-be underestimate the power of a known brand to generate sales. *On the contrary,* a little-known franchise is often much more challenging and less rewarding to operate than a large brand-name one.

Lack of coherence: The quickest way to tell if a franchisee association has any clout is to study the company's franchise agreement. Don't just rely on the contract.

Coherence: The quickest way to tell if a franchisee association has any clout is to study the company's franchise agreement, *but* don't just rely on the contract.

Different transitional expressions signal to the reader how one idea is linked to the others. Using the appropriate transitions helps you convey your ideas smoothly and clearly.

The following chart lists some of the most useful transitions. The relationships are listed on the left, the transitions on the right.

Signal	Transitions	
Addition	also	in addition
	too	and
	besides	further
	next	then
	finally	moreover
Example	for example	for instance
	namely	specifically
Chronological order	first	second
	third	fourth (etc.)
	next	subsequently
	immediately	later
	eventually	in the future
	currently	now
	during	meanwhile
	before	soon
	afterward	at length
	finally	then
Contrast	nevertheless	nonetheless
	yet	in contrast
	on the contrary	still
	however	on the other hand
Comparison	in comparison	similarly
	likewise	in the same way

Concession	naturally	granted
	certainly	to be sure
	of course	
Place	nearby	in the distance
	here	there
	at the side	next to
	adjacent	in the front
	in the back	
Result	due to this	so
	accordingly	consequently
	as a result	therefore
Summary	finally	in conclusion
	in summary	in brief
	as a result	hence
	on the whole	in short

Sentence Sense

Clear writing uses sentences of different lengths and types to create variety and interest. Craft your sentences to express your ideas in the best possible way. Here are some ways you can vary your sentences to create an effective, readable, interesting style.

* Keep the subject and verb close together in very long sentences to make the sentences easier to read and understand.

* Vary the length of your sentences. The unbroken rhythm of monotonous sentence length can lull a reader into unconsciousness.

* When your topic is complicated or full of numbers, use simple sentences to aid understanding, and keep them short!

* Use longer, more complex sentences to show how ideas are linked together and to avoid repetition.

Style and Punctuation

Your choice of punctuation also has a critical influence on your writing style because it determines the links between sentences. Further, it suggests whether sentence elements are coordinating or subordinating. Here are some guidelines:

* A period shows a full separation between ideas. It's a complete stop.

* A comma and a coordinating conjunction show addition, choice, consequence, contrast, or cause.

❖ A semicolon shows that the second sentence completes or adds to the first sentence. The semicolon suggests a link but leaves it up to the reader to make the connection.

❖ A semicolon and a conjunctive adverb (a word such as *nevertheless, however,* etc.) show addition, consequence, contrast, cause and effect, time, emphasis, or addition.

Style Wars

What happens if your boss likes an ornate, flowery style with big words and windy sentences? Or take a less extreme case: What if your company prefers writing in the passive voice to the active voice? In either case, you have several choices:

1. Write clearly and logically, based on what you learned in this chapter. Seeing effective writing may change your supervisor's mind.

2. Conference with your supervisor about changing writing styles. People may be using weaker writing models because they don't have anything better to use.

3. Recognize that writing style serves to unify a company as well as communicate ideas. Even if the style isn't as strong and effective as clear writing, it may bring people together in a corporate culture.

Summary

❖ A writer's *style* is his or her distinctive way of writing. Style includes word choice, sentence length and structure, tone, voice, diction, and overall structure.

❖ When you select a writing style, your three main considerations are the subject, purpose, and audience.

❖ All effective business writing is clear, concise, and coherent.

❖ Write clearly by using the active voice, emphasis, and strong verbs.

❖ Write concisely by deleting redundant words and phrases, revising sentences that start with expletives, and combining sentences that repeat information.

❖ Write coherently by using transitions.

❖ Punctuation also affects writing style because it determines the degree of linkage between sentences.

❖ Clear writing uses sentences of different lengths and types to create variety and interest.

❖ Writing style serves to unify a company as well as communicate ideas.

Chapter 7

Selecting Words That Work

In this chapter, you'll learn all about diction. I'll show you which words usually work in business writing, and which ones don't. But first, an important warning: Remember to violate any of the guidelines in this chapter to suit your audience and purpose. Also break the rules to avoid saying anything silly, awkward, or downright convoluted. When it comes to language and business, always let logic rule the day.

What Is *Diction*?

Diction is word choice. The words you select as you write make up your *diction*. Diction ranges from *formal* to *informal*. *Formal diction* is marked by long, "difficult" words; *informal diction* is characterized by shorter, easier words. Neither level of diction (or any level in between) is good or bad; rather, each one is appropriate in different writing situations. Your diction affects the clarity and impact of your message.

English is an unusual language in that it comes from two main language families, Latinate and Germanic. Over time, the two vocabularies began to merge. Even today, hundreds of years after modern English developed, words often retain traces of their origins:

❖ German-based words tend to be shorter, more direct, and more blunt.

❖ Latin-based words tend to be long and scientific.

The word you want in a specific instance depends on the context: the audience, purpose, and tone. You'll sound more straightforward and forthright if you draw your words from Germanic roots. A Latin vocabulary, in contrast, suggests a more elevated level of diction. Choose your words carefully, with constant attention to your audience and to the effect you want to have on them. Use a thesaurus or dictionary to help you find the words that make your meaning as clear as possible.

Selecting Words

In general, always use words that are *precise, appropriate,* and *familiar.*

1. *Precise* words say what you mean.

2. *Appropriate* words convey your tone and fit with the other words in the document.

3. *Familiar* words are easy to read and understand, which helps you communicate your message.

Let's explore each of these criteria in detail.

Use Precise Words

Precise words capture the exact meaning you wish to convey. For example, instead of using the vague noun *thing* to indicate an object, name the object. In the same way, instead of using the vague adjective *nice,* use the adjective that conveys your exact shade of meaning, such as *superior, acceptable,* or *satisfactory.* Ditch empty phrases such as *apparent significant financial gains* in favor of clear words and phrases such as *a lot of money* or *large profits.*

Be extra picky when you select words for a business document. Remember what you learned in Chapter 5 about *denotation* (a word's dictionary meaning) and *connotation* (a word's overtones). To communicate effectively, you have to consider a word's connotations as well as its denotations.

Also weigh the importance of context and connotation. Words carry different connotations depending on how they are used, especially where gender is concerned. For example, an *aggressive* man and an *aggressive* woman are often perceived differently: The former description has a positive connotation; the latter, a negative one.

Use Appropriate Words

Words that sound alike or are spelled alike are often mixed up with each other. Other pairs of words are misused because they have special uses and meanings. The following chart lists some of the most often confused words used in business writing.

Word	Definition	Example
accede	to yield	We accede to your order.
exceed	to surpass	Don't exceed the cost.
access	right to use	Give us access to the files.
excess	surplus	There's excess paper.

adept	skilled	They are adept workers.
adopt	take up	Please adopt the budget.
advise	to give counsel	Advise me.
advice	counsel (noun)	Reject the advice.
amount	measurable	amount of debt
number	countable	number of folders
between	two choices	between you and me
among	three or more choices	among the three of us
confuse	puzzle	You confuse me.
complicate	make complex	The report complicates the situation.
discreet	tactful	Discreet people are politic.
discrete	separate	Two discrete rules must be followed.
eminent	distinguished	eminent official
imminent	about to happen	imminent storm
fewer	countable	fewer vacation days
less	not countable	less pleasure
forward	ahead	Walk forward.
foreword	introduction	The book's foreword was written poorly.
good	nice (adj.)	Do a good job.
well	nice (adv.)	My department is doing well.
it's	it is	It's quitting time.
its	belonging to it	The car lost its muffler.
moral	ethics; good	moral of the story
morale	attitude	employee morale
personal	individual	My personal decision is to stay.
personnel	employees	All personnel get raises.
precede	to go before	Precede me through the door.
proceed	to continue	Proceed to the exit.
proceeds	money (noun)	The proceeds from the sale were stolen.
quite	very	quite an accomplishment
quiet	not noisy	a quiet day
regulate	control	regulate the cost
relegate	put in order (usually lower)	relegated to the back office

Use Familiar Words

If there's one product American business can easily produce in vast amounts, it's *doublespeak*. Doublespeak comes in many forms, from the popular buzzwords that everyone uses but no one really understands—globalization, competitive dynamics, reequitizing, and empowerment—to language that tries to hide meaning, such as reengineering, synergy, and restructure.

Remember that your primary goal is to communicate clearly and concisely, so use words that your readers will know and understand. Strive to avoid any language that hides, evades, or misleads. This includes *doublespeak, inflated language, jargon, bureaucratic language*, and *buzzwords*. Let's look at each of these in turn.

Avoid Doublespeak

Have you seen the "personal manual databases" advertised on late-night television recently? Maybe you thought you couldn't figure out what was being sold because you were so tired. It wasn't you; it was the language. What's a "personal manual database"? It's a *calendar*. It's also an example of *doublespeak*, a convoluted phrase that deliberately hides meaning.

At the least, doublespeak is confusing and annoying. At the most, though, deliberately misleading language can be cause for litigation. For example, in a recent case, a woman was initially thrilled to get a certificate stating she had won an "all-terrain vehicle" as a prize for visiting a vacation resort. She had to pay $29.95 for "handling, processing, and insurance," the prize voucher read. She paid the money and got her prize: a four-wheeled lawn chair that converted to a cart. Not surprisingly, the company claimed that the language wasn't deliberately misleading. The matter is currently in court, and serves to illustrate the legal as well as moral ramifications of using deliberately confusing words and phrases.

Here are a few more examples of doublespeak that I've culled from recent business publications:

Confusing Phrase	Meaning
a personal time control center	watch
writing fluid	ink
underground condominium	grave
vertically challenged	short person
revenue enhancement	tax increase
unauthorized withdrawal	robbery
outplaced	fired
nonpositively terminated	fired
career change opportunity	fired

involuntarily leisured	fired
mechanically separated meat	salvaged meat
cheese analogs	fake cheese
greenmail	economic blackmail
takeover artists	corporate raiders
social expression products	greeting cards
learning facilitators	teachers
compromised susceptible host	a sick person
automotive internists	car mechanics
vertical transportation corps	elevator operators
nonperforming assets	bad loans
nonperforming credits	bad loans
negative cash flow	corporate losses
deficit enhancement	corporate losses
negative contributions to profits	corporate losses

Since it evades and obscures meaning, doublespeak is dishonest language. Steer clear of it.

Avoid Inflated Language

Doublespeak is obvious and relatively easy to eliminate. *Inflated language* can be harder to spot, however, because it's more subtle. It consists of words and phrases used in business communication because they are thought to sound businesslike. *That's* why you're having trouble understanding what everyone's writing!

The following chart lists some of the most common examples of unnecessarily inflated words and phrases. Use the words from the column on the right to make your writing more powerful and effective. Your readers will thank you for it.

50 Chief Offenders—and Their Replacements

Inflated Language	Better Communication
accede	agree
accordingly	so
acquiesce	agree
admonish	warn
affirmative	yes
aggregate	total
allay	calm

alleviate	reduce
allocate	assign
append	add, attach
ascertain	determine
attain	gain
authenticate	prove
cognizant	aware
commence	begin, start
concurrent	parallel
consolidate	join, combine
curtail	shorten
defer	postpone
definitive	final
delineate	outline, describe
disseminate	distribute
elucidate	clarify
endeavor	try
entail	involve
enumerate	list
equitable	fair
exhort	urge
hereabouts	here
impacts on	affects
liaise	meet, connect
manifest	show
modicum	bit
penchant	ability
permutation	change
perusal	study
preamble	introduction
predicated	based
predilection	preference
promulgate	promote
rationale	reason

recapitulate	review, summarize
relinquish	give up
remunerate	pay
repercussion	effect, results
sanction	approve
stipend	payment, wage
terminate	end
utilize	use
viable	practical

Avoid Jargon

Jargon is the specialized vocabulary of a particular group. Jargon features words that an outsider unfamiliar with the field might not understand. There's medical, legal, educational, and technological jargon. All sports, hobbies, and games have their own jargon, as do the arts.

As you write, consider your purpose and audience to decide whether a word is jargon in the context of your material. For example, if you're writing for a group of computer specialists, using the technical terms your audience expects—their jargon—is okay. Also, using a little jargon in a job application letter suggests that you know the language of the specialty so you're the right person for the job. Using jargon with the appropriate audience communicates your meaning, but using jargon unnecessarily confuses readers. Here's the rule: If a technical term has an equivalent in plain English, use the simpler term.

Avoid Bureaucratic Language

Bureaucratic language is overly complex and hard to decipher. Here's an example:

> The initial fax already distributed through appropriate channels should be disregarded and retracted and instead substituted by the fax sent before the foregoing one was distributed. The fax at the present instance being held by the designated company officers should be allied with the antecedent one to direct attention to the fact that the preceding fax should be disregarded by the recipient.

Here's how the memo reads without the bureaucratic language. Notice how much more clearly and forcefully it communicates:

> Replace the first fax you received with the one that followed it. Please attach this notice to the canceled fax.

Does this mean you can't use any words with more than two syllables? There's nothing inherently wrong with long words, but too many business executives think a long word is always better than a short one. No doubt this tendency comes from a desire to impress, to sound more authoritative, but it usually ends in imprecision and gracelessness. Even worse, if you use long words improperly you sound foolish. Use a long word only if it expresses your meaning most precisely.

Avoid Buzzwords

Buzzwords are empty words and phrases that add nothing to your writing and so should be cut. Buzzwords have been so overused that they have lost their meaning. Here are some examples:

Sample Buzzwords

quite	very	basically	really
central	major	field	case
situation	kind	scope	sort
type	thing	area	aspect
factor	quality	nice	central
major	good	excellent	fine

Here's how they look in context:

Wordy: These **types** of administrative problems are **really quite** difficult to solve.

Better: Administrative problems are difficult to solve.

Check-Up

Use the following checklist as you edit your writing to identify doublespeak, inflated language, jargon, bureaucratic language, and buzzwords:

❖   What does the word or phrase mean?

❖   Can it be stated more clearly and simply?

❖   Does the phrase fit the audience and purpose?

❖   Is there a better choice that would make my meaning clearer?

Use Nonbiased Language

Biased language assigns qualities to people on the basis of their gender, appearance, age, race, or physical condition. It reflects prejudiced attitudes and stereotypical thinking. We all know that obviously biased attitudes aren't acceptable in today's world. But biased language can be much less obvious, and every bit as offensive. Fortunately, most of the time it requires only a little sensitivity to avoid offending people with your choice of words.

For example, women accounted for 59 percent of labor-force growth between 1985 and 1995, the most recent year for which statistics are available. Because more than half the women in America are in the workforce, women are an economic and political power that can't be ignored. Modern women get angry at writers and speakers who stereotype and patronize them with biased language.

In addition, one in every six Americans has a disability, defined as a physical, emotional, or mental impairment. Expect the ratio to increase as the population ages, and be especially aware of the terms used to describe people with disabilities.

Finally, the law is increasingly intolerant of biased documents and hostile work environments. Because federal law forbids discrimination on the basis of gender, age, race, or physical condition, people writing policy statements, grant proposals, or any other official documents must be very careful not to use any language that could be considered discriminatory. Otherwise, they're courting legal action.

Therefore, you want to use nonbiased language in all your business writing and speech. Here are some guidelines to help you use fair and impartial language in business communication.

1. Don't use *he* or *man* to refer to both men and women. You can often circumvent awkward constructions by using the plural form of the pronoun or noun.

    Biased: *He* must approve all *his* employees' vacation requests.

    Nonbiased: *Supervisors* must approve all employees' vacation requests.

2. Avoid expressions that exclude one sex.

    Biased: **man**kind   fore**man**

    Nonbiased: humanity   supervisor

3. Don't use language that denigrates people.

    Biased: cripple   old **wives'** tale

    Nonbiased: wheelchair user   folklore

    Further, don't use phrases that suggest women and men behave in stereotypical ways, such as *talkative women* or *rowdy boys*.

4.   Use the correct courtesy title.

Use *Mr.* for men and *Ms.* for women, but professional titles take precedence over either. For example, in the classroom, I am *Dr.* Rozakis rather than *Ms.* Rozakis. Always use the title the person prefers. If you aren't sure what courtesy title to use, check in a company directory or on previous correspondence to see how the person prefers to be addressed.

5.   Refer to a group by the term it prefers. Language changes, so be aware of the current preferred terms. Here are some current terms to use:

Asian is preferred over Oriental.

Inuit is preferred over Eskimo.

Latino is the preferred designation for Mexican Americans, Puerto Ricans, Dominicans, and other people with Central and Latin American backgrounds.

6.   Focus on people, not their conditions.

Biased:	mentally retarded
Nonbiased:	people with mental retardation
Biased:	cancer patients
Nonbiased:	people being treated for cancer

A Note on the Third-Person Indefinite Pronoun

Perhaps the most confusing issue is the use of the third person indefinite pronoun, as in "Each director is responsible for writing [his/her/their/one's] employee evaluations." Which pronoun is correct? This is a delicate question, and there's no one solution. Language, like life, is rarely that clear-cut.

Each director is singular, as the verb *is* instead of *are* indicates, so *their* (a plural) doesn't agree with the verb and isn't grammatically correct. Nonetheless, we use this construction often in speaking, as in, "A friend of mine called me," and, "What did they say?" Even though many writers use it as well, grammar purists consider it incorrect for formal business writing.

"Each director is responsible for writing *his* employee evaluations" is the traditional usage. This assumes the masculine pronoun stands for everyone, but today this construction is considered biased because it suggests that all executives are male. "Each director is responsible for writing *his or her* employee evaluations" is grammatical and nonbiased, but it is awkward and wordy, especially when you use "his or her" over and over.

There are several ways out. One is to mix the occasional *his* or *her* together with *his and her*. It's not a bad solution because it cuts down on suggestions of bias without making your writing clumsy. However, I favor a sidestep; avoid the problem altogether and make your subject plural whenever possible: "All directors are responsible for writing *their* employee evaluations."

Summary

❖ *Diction* is word choice. The word you want in a specific instance depends on your audience, purpose, and tone.

❖ In general, always use words that are precise, appropriate, and well-known.

❖ Avoid doublespeak, inflated language, jargon, bureaucratic language, and buzzwords.

❖ Use nonbiased language in all your business writing and speech.

Chapter 8

Intercultural Communication

All the challenges of communicating in one culture and country increase sharply when people communicate across cultures and countries. However, succeeding in today's global market requires intercultural skills. You've got to master the ability to communicate skillfully with people from different cultures and countries, based on an understudying of cultural diversity. That's what you'll learn in this chapter.

The Changing Face of Business

Who is the "average" American worker today? According to the most recent census, America boasts about 264.6 million citizens. Nearly a third of us chose to identify ourselves as minorities. Here's how we describe ourselves:

- ❖ 33.5 million (13 percent) of us are black.
- ❖ 27.7 million (11 percent) of us are Hispanic.
- ❖ 9.5 million (4 percent) of us are Asians and Pacific Islanders.
- ❖ 2.3 million (1 percent) of us are Native American/Inuit.

All told, 23 million of us are foreign-born, the highest level since before 1945. Just how diverse are we? Here are some statistics to set your head spinning:

- ❖ Employees in the Digital Equipment Corporation plant in Boston come from 44 countries and speak 19 languages; the plant's announcements are printed in English, Chinese, French, Spanish, Portuguese, Haitian Creole, and Vietnamese.
- ❖ More than 30 million Americans speak English as a second language, which means that roughly 14 percent of the American population speaks about 140 different languages.
- ❖ More than 100 languages are spoken in the school systems of New York City, Chicago, Los Angeles, and Fairfax County, Virginia.

❖   Over 25 percent of America's immigrants—6.7 million—were born in Mexico. Other common immigrant homelands include the Philippines (1.2 million Americans hail from there), China/Taiwan (816,000); Cuba (797,000), Canada (695,000), El Salvador (650,000), Great Britain (617,000), Germany (598,000), Poland (538,000), Jamaica (531,000), and the Dominican Republic (509,000).

❖   More than 40 percent of Californians are black, Hispanic, or Asian.

❖   There are more than 2,000 Hmong from Laos living in Wisconsin alone. [source: 1998 World Almanac]

The Census Bureau doesn't have a lock on the future, but their data does suggest that 50 years from now, America will be even more diverse. For example, the Census Bureau predicts that ...

❖   The non-Hispanic white percentage of the population will decrease from the current 73 percent to 53 percent.

❖   At the same time, citizens of Hispanic origin will increase 13 percent.

❖   Asians and Pacific Islanders will see their numbers more than double.

❖   There will be an increase in the number of black Americans as well.

Business Trends and Intercultural Interplay

Business and business communication are changing with dizzying speed. Here are the most significant trends already in place:

1.   *Focusing on the customer.* Increasingly, American firms are embracing "Total Quality Management" as a means of being responsive to consumer needs. Standing still means falling behind. And as the world changes faster and faster, it can be challenging—and stressful—to deal with differences.

2.   *Dealing with diversity.* Women and people of color have always been a part of America's workforce, but in the past, they were usually relegated to support positions. Now, American businesses are tapping *all* talent rather than simply falling back on gender and tradition. In addition, business has become increasingly aware of diversity that comes from age, religion, class, regional difference, sexual orientation, and physical disabilities. Helping your staff reach its potential calls for flexibility as well as an awareness of diversity and intercultural communication. Treating people with respect has always been good business. The realities of diversity makes it a necessity.

3.   *Conducting business abroad.* More and more of the products we purchase are made overseas. Therefore, even if a company doesn't try to market its

products to other countries, it must still deal with international competition.

The web of international business is not confined to exports and imports, however. For executives in global companies, international experience is often essential for career advancement. Companies such as Dell Computer, Gerber, General Motors, and Motorola are sending more and more executives overseas as they expand into new markets. And after the passage of the North American Free Trade Agreement (NAFTA), there are more and more interchanges between Canada, the US, and Mexico.

4. *Conducting international business from home.* Even executives and workers within the United States may have international ties. The market for buses in Mexico City, for example, is greater than the entire market for buses in America. Honda makes cars in Ohio and Toyota makes cars in Kentucky. Meanwhile, Ford builds some of its cars with parts from Mexico and Europe.

5. *Working in teams.* To produce high-quality goods at the most competitive prices, more and more companies are relying on teamwork. The rise of teams means that a premium is placed on executives who can work *with* people rather than just delegating work *to* people.

And since the people you'll be working with are so diverse, you're going to need special skills to adapt to the new working conditions.

While people from other backgrounds can vastly enrich our lives, it is inevitable that misunderstandings will occur in the office over customs and culture. Read on to find out how you can minimize these potential hazards in the workplace through your writing and other business communication.

Accepting Different Values and Traditions

Our values and traditions affect the way we respond to people and situations. Our responses can be completely unconscious, which makes them even more challenging to recognize. This is especially crucial in today's business setting, where success is predicated on communication and cooperation. Here are some examples:

❖   In North America, messages are supposed to build goodwill while doing business—but the message must be concise. In Japan, however, building goodwill is far more important than saving words and time. As a result, Japanese and American business writing take markedly different forms.

❖   Most North Americans believe that employees should be treated fairly and equally; in some other countries, in contrast, it is expected that certain groups will receive preferential treatment. This is also reflected in writing.

❖ Most North Americans embrace competition; the Japanese, however, traditionally believe that competition leads to discord. Both American and Japanese business documents are designed to accomplish these diverse cultural goals.

❖ Most North American executives pride themselves on promising action by a specific date. Among some Asian and Muslim cultures, however, this is considered presumptuous. Letters, faxes, and E-mails are crafted accordingly.

❖ America executives believe that success is based on individual achievement; in many European countries, success is traditionally linked to social class.

❖ In the Northeast, business calls tend to get to the point right away. This directness is often considered rude in the South, where small talk comes before business. It's not surprising that business letters tend to be more direct in the Northeast, less so in the South.

Business Writing and Cultural Difference

In what other ways do cultural differences affect business writing? Here are some examples:

❖ Asians put their family names first; North Americans and Europeans place their family names last.

❖ Arabic writing reads from right to left; North American and European writing reads from left to right.

❖ Since Japanese reads from right to left and bottom to top, Japanese and English documents start at opposite ends.

Here are some guidelines to consider when you draft documents for multicultural audiences:

1. Never assume that your colleagues and clients speak the same "English" that you do. English is not the same around the world. Many Americans born in Europe, Asia, India, Africa, and the Caribbean have learned British English, not the American variety. For example, a British "barrister" is an attorney who handles non-court work such as real estate, while a "solicitor" represents clients in court. American English uses the terms "attorney" and "lawyer" interchangeably for all legal representation.

2. Assume that most cultures are more formal than American culture. As a result, with international business writing, it's safer to err on the side of formality than on the side of informality.

3. When you write international business correspondence for your company, always use the recipient's title before his or her name. Don't address the recipient by his or her first name alone, unless you're close personal friends (and then why would you be writing a business letter in the first place?)

4. Adopt a formal tone in all business correspondence. Don't use contractions and slang. Also avoid *idioms*, phrases whose literal meaning doesn't match their figurative meaning, such as "it's raining cats and dogs."

5. Consider your audience very carefully when you're planning your document. In most instances, you'll have to make negative requests far more indirect. You can accomplish this in part by including buffers before you deliver the negative news.

6. Decide whether appeals that work for some audiences would be equally successful in other cultures. This holds true within America as well as abroad.

7. In international business correspondence, list the date with the day first, not the month. Also drop the comma. For example:

   American style: July 4, 1776
   International style: 4 July 1776

8. Spell out the month to avoid confusion.

9. If you're writing a text that is going to be translated, allow more space than you would on an English document. When English is translated into other languages, it often takes up one-quarter to one-third more space.

10. Be aware of holidays celebrated by people whose traditions and culture are different from your own. For example, you wouldn't do business with an Israeli firm on Yom Kippur, the holiest day of the Jewish calendar. Any document sent that day would reveal cultural insensitivity.

The following chart summarizes some of the most effective writing strategies to reach different cultures. All generalizations are dangerous, so carefully consider your audience as you draft your business documents.

Writing Strategy	Cultures
indirect requests	Japanese, Arabic
polite tone	Japanese, Arabic
ambiguous requests	Japanese, Arabic
direct requests	North American, German
clear and precise	North American, German
confrontational stance	North American, German
attention to detail	North American, German

Checklist

You can use the following checklist to evaluate each document you draft. It will help you evaluate your writing for cultural sensitivity.

❖ Am I aware of my colleagues' and clients' cultural values and beliefs?

❖ Am I sensitive to cultural differences?

❖ Am I aware that my preferred values and values are influenced by culture and not necessarily "right"?

❖ Am I flexible and open to change?

Summary

❖ Succeeding in today's global market requires intercultural skills, the ability to communicate skillfully with people from different cultures and countries, based on an understanding of cultural diversity.

❖ Nearly a third of all American workers identify themselves as minorities. This percentage is expected to increase as we move into the 21st century.

❖ Today's most important business trends include focusing on the customer, being aware of diversity, marketing internationally, and working in teams.

❖ Our values and traditions affect the way we respond to people and situations.

❖ Always consider your audience, especially with intercultural communication. Recognize that appeals and writing strategies must be adapted to a specific market.

❖ Check each document you draft for cultural awareness and sensitivity.

Chapter 9

Document Design

So far, I've concentrated on the *content* of your business writing, but the *form* also matters a great deal. Successful executives are a savvy lot. They know that effective documents read well *and* look well. Good document design is another element in good business because it builds goodwill as it saves time and money. In this chapter, learn how to design your documents to make them more accurate, usable, and effective.

Stack the Deck

Below are two documents that contain the identical information. Which document is easier to read—and why?

Document #1

Your Supercool Refrigerator-Freezer is protected by these Supercool warranties. Full one year warranty (excluding Alaska). Supercool Company warrants that Supercool will repair, without charge, any defect or malfunction occurring in this refrigerator-freezer during the first year after the original date of delivery to the consumer. Full four-year refrigerating system and cabinet warranty. During the second through the fifth years, Supercool will repair, without charge, any defect or malfunction occurring in the cabinet liner or Refrigerating System. The Refrigerating System consists of these parts: the compressor assembly, condensers, refrigerating or cooling coils, inter-connecting tubing. These warranties do not apply: 1. To conditions resulting from improper installation or incorrect electric current. 2. To conditions resulting from consumer damage, such as improper maintenance or misuse and accidental alteration. 3. If the original serial number cannot be readily determined. 4. To service calls not involving malfunction or defects in materials and workmanship, and naturally the consumer shall pay for such calls. 5. To Refrigerator-Freezers installed outside the continental United States and Hawaii. 6. To light bulbs.

Document #2

Your *Supercool* Refrigerator-Freezer is protected by these *Supercool* warranties

FULL ONE YEAR WARRANTY (Excluding Alaska)

Supercool Company warrants that Supercool will repair, without charge, any defect or malfunction occurring in this refrigerator-freezer during the first year after the original date of delivery to the consumer.

FULL FOUR-YEAR REFRIGERATING SYSTEM AND CABINET WARRANTY

During the second through the fifth years, *Supercool* will repair, *without charge,* any defect or malfunction occurring in the cabinet liner or Refrigerating System. The Refrigerating System consists of these parts:

❖ the compressor assembly

❖ condensers

❖ refrigerating or cooling coils

❖ inter-connecting tubing

THESE WARRANTIES DO *NOT* APPLY:

1. To conditions resulting from improper installation or incorrect electric current.

2. To conditions resulting from consumer damage, such as improper maintenance or misuse and accidental alteration.

3. If the original serial number cannot be readily determined.

4. To service calls not involving malfunction or defects in materials and workmanship, and naturally the consumer shall pay for such calls.

5. To Refrigerator-Freezers installed outside the continental United States and Hawaii.

6. To light bulbs.

The second document is obviously much clearer. Notice how the important information jumps right out, highlighted by capital letters, bold-face type, headings, bullets, and spacing. The arrangement of words on the page and the use of "white space"—empty space—also contributes to the effectiveness of the second document.

Letter Perfect

There are several differences between written and verbal communication but here's the key one: with written communication, people can read each section in whatever order they want. With spoken communication, however, the listener receives information in the sequence determined by the speaker.

As a result, when you're creating a written document, you must guide your readers along to page to help them gather the information the way you want it gathered. That's where page design and layout come in. These two elements are the only way you can direct to the reader through your writing.

Use the following guidelines to create visually effective documents that achieve your purpose:

1.   Use headings to direct the reader's eye.

2.   Use typefaces to highlight key information.

3.   Use lists to make items easy to read.

4.   Select margins that suit the audience and purpose.

5.   Use white space to point out important points.

6.   Place key information in specific areas.

7.   Use visuals, clip art, and color judiciously.

8.   Consider cultural expectations.

Use Headings to Direct the Reader's Eye

You know that we're in the midst of the greatest information explosion the world has ever known. There's just too much material to absorb—but we have to assimilate it anyway. Large amounts of information are always easier to grasp when they're divided into smaller pieces. That's the philosophy behind the use of *headings*.

Headings are words or phrases that group points and divide your document into sections. Headings allow your reader to get a quick overview of the document and isolate the key points. In addition, headings break up a page and make it look less intimidating. Use headings effectively and you'll get fewer readers sighing, "What *is* this—a novel or a memo?"

Here's how to use headings:

❖   Make headings specific. BORROWING FROM YOUR RETIREMENT FUND is better than BORROWING, for example. "Borrowing" could mean just about anything from hitting your neighbor up for some artificial sweetener to asking your colleague for a tranquilizer. "Borrowing from Your Retirement Fund," in contrast, relates directly to a retirement fund.

❖ Headings can be arranged in a hierarchy, from overviews to more specific subheads. These are indicated by size and type face. The more important the heading, the larger and bolder it will be. For example:

LEARNING ABOUT YOUR MEMBERSHIP

    Member Annual Statement

    Consultation Service

    Video Consultations

    Preretirement Planning Seminar

    Retirement Hotline Service

    Retirement Website

You can tell "LEARNING ABOUT YOUR MEMBERSHIP" is the key head because it is the largest, all capital letters, and bold face. You can tell that the other heads are important but to a lesser extent because they are bold-face but not all caps or 14-point type.

❖ Center the most important headings in the middle of the page. This tells your reader that they *are* the key headings.

❖ Each heading is usually followed one or more paragraphs of text. As you decide how much text to include under each heading, always focus on your subject and audience. With complex subjects and a general audience, use short paragraphs. With easier subjects and a more informed audience, you can make the paragraphs longer. Here's a model, based on a complex subject and general audience.

LEARNING ABOUT YOUR MEMBERSHIP

Member Annual Statement

A summary of your membership and projection of present and future benefits is mailed to your home each January. See pages 12-13.

Consultation Service

Individual meetings with System Information Representatives are available in locations throughout the country during the year. Consultation schedules are posted in your office each September.

Video Consultations

Call to set up a meeting with a System Information Representative via a computer-to-computer connection.

1-800-555-1234

Preretirement Planning Seminar

These day-long programs, for members age 45 and older, present general information on a variety of retirement-related topics. Schedules are posted in your building and on our website.

Retirement Hotline Service

Call our 24-hour toll-free number to request System forms and get up-to-date recorded messages with the latest benefit information.

1-800-555-1234

Retirement Website

Check out our services, schedules, and latest information at: **www.retirement.org**

Use Typefaces Effectively

Among other things, computer software has given us a dazzling array of *fonts*—different typefaces. There is everything from Albertus Extra Bold to Wingdings on the program I'm using right now.

Fonts come in different sizes, too, from itty-bitty to monster-sized. The shape of the letters also varies. *Fixed fonts* such as Courier assign a space to every letter. An *m* takes the same space as a *p*, for example. *Proportional fonts* such as Times New Roman have letters of different sizes. Some letters take up more or less space than others. In Times New Roman, for instance, the letters expand and contract to fill the allocated space.

Some fonts have extensions, called *serifs*. The little "foot" on the bottom of an "r" in Courier is an example of a serif. Fonts such as Geneva and Helvetica are called *sans serif* since they do not have these extensions.

This wide variety of fonts is a double-edged sword, however. On one hand, many fonts allow busy executives to create well-designed documents quickly and easily. On the other hand, too many typefaces allow people to produce cluttered and fussy documents that are difficult—if not impossible—to read. This isn't going to happen to you—not if you use the following guidelines:

❖   Select a standard font. The most commonly used fonts for business writing are Times Roman and Helvetica. Stay away from unusual fonts because they'll distract your reader from your message. Remember: You want the words to be the focus of your document, not the typeface itself.

❖   In general, use one font per document. More than one font creates a messy, hard-to-read document.

❖   Use san serif typefaces for titles and labels because they are crisp and easy to read.

❖ If you must use two different fonts in one document, choose one serif and one sans serif. Your reader will find it easier to distinguish between them.

❖ Create emphasis and level of headings by using bold, italics, and different sizes of the same font, as you learned earlier in this chapter.

❖ Boldface type is easier to read than italics. Use bold face if you need to emphasize only one element in the text.

❖ Avoid shadow or outline fonts in the text. They're hard to read, especially when they're small. You might want to use these fonts for posters, however.

❖ Use 10-12 point type for the text of a letter or other document. Anything smaller is difficult to read; anything larger is distracting in the body of the document, although larger type is ideal for heads.

❖ Avoid tiny type (anything under 8-point font). "Small print" has become a synonym for disreputable business practices—and with cause. It's too easy to bury important information in small print. Small print *can* help you fit in the material you feel you must include, but it will inevitably create ill-will for you and the company you represent.

Use White Space

Effective public speakers know that pauses count as much as words. In the same way, *white space*—the empty space on a page—counts as much as text. Judicious use of white space makes a document easier to read by highlighting the text. When used thoughtfully, white space separates and emphasizes key points.

How can you use white space effectively in your documents? Try these ideas:

❖ Mix short, medium, and long paragraphs. This makes a page more visually exciting.

❖ Provide sufficient white space around paragraphs, too. Figure one inch to one-and-a-half inches on all sides.

❖ Keep the first and last paragraphs short—between three and five lines. One-line paragraphs are fine, especially in the beginning and end of a document.

❖ Realize that effective design takes up space on a page. When you're short on space, it's better to trim the text and keep all the white space. Remember that your overall goal is to create goodwill and make the document easy to read. This enhances your credibility and your company's reputation.

Notice how the white space between the lines makes each item stand out in the previous list.

Use Lists

To help readers locate key elements, use indented lists, bullets, or numbers — just as you see on this page (and throughout this book in general). An effective way to highlight important material in business documents, lists work equally well for words, phrases, sentences, and even paragraphs.

In general, lists are aligned to the left margin, although they can be set in the middle of the page to make them really pop out of the document.

❖   Use bullets, as you see here, or numbers, depending on the way you decide to set off the items. Traditionally, bullets are used when the sequence of items doesn't matter; numbers when it does. Increasingly, however, the demands of page design take precedence over this guideline.

❖   All word processing programs have icons for bullets, but if you're baffled and bullet-less, just type a bullet the old-fashioned way. Type a lower-case o and fill it in with a pen or pencil. Skip three or four spaces between the o and the first letter of the word that follows.

❖   Whether you set off the items with bullets, numbers, or other dingbats (pre-made designs), make sure that all the items are in parallel form. Here's an example:

Not Parallel: You can accrue service credit by:
- *render* service as a member.
- *received* prior service credit.
- *to transfer* credit from another retirement system.
- *receiving* credit for service in the active military which interrupted your career.

Parallel: You can accrue service credit by:
- *rendering* service as a member.
- *receiving* prior service credit.
- *transferring* credit from another retirement system.
- *receiving* credit for service in the active military which interrupted your career.

❖   Also make sure the items fit with the *stem,* or part of the sentence that introduces the list. The stem in the above list is: "You can accrue service credit by."

Use Margins

Margins can be *justified* or *ragged.* Justified margins are evenly lined up; ragged margins are not. All documents are left-justified; that is, the left margin is even.

Computer software allows you to justify the right margin as well. As a result, the text will be even on both sides, as with a newspaper or magazine article. Justified margins have advantages and disadvantages, as this chart shows:

Justified Margins

Advantages	*Disadvantages*
allows 20% more text on page	can create big gaps in text
creates a polished look	adding or deleting a word affects the whole paragraph
	can be harder to read
	doesn't work as well with nonproportional typefaces
	looks odd with a short document or short paragraphs

Justify the right margin when you want the document to look more professional and polished. Justifying the right margin can also help you get more text on the page.

Arrange Information to Advantage

Since English is read from left to right, top to bottom, our eyes are accustomed to scanning the page in a very specific way, a "Z" pattern. As a result, different sections of the page create different visual impact. Here's how it breaks down:

Most Important
Part of the Page

Second Most
Important Part
of the Page

As a result . . .

- ❖   Place titles and other top elements in the top left part of the page.
- ❖   Place reply coupons and other important elements at the bottom right part of the page.

Use Visuals, Clip Art, and Color

Visuals, clip art, and color, like fonts, allow busy executives to create professional-looking documents with the flick of a finger. Today's desk-top publishing packages help people design and produce documents that it used to take a printer to assemble. But like the abundance of fonts, this wealth of clip art, color, and other add-ons can do more harm than good.

Visuals, especially charts and graphs, are a superb way to present a great deal of information in a condensed form. One picture *can* be worth a thousand words when it comes to getting your message across in a business document, but the visual must be clear and easy to understand to be effective. No visual is always better than a confusing one.

Used judiciously, visuals, clip art, color, and other design elements can help you communicate your message and build good-will. However, it's tempting to overdo it. Think of these elements as hot peppers—a little goes a long way in a dish. In a similar way, a few well-chosen design elements go a long way in a document.

Consider Cultural Expectations

When you plan a document, consider the variety of culturally sensitive issues. As you learned in Chapter 8, even an exclusively domestic business is dealing with people from a wide variety of backgrounds. What people consider esthetically pleasing is culturally linked.

Always consider your audience's needs and expectations. Show that you understand the purpose for the business communication and the context in which it takes place.

Here are some questions to ask yourself as you plan your document design:

- ❖   What are the design characteristics of books, magazines, and newspapers in the target culture?
- ❖   How are cartoons and graphics drawn?
- ❖   Which way is the text going to be read: left to right, right to left, or vertically? Sometimes it's both; classic examples are Arabic and Hebrew.

❖ Although 8.5 × 11 paper is standard in America, paper size does vary in other countries. When designing a page or instructing translators, consider this factor as well.

❖ Color considerations are sometimes complex; here are a few examples to think about:

Color	Country	Connotations
Red	China	prosperity, good fortune
Red	Ivory Coast	mourning
Red	Malaysia	strength
Blue	Ghana	joy/happiness
Blue	Hopi Indians	religious significance
Yellow	Malaysia	royalty
Yellow	America	caution

Use this information as you select ink and paper colors.

The Proof Is in the Pudding

How can you tell if your page layout is effective? One of the most effective ways to evaluate a document design is to run it by a test audience. Watch as your readers scan the document. Where do they pause? Where do they reread? Do they seem confused?

Have representatives from all possible segments of your audience read the document, especially if it is an important communication with wide-reaching ramifications.

Document design is key to the success of all written communication in a business environment. As a result, it's a factor to consider from the very beginning of the writing process, not something to play with when you're all done writing.

Always consider your audience and purpose as you design your documents. Add in the headings and subheadings as you draft, keeping your readers' needs in mind. Make visuals a part of your presentation.

Summary

❖ Use specific headings to direct the reader's eye.

❖ Use typefaces effectively. Select a standard font, use one font per document, and avoid tiny print.

❖ Use white space effectively.

❖   Use lists to help readers locate key elements.

❖   Use justified or ragged right margins, depending on your audience and purpose.

❖   Place key information in the top left quadrant and secondary information in the bottom right quadrant.

❖   Use visuals, clip art, and color judiciously.

❖   Consider cultural expectations when you design documents.

❖   Get feedback from test audiences.

Part 3
COMMONLY USED DOCUMENTS

Chapter 10

Letter Perfect (Resumés and Cover Letters)

Sharp executives know that the only certainty in the corporate world is uncertainty. As a result, it's always wise to have your resumé up-to-date. This chapter introduces the main types of resumés and helps you decide which format is best suited to your needs. Then you'll learn how to write a powerful cover letter to introduce your resumé—and you.

What's a Resumé and Why Do I Need One?

A *resumé* is a persuasive summary of your qualifications for employment. An effective resumé opens the door for an interview.

A resumé is always accompanied by a *cover letter*. A successful cover letter and resumé are tailored to suit the employer's needs and your qualifications as closely as possible. For that reason, many people have several different versions of their resumé, depending on the specific job for which they are applying.

Effective resumés and cover letters must be neat, accurate, free from any writing errors, and usually no more than one page long. If you do use more than one page, the second page should have at least 10 to 12 lines, or it will look skimpy. Let's start with the different formats available.

Types of Resumés

There are two basic types of resumés, the *work history resumé* and the *functional (skills) resumé*. The work history resumé is the traditional format, expected from executives with years of work experience. The functional resumé is more suited to a newcomer or someone changing fields. It also gives you more wiggle room to explain an unconventional work history. Here's each type of resumé in detail:

Work History Resumé

This type of resumé summarizes your accomplishments in reverse chronological order (starting with the most recent accomplishments and working backwards). It stresses academic degrees, job titles, and dates. Use a chronological resumé when …

❖ your education and experience are logical preparation for the job you want;

❖ you have an impressive education or job history.

Below is a model resumé for an executive with about twenty years of experience:

Christopher Hobart
321 Maple Street
Foster's Meadow, Illinois 66217
phone: (312) 555-9876   fax: (312) 555-4321   e-mail: CHobart1234@aol.com

Work Experience

Multi-National Publishers   1994-present Vice President - Manufacturing

Multi-National Publishers produces 12 four-color monthly magazines, along with 10 trade paperback collections annually, a variety of custom publications for government, and a variety of catalogues and promotional materials.
- supervised purchasing and manufacturing departments
- negotiated contract terms with major suppliers
- approved all purchasing and print runs
- determined or approved specifications for all custom publications

One Nation Publishing   1988–1993   Director of Manufacturing
- managed department through major expansion of line
- introduced computerized scheduling system
- cut production costs by 33% in each of first three years

Big City Publishing   1985–1988   Production Manager
                         1981–1985   Assistant Production Manager

Related Activities

U.S. Manufacturing Alliance 1998   Keynote Speaker
- Topic: "Publishing in the World of Tomorrow"

World Publishers Conference 1997   Speaker
- Topic: "Buy It Now or Don't Buy It At All!"

Publisher World Profiles   1995   Profiled
- Named one of "Publishing's Top Ten Buyers"

Education

VanderClef University   1981   MBA Manufacturing
Harston University   1980   BA Communications, Cum Laude

The following job seeker is a manager with ten year's experience:

Gloria Ramirez
2468 East 17th Street—Apt. 2B
Baltimore, Maryland 21205
phone: (410) 555-1234   fax: (410) 555-6789   e-mail: GloRamirez@juno.com

Employment Experience

Aero-Mobile Services   1996-present   Manager–Accounts Receivable

Aero-Mobile is a major provider of limousine services for Fortune 500 Companies executives, with billings of over $3 million annually

❖ supervised Accounts Receivable Department of twelve employees

❖ coordinated transition of systems to 100% computerized billing

❖ was responsible for collecting over 65% of delinquent accounts

Gerber's Glove Company 1992–1996   Assistant Manager
                                                                Accounts Payable

❖ assisted Manager in installing computerized billing system

❖ responsible for managing payables to all suppliers

Turner Tops Kitchens   1989–1992   Accounts Payable Clerk

Mary B's Fine Clothes   1986–1989   Bookkeeper

Education

Waldorf Business School   1992   MBA Accounting

❖ Graduated in top 10% of class

Cornwall University   1989   BBA Public Accounting
                                                             High Honors

❖ named to "Who's Who Among Business Majors—1988"

❖ co-president, Cornwall School of Business Honor Society

❖ editor of Accounting Honor Society newsletter

References

Upon request

Functional (Skills) Resumé

This type of resumé emphasizes your skills. Use this format when ...

❖   your education and experience are not the usual preparation for the job you want;

❖   you lack an impressive education or job history;

❖   arranging your recent work history in reverse chronological order would create the wrong impression (perhaps because you have been demoted, fired, or hopped from job to job).

Recently, an executive recruiter (a "headhunter") invited me to interview for the position of Vice-President of Educational Services for a world-class provider of supplemental education. The position called for a strategist to oversee more than 500 learning centers, design and develop course offerings, create and manage partner relationships, and integrate curriculum and technology.

The executive placement recruiter and I decided to present my qualifications in the resumé format shown on pages 105-107 because I had an impressive background in education and curriculum development but virtually no management skills.

Notice that this resumé is three pages long. This is expected with a job in the six figures and an applicant with more than 20 years' experience in the field.

As you can see from these models, whether you select the *work history resumé* or the *functional (skills) resumé,* all resumés include the following information:

❖   *Heading* (name, address, telephone number, e-mail address, if you have one)

❖   *Education* (college, university, additional training and course work)

❖   *Experience* (positions held, including titles, responsibilities, and length of service. Try to include only relevant experience, the jobs that will convince the prospective employer that you will be an asset to the company.)

❖   *Extras* (Possibilities include military service, computer skills, foreign languages, honors and achievements, references, etc.)

If you are just starting out, it is expected that you will also include a *Career Objective* line to zero in on the position you want. Think of this as a "position wanted" ad for yourself. It's placed right after the heading. For an executive moving up, however, the career objective is usually omitted, since it is obvious where you're trying to go.

Laurie Rozakis, Ph.D.
123 Main Street
Anytown, USA 11550

phone: (555) 555-5555   fax: (555) 555-5551   email: Rozakile@aol.com

Teaching Experience

The Johns Hopkins University Institute for the Academic Advancement of Youth (IAAY)	1993–present	*Summer writing instructor* • created the young students' writing program, *Writing and the Imagination* • designed and developed individualized curricula
The State University of N.Y. at Farmingdale	1986–present	*Associate Professor of English* Chancellor's Award for Excellence in Teaching • instruct students in English, Language Arts • tutor students in the learning center • developed the University's *Writer's Guidebook*
Hofstra University	1979–1986	*Adjunct Assistant Professor of English*
Commack UFSD #10	1973–1984	*English/Writing Teacher,* Grades 9–12 • trained student teachers • analyzed and purchased curricula • negotiated text purchases
Private tutoring	1973–present	• evaluate and teach ESL students, at-risk learners, learning-disabled children, and gifted students. • design personalized SAT, ACT study programs • boost students' self-esteem through individualized study skills classes • create diagnostic assessment vehicles for personalized learning

Education

SUNY Stony Brook	Ph.D.	1984	American and British Literature; Writing Degree awarded with highest honors
Hofstra University	MA	1975	American and British Literature; Writing
Hofstra University	BA	1973	English/Secondary Education/ Summa Cum Laude Degree earned in 3 years/Full merit scholarship NY State Teaching Certificate, English, grades 7–12

Publishing and Curriculum Development

As a recognized expert in reading, language arts, and math curricula, I have been writing materials for educational publishers since 1980. I am especially well respected as a writer of elementary materials that target remedial learners. I have also created authoritative secondary curriculum materials, standard testing and assessment packages, successful remedial education workbooks, challenging materials for gifted and talented education, and useful ESL features. I have developed, created, and edited more than 100 books; nearly 50 are carried on-line by Amazon.com. Here is a representative sampling of my recent work:

Elementary Curriculum Materials

Addison-Wesley/Scott Foresman

❖ analyzed existing text, ancillary materials, and assessment packets and developed over 20 units of teacher and student material for *Addison-Wesley Quest 2000* math program

❖ created materials for classroom and learning center use and designed testing materials for *AW Science*

Harcourt, Brace and Company

❖ wrote 30 phonics lessons (games, puzzles, and cooperative learning exercises) for Harcourt *Spelling*

❖ integrated traditional techniques with contemporary approaches to create more than 25 lessons, including testing apparatus, for Harcourt *Reading*

Secondary Curriculum Materials

Macmillan/Mc-Graw Hill

❖ wrote prototype lessons for the entire text and produced more than 10 units of lessons for *Writer's Choice*

❖ created 20 core lessons and assessment material for *Effective Speech*

Prentice Hall

❖ created literature lessons, grammar and spelling lessons, testing material, and novel study guides for *Prentice-Hall Literature* (grades 6–12)

Testing and Assessment

Barron's Educational Publishers

❖ revised the *English Composition CLEP* exam workbook

❖ created the English review section for the Barron's review text on the *National Teacher's Exam*

Educational Testing Service

❖ scored AP English exams since 1987; invited to score SAT and GMAT exams on-line

Macmillan

❖ wrote *The Advanced Placement Exam in English.* In print for more than 15 years, the book sparked Macmillan's entire AP exam line.

❖ wrote *The Verbal Workbook for the ACT*

❖ wrote *The College Writing Placement and Proficiency Examination* workbook

Management Experience

Farmingdale Library Board of Trustees

In 1984, I was elected to the Farmingdale Library Board of Trustees, part of a five-member board. I was reelected in 1989 and again in 1994. We currently have 62 employees.

❖ I am directly responsible for the construction of one of the largest public libraries in Nassau County, Long Island, New York. As Board President from 1990 to 1994, I initiated the $8.8 million bond issue, campaigned for its passage, and then supervised the construction of the new building.

❖ I then supervised the sale of our two previous buildings, interfaced with town officials, prospective buyers, and financing corporations

❖ As Chair of the Budget Committee, I prepare our annual $2.4 million budget. I decide how much money to allocate for books, videos, electronic media, periodicals, travel, computers, furniture, repairs, salaries, and employee benefits.

Advertisements for Myself

Your resumé is a type of persuasive writing, since you're trying to convince the human resources department to pass you up the ladder, to grant you an interview, to get your foot in the door. A resumé is an advertisement for yourself, so don't sell yourself short. Be sure to put yourself in the best possible light by describing all your relevant strengths. Modesty is indeed a virtue, but not when it comes to resumé writing.

As you write your resumé, emphasize the things you've done that are most relevant to the position for which you're applying and show how you're superior to other candidates. Be realistic, use the layout to emphasize key points, and relate your experience to the job you want. Here are some additional guidelines:

1. *Be truthful.* You're expected to put your accomplishments in the best possible light, but *always* tell the truth. Background checks are a hot topic in personnel circles today. Experts say a decade of litigation has nervous employers turning more and more to professional background checkers, who report that caseloads are growing at 30 percent a year. Investigators find discrepancies or outright lies in about one-third of the resumés they check.

2. *Be concise.* As a rule of thumb, resumés reflecting five years or less experience should fit on one page. More extensive experience can justify usage of a second page. Consider three pages (about 15 years or more experience) an absolute limit. Avoid lengthy descriptions of whole projects of which you were only a part.

3. *Be strong.* You're an executive, a recognized leader, so show it with your language by beginning sentences with action verbs. This helps you portray yourself as someone who is active, smart, and efficient. Stuck for a verb? Here's a list of active verbs to enhance your resumé.

   A

achieved	acquired	adapted	added
administered	advanced	advertised	aided
advised	advocated	arranged	assigned
analyzed	answered	anticipated	assembled
appointed	appraised	attracted	attained
approved	arbitrated	assessed	assisted
audited	augmented	authored	addressed
authorized	automated	awarded	allocated

   B

balanced	bargained	bought
broadened	budgeted	built

C

calculated	capitalized	commissioned	created
cataloged	centralized	combined	chaired
changed	charted	counseled	conducted
co-authored	collaborated	compared	contracted
corresponded	coordinated	computed	consulted
constructed	contributed	controlled	compiled

D

debugged	defined	delivered	drafted
demonstrated	designated	designed	doubled
determined	developed	devised	directed
diagrammed	distributed	discovered	divested
dispatched	displayed	diversified	documented

E

earned	edited	effected	extended
elected	employed	encouraged	explained
enforced	engineered	enhanced	expedited
enlarged	enriched	established	expanded
estimated	evaluated	examined	exceeded

F

facilitated	familiarized	financed	fulfilled
forecasted	formalized	formed	framed

G

gained	gathered	gauged	guided
generated	governed	graded	granted

H

handled	headed	hired	hosted

I

identified	illustrated	implemented	issued
improved	increased	incurred	involved
influenced	informed	initiated	insured
inspected	inspired	installed	invested
instituted	instructed	investigated	invented
interfaced	interpreted	interviewed	introduced

J

joined	judged

L

launched	led	litigated
lobbied	located	

M

maintained	managed	mapped	monitored
marketed	maximized	mediated	motivated
met	minimized	modernized	multiplied

N

named	negotiated

O

obtained	offered	offset	oversaw
opened	operated	ordered	overhauled

P

paid	participated	passed	purchased
pinpointed	pioneered	planned	published
prepared	presented	preserved	provided
printed	probed	processed	proved
produced	profiled	programmed	publicized

R

raised	ranked	rated	routed
received	recommended	reconciled	reviewed
recovered	recruited	rectified	refined
redesigned	reduced	remodeled	replaced
regulated	reinstated	revitalized	reversed
renegotiated	reorganized	revised	revamped
repaired	represented	researched	restored
restructured	resolved		

S

safeguarded	scheduled	screened	surveyed
secured	selected	shaped	surpassed
simplified	sold	solved	supported
spearheaded	specified	stabilized	supplied
staffed	standardized	steered	supervised
streamlined	strengthened	structured	studied

T

targeted	taught	tested	tripled
traded	trained	transformed	traveled
translated	transported		

U

uncovered	undertook	unified
united	updated	upgraded

V

validated	valued	verified

W

weighed	won	wrote

4.   *Be ruthless.* I know you want to give an exhaustive picture of your life and experiences, but this is the time to pay close attention to what you do and do not include. If a job, talent, or skill doesn't directly relate to the position you're seeking, leave it off your resumé. Here's a list of irrelevant information:

   ❖ social security number

   ❖ marital status

   ❖ health status

   ❖ citizenship

   ❖ age

   ❖ irrelevant awards

   ❖ irrelevant associations and memberships

   ❖ irrelevant publications

   ❖ irrelevant recreational activities

   ❖ a second mailing address ("permanent address" is confusing and never used)

   ❖ previous pay rates (they'll make an offer if they're interested)

   ❖ reasons for leaving previous jobs

   ❖ parts of your name which you really never use (i.e., middle name)

   Some information is actually forbidden by law, so it doesn't rate a place on your resumé either. Below are some items forbidden by law:

   ❖ your age

   ❖ marital status

   ❖ race

   ❖ sex

   ❖ health (any medical conditions)

   If you include any of this information, large companies will delete it from your resumé so they cannot be accused of discriminating. Include height information only if the job has a minimum height requirement (such as the police department).

5. *Be careful.* Have a trusted friend review your resumé. Be sure to pick someone who is attentive to details, can effectively critique your writing, and will give an honest and objective opinion. Seriously consider their advice. Get a third and fourth opinion if you can.

    Proofread, proofread, proofread. Be sure to catch all spelling errors, grammatical weaknesses, unusual punctuation, and inconsistent capitalization. Proofread your resumé numerous times over at least two days to allow a fresh eye to catch any hidden mistakes.

6. *Be professional.* When it comes to job seeking, appearance is often reality. Make your resumé look as good as you are, so laser print it on plain, white paper. Typing, dot matrix printing, and even ink jet printing look pretty cheesy.

The Cover Letter

Once your resumé has been assembled, laid out, and printed to your satisfaction, it's time to write your cover letter. Though there may be instances where you deliver your resumé in person, most often you will be sending it through snail mail, and increasingly, through E-mail. Resumés sent through the mail (conventional or electronic) *always* need an accompanying letter that briefly introduces you and your resumé. It's never a bad idea to include a cover letter if you deliver your resumé in person, too.

Your cover letter is designed to get a potential employer to read your resumé, just as the purpose of your resumé is to get that same potential employer to call you for an interview. So don't attempt to tell your life story in the cover letter. Instead, highlight your major accomplishments—the ones that make you best suited for the job—and convey a sense of your personality.

Cover Letters versus Resumés

Although a resumé and a cover letter do overlap in certain areas, there are three crucial differences:

❖   A *cover letter* is adapted to the needs of a particular organization; a *resumé* is usually adapted to a position.

❖   A *cover letter* shows how your qualifications can help the organization meet its needs; a *resumé* summarizes all your relevant qualifications.

❖   A *cover letter* uses complete sentences and paragraphs; a *resumé* uses short phrases.

How to Write a Winning Cover Letter

Here's your basic carved-in-granite rule: *Never, never, never* use a form letter for your cover letter. Each cover letter must be as personal as possible. If you can substitute another inside address and salutation and send out the letter without any further changes, it isn't specific enough.

Of course, once you have written your first great cover letter, you certainly can use similar wording in subsequent letters.

Like your resumé, your cover letter should be clean, neat, and direct. A cover letter usually includes the following information:

❖ Your name and address (unless it already appears on your personal letterhead)

❖ The date

❖ The name and address of the person and company to whom you are sending your resumé

❖ The salutation ("Dear Mr." or "Dear Ms." followed by the person's last name, or "To Whom it May Concern" if you are answering a blind ad.)

❖ An opening paragraph explaining why you are writing (in response to an ad, the result of a previous meeting, at the suggestion of someone you both know) and indicating that you are interested in whatever job is being offered.

❖ One or two more paragraphs that explain why you want to work for the company and what qualifications and experience you can bring to that company. Include facts and examples that show how you can do the job, details that show your knowledge of the company, and qualities that employers seek: the ability to read and write well, think critically, speak effectively, and get along with others.

❖ A final paragraph that closes the letter and requests that you be contacted for an interview.

❖ The closing, "Sincerely," or "Yours truly," followed by your signature with your name typed under it. (Notice that only the first letter of the close is capitalized.)

Get all this information in one page. Use a polite, professional, and concise style.

Get the Scoop!

Try these suggestions to create more effective cover letters:

❖ Send letters to individuals, not just to companies or departments. Call the company and find out the name and title of the person to whom to address your letter. Addressing a letter to an individual shows initiative and resourcefulness. It also helps make sure your letter lands on the right desk.

❖   While we're on this theme, whenever possible, target your letters to department heads and hiring managers. Your goal is to get your letter to the person who actually does the hiring and for whom you would be working.

❖   If you've been referred by someone, make the most of your connection. Name the person who referred you in your opening sentence. The name will grab your reader's attention, and your letter and resume will get more careful consideration. Of course, always make sure that the tip is a good one, not someone just indicted for fraud, insider trading, or cross-dressing. And be sure to get prior permission from the person to mention his or her name.

❖   Focus on your readers' needs, not yours. Make your qualifications clear and emphasize how you can use them to help their organization.

❖   When describing your qualifications, don't quote from your resume. Instead, include examples from your work experience that demonstrate your skills.

Last Licks

1.   Take the time to know the company or organization you're contacting.

2.   Know what you have to offer. Analyze your strengths and weaknesses.

3.   Be prepared to show the employer that you can do the job—and do it well.

4.   Target your letter to an individual rather than a position.

5.   Spend the time getting it right. You have no chance of getting an interview if your letter contains errors.

Here's a sample cover letter:

72-12 Ashford Avenue
San Diego, CA 23456

February 28, 1999

Ms. Tracey Algieri
Purchasing Director
1234 Big Building
Los Angeles, CA 34981

Dear Ms. Algieri:

I am writing in response to your advertisement for a Production Manager which appeared in the *LA Times* on Sunday, February 28, 1999. After speaking with your assistant, Justin Tyme, I decided to fax my resumé to you. As it shows, my experience and background very closely match the requirements for this position.

I have been working for the past three years as Assistant Production Manager at Computer One, the world's leading computer magazine publisher. Recently the decision was made, however, to close the department and have individual departments absorb its functions. As a result, I am looking for an opportunity that could take full advantage of my abilities.

I have been responsible for overseeing the purchasing and printing of over $1 million annually of marketing, advertising, and promotional materials. I have been working closely with the marketing departments of many of Computer One's publications simultaneously, to ensure their print production needs are met. To this end, I maintain constant contact with a wide variety of vendors to establish deadlines and ensure cost estimates are met. I am familiar with multicolor printing techniques, often being responsible for on-site press approvals. Additionally, I am at home in a Macintosh computer environment, proficient in Microsoft Word, Excel, Lotus Notes, and knowledgeable in QuarkXPress and Illustrator. I have top-notch interpersonal skills and am able to manage a variety of projects and tasks at once. I am open-minded and flexible.

I look forward to meeting with you to discuss the position as Production Manager. I can be reached during the day at 555-555-555, or evenings at 555-555-1234.

Sincerely,

Smart Executive

Smart Executive

Thank-You Notes

You should always write a business thank-you letter when you've ...

❖ had a phone conversation with someone at the company about an actual job opening or any matter relating to employment.

❖ been granted an informational interview.

❖ had an actual job interview.

❖ been offered a job and declined it.

In the highly competitive upper end of the job market, many employers expect applicants to be more aggressive. Following up after an interview can give you the winning edge. In this situation, a "thank-you letter" really functions as a follow-up. The letter should remind the interviewer:

❖ who you are

❖ what position you want

❖ your outstanding qualifications

❖ what he or she liked in you

❖ what new information you learned about the company during the interview

Also use the thank-you letter as a chance to counter any negative impressions that came up during the interview. Be very sure that letter is well-written and completely free of errors.

Summary

❖ A *resumé* is a persuasive summary of your qualifications for employment. An effective resumé opens the door for an interview.

❖ A *work history* resumé summarizes your accomplishments in reverse chronological order (starting with the most recent and working backwards). It stresses degrees, job titles, and dates.

❖ A *functional (skills) resumé* emphasizes your skills.

❖ All resumés include a heading, education, experience.

❖ Send a thank-you letter when you've had a phone conversation with someone at the company about an actual job opening, have been granted an interview, or have been offered a job and declined it.

Chapter 11

Persuasive Messages: Performance Appraisals and Letters of Recommendation

The business of business is selling—and whatever you're selling, your pitch will be most effective when it is based on logic, credibility, and trust. You can achieve these goals in a variety of ways. That's what you'll learn in this chapter.

See It My Way: Persuasive Messages

Here are the Big Three: *logic, credibility,* and *trust. Logic* comes from the strength of your argument. Sometimes you'll have strong, logical arguments; other times, however, the obstacles may be very difficult to overcome.

Credibility is how the audience responds to you. People are more likely to be convinced by someone they see as powerful, expert, or attractive. Credibility builds *trust,* which makes it easier to persuade your audience. How can you build credibility and trust? Try these ideas:

- ❖ *Be specific.* If you claim one product is better than another, provide facts, details, and examples to prove it. Give the reader something specific to chew on.

- ❖ *Tell the truth.* Don't exaggerate or put yourself in the position of being called, "Liar, liar, pants on fire."

- ❖ *Deal straight.* If something isn't what you expect it to be, get it out in the open. Once you violate a client's or colleague's trust, it's almost impossible to win it back.

But remember that people don't make decisions based on logic alone. Were that the case, we couldn't explain love in general and some of the odder couplings in particular that we see around us. *Emotional factors* can be every bit as persuasive as logical ones. People react to the emotional overtones of a persuasive appeal, the feelings it generates.

Now, let's turn to the two most effective persuasive appeals, the *direct request pattern* and the *problem-solving pattern.*

When the Audience *Is* on Your Side ...

When you expect your audience to agree with your appeal, use the *direct request pattern* to organize your ideas. With this approach, you ...

1. *Make your request up front.* You can delay the message briefly if you don't want to seem too abrupt, but usually you can plunge right in. After all, the audience is on your side.

2. *Provide all necessary information.* For example, if the customer claims that a package wasn't delivered on a specific date, cite the day the package was mailed, the method of shipping, and the proof that it was indeed received (the signature).

3. *Make your request clear.* You're trying to persuade your readers to take action—*what* action? Specify whether they should return the item for a refund, send a check, respond by a specific date, attend a meeting, complete a proxy form, and so on. There's no reason to be coy or make the reader play 20 Questions.

Here's a direct request letter I received about working with disadvantaged children. The writer, a millionaire businessman, had carefully analyzed his audience—me!—and knew that I would be very likely to agree to his request. Since I wouldn't be hard to persuade, he decided to use the direct request pattern. Notice that his request is in the very first paragraph.

RGE Inc.
1234 Business Quadrangle
Big City, Nice State 76283

October 4, 1997

Dear Dr. Rozakis:

Request made up front

In September, I enjoyed reading an article about your publishing career in *The New York Times.* I'm sure your "wonderful light touch" and "high energy" have contributed to your success and your demanding life as a writer, professor, wife, and mom. I am sending this letter to ask if you would like to share your life experiences and great sense of humor with a group of children from disadvantaged backgrounds who participate in a program with which I am involved.

The name of the program is "I Have a Dream." I am the sponsor of the Big City chapter of this national program. We work with at-risk students in the Big City school district. In 1992, I made a commitment to forty-six

Necessary information

"Dreamers" (at-risk students) by offering them financial, emotional, and educational support to stay in school and attend college or vocational school. We provide mentoring, tutoring, curriculum enrichment, and a host of other social and recreational programs to help achieve our goals. This goal is to have children "drop in" on society rather than "drop out."

We are always on the lookout for role models to provide children with positive values to stand in counterpoint to the many negative influences in their lives. I am sure, Dr. Rozakis, that our children would delight in meeting you and perhaps discussing a few of the books you have written. We would be delighted if you were able to find the time to come and meet the Dreamers and visit with the IHAD program.

I have enclosed a recent article from the local newspaper to give you some additional background information about the program.

> Request
> made
> clear

I would be happy to speak to you in greater detail about IHAD. I hope you can find the time to meet with the youngsters.

Sincerely,

Jeffrey Smith

Jeffrey Smith

JS/cg

Enclosures

When the Audience *Isn't* on Your Side ...

What happens when your request is likely to be met with resistance? In these instances, the direct request pattern is likely to fall as flat as some of my cakes. When you expect audience resistance, use the *problem-solving pattern*. This format allows you to disarm opposition by piling on good reasons before your reader can say "No." Here's how it works:

1. *Start on common ground.* From the very beginning, show that your request will help the reader. If you're feeling especially optimistic, start with a negative point—that you'll later show is really a positive side.

2. *Define the shared problem.* This is the situation your request will solve. Always be straightforward; don't assign blame or drag in personalities. It's important to convince your readers that action must be taken before you can persuade them that you have the best solution.

3. *Show why other solutions aren't valid.* Without using the words *I* or *me*, show why other solutions aren't valid. You can't bring in your solution before you sweep away the others.

4. *Describe your solution.* Now bring in your solution, summarizing the primary and secondary benefits. As you argue your point, show that any negatives are outweighed by positives. While you're concentrating on the key benefit, don't neglect minor advantages as well.

5. *Make your request.* Now that you've made your case, make your request. Don't be shy about stating what action you want your reader to take; unless your point is clear, your reader won't be able to act as you wish.

6. *Proofread.* Make sure you're saying what you think you're saying. The following absurd persuasive subject lines appeared on various letters, memos, and appeals:

    ❖ Safety Experts Say School Bus Passengers Should Be Belted

    ❖ Include Your Children when Baking Cookies

    ❖ If Strike Isn't Settled Quickly, It May Last a While

    ❖ New Vaccine May Contain Rabies

    ❖ Cold Wave Linked to Temperatures

    ❖ Red Tape Holds Up New Bridges

    ❖ Astronaut Takes Blame for Gas in Spacecraft

    ❖ Kids Make Nutritious Snacks

Here's a model memo that uses the *problem-solving pattern* to persuade readers. It addresses the issue of the increasing informality among many employees, shown by a more relaxed dress code.

August 22, 1999

To: Senior Staff

From: S.L. Minton

Re: Dress-Down Fridays

Allowing employees to dress comfortably is a very important element in creating a productive work environment. Our employees enjoy being able to "dress down" on Fridays by wearing casual clothing. Recently, however, a number of employees have extended the "dress down" privilege to the entire work week.

> Common ground

> Shared problem

We need to maintain a professional atmosphere because clients and potential clients visit the office daily. Last week, for example, the CFO of Mongo Bank stopped by for a meeting and noticed two middle-managers wearing shorts, sandals, and T-shirts. Naturally, the CFO was perturbed at the casual tone and wanted to know "What kind of outfit we were running here?" Inappropriately dressed employees damage the professional, business-like atmosphere we strive to create. They erode customer confidence and may cost us business, as well.

> Eliminate other solutions

Since "dress down" Friday has extended to include the entire week, it is impractical to continue this program. Starting Monday, August 25, all employees will dress in a professional manner at all times. Shorts, T-shirts, sandals, and other beach wear will no longer be consider appropriate business attire.

> Your solution

Please help us maintain our reputation as a respected supplier of top-notch financial services by dressing in a business-like, appropriate manner when you are in the office.

> Your request

Performance Appraisals

As an executive, you're no doubt called upon to evaluate or appraise your subordinates' performance. In most companies, employees have access to their files; usually, they must sign the appraisal to show that they've read it.

When you write an appraisal, you're automatically thrust into a delicate situation, because this type of persuasive writing must motivate the employee to work harder and still protect the company. It's a double-edged sword because praise that doesn't succeed in motivating the employee can backfire if the employee doesn't improve. A company can get into serious legal trouble if it tries to fire someone whose evaluations never mention the employee's mistakes. The executive who wrote the appraisal can get sucked right into the legal mess.

To protect yourself and the company, focus on specific observations, not inferences. For example:

Inference: Rick has a problem with punctuality.

Observation: On March 12, Rick was 30 minutes late to the regularly scheduled Thursday morning department head meeting. On April 5, Rick was 45 minutes late to the announced Quality Teams meeting.

To avoid problems with poor writing, many companies use a preprinted Performance Review form. The sample printed below has been compiled from samples gathered from several large and small companies. It leaves room for executives' comments but carefully sets forth the categories to be evaluated.

PERFORMANCE REVIEW

Employee Name _____

Employee's Present Rank and Title _____

Date _____

Manager/Supervisor's Name _____

Instructions: Rank the employee in each category according to the following scale. Include relevant supporting detail.

   1 = unsatisfactory

   2 = needs improvement

   3 = competent

   4 = exceeds responsibilities

   5 = outstanding

Performance Standards	**Ranking and Details**

1. *Job Skills*

applies skills appropriately _____

understands tasks _____

understands role within company _____

continues training _____

takes initiative _____

2. *Oral Communication Skills*

verbal expression clear _____

listens well _____

solicits responses _____

3. *Written Communication Skills*

written expression clear

writes concisely and clearly _____

4. *Interpersonal Skills*

interfaces well with others _____

effective team member _____

promotes open communication_____

manages diversity _____

5. *Leadership Skills*

inspires teamwork_____

positive role model _____

confident _____

encourages idealism_____

resolves conflicts well _____

6. *Ability to Make Decisions*

analyzes and evaluates choices_____

makes and implements decisions_____

accepts responsibility _____

7. *Ability to Solve Problems*

identifies problems _____

analyzes solutions_____

chooses best course of action _____

seizes opportunities _____

8. *Organizational Skills*

staff selection skills _____

policy management ability _____

evaluation skills_____

delegates responsibility _____

budget planning_____

expense control _____

maintains deadlines _____

achieves goals _____

9. *Planning Skills*

implements change _____

establishes priorities _____

coordinates resources _____

sets schedules _____

maintains schedules_____

manages time well _____

10. *Creativity*

innovative thinking _____

original concepts _____

fresh approaches _____

Overall Performance Rating _____

Summary

1. Strengths

   _____

   _____

   _____

2. Areas for Improvement

   _____

   _____

   _____

3. Personal Growth and Development

   _____

   _____

   _____

4. Next Year's Goals

   _____

   _____

   _____

Employee Response (Attach additional pages, if necessary)

   _____

   _____

   _____

Employee's Signature   Date

_____   _____

Supervisor's Signature   Date

_____   _____

Letters of Recommendation

Like a performance review, a letter of recommendation must be specific if it is going to be persuasive. An effective letter of recommendation can often clinch the deal for a promotion, raise, or new position.

However, as a result of today's litigious society, some companies now refuse to write letters of recommendation. Instead, they will only state how long they employed someone and in what capacity.

If you do write a letter of recommendation, begin by summarizing the person's qualifications. Follow this with specific details about the person's performance. Conclude with your overall recommendation and additional words of praise.

Should you include negative comments? Some people feel that negative comments weaken the letter and open the corporation to lawsuits. Other companies, in contrast, feel that a few honest negatives make the praise more convincing. It's your call. In any event, understand that the phrase, "Call me if you need more information" is often a code for "I have negative comments that I'm not willing to put in writing. Call me and I'll give you the *complete* picture."

Here's an excerpt from a letter written on behalf of a teacher seeking promotion.

. . .

From the very beginning of her tenure at Harston University, Dr. Fortunato has enjoyed a reputation as an exceptional instructor. Indeed, a former chairperson stated that she was one of the two best instructors in our department—at a time when it numbered thirty members. A perusal of Dr. Fortunato's observations show that the chairperson's assessment was a very astute one.

What Dr. Fortunato brings to the classroom is a deep concern for her students, unflagging vitality, and innovative techniques. She has the rare ability to make each student feel that he or she is the instructor's prime focus. I should note that much of this praise comes from students in two very difficult courses to teach— English 097 and English 101, courses which Dr. Fortunato has personally made her own. In addition, she has taught literature, electives, and technology courses.

As chair, I can attest to the fact that Dr. Fortunato has helped a number of students in critical situations. In fact, one of Dr. Fortunato's students made it a point to find me and tell me how important Dr. Fortunato had been to the student's remaining in college. Last, Dr. Fortunato has earned the recognition of the university by winning the prestigious Chancellor's Award for Excellence in Teaching . . .

Summary

❖ Build logic, trust, and credibility in all your persuasive appeals.

❖ When you expect your audience to agree with your appeal, use the *direct request pattern* to organize your ideas.

❖ When the audience *isn't* on your side, use the *problem-solving pattern*.

❖ When you write performance appraisals and letters of recommendation, focus on specific observations, not inferences.

Chapter 12

Persuasive Messages: Flyers, Brochures, Press Releases

In this chapter, you'll learn how to design flyers, brochures, and press releases that convey logic, credibility, and trust.

Planning a Flyer

Flyers are an effective and low-cost way to announce an event, from a conference to a workshop. You can use flyers to recruit volunteers, raise awareness about an issue, or advertise a new product or service. *Brochures* serve the same purpose, but are larger and thus cost more. The option you select depends on your audience, purpose, and budget. Let's look at each choice in more detail, starting with the economical alternative, flyers.

What's a Flyer?

Flyers are one-page announcements or advertisements. Flyers can come in all shapes and sizes, but because cost is usually the primary factor, most flyers are printed on $8^1/_2 \times 11$-inch paper, on one side only. There are two ways to arrange the text: *portrait* and *landscape*.

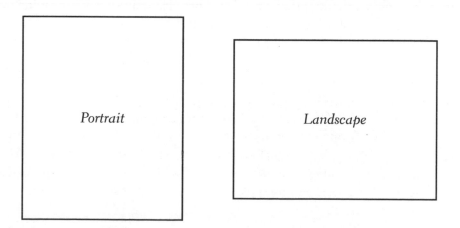

Portrait

Landscape

Whether you print the text vertically or horizontally, flyers follow this format:

Visuals	One picture is worth a thousand words, especially when it comes to flyers. With the advent of low-cost computer graphics, it's easy to add clip art that conveys your theme and helps draw attention to the text. Be sure the composition is visually balanced. None of the elements should overpower the page and prevent the audience from reading the text and getting the message.
Head	In bold, large type (at least one-half inch to one-inch high), announce the topic. The head can be in the form of a question or a statement.
Subheads	Boldface the key subheads so they stand out on the page.
Text	Your audience should be able to read the text very quickly, in less than a minute. Arrange the text in small chunks, using bullets to dramatize the main points. Keep it simple; don't clutter the page with too much text.
Foot	Conclude with a final statement to remind readers that the issue is urgent.

As with many types of business writing, much of the impact your flyer will have will depend on its design. The effect depends not only on the text and tone, but also on graphics and color.

Always keep your audience in mind. For example, the flip phrasing, bright colors, and cartoon drawings ideally suited to a flyer for a corporate day care center would be a flop in a flyer announcing a bank opening.

Come Flyer with Me

Consider these suggestions as you plan a flyer:

- ❖ Flyers are usually posted on bulletin boards. As a result, the heading must be easily read from a distance of five to ten feet. You may even want the type to be large enough so people can read it from a passing car.

- ❖ Use a simple font. Ornate fonts like this, *this*, or **this** are too hard to read from a distance.

- ❖ Be sure the design is appropriate to the organization and topic. A crisp, clean, high-tech look with a bold border might be ideal for an up-and-coming software retailer, but not for a financial investment company.

- ❖ Be sure the graphic matches the theme. Be very obvious. Remember, people are reading your flyer quickly. A flowering branch works for a series of seminars on spring planting, but does not suggest a spring sale of mattresses.

❖ Keep the words to a minimum. Rely on action verbs and lists.

❖ Remember that a flyer is a type of persuasive writing, so make sure the text of your document convinces people to take the action you're advertising: attend the event, buy the product, use the service, and so on.

Here's a sample flyer:

WILL YOU BE READY FOR RETIREMENT?

Did you know ...

❖ Nearly 50% of all Americans ages 30–49 say they won't be prepared for retirement.

❖ Half of all households have less than $1,000 in net financial assets.

Find out how you can make sure *you* have the money you need to retire comfortably. Speak with registered financial advisors—*free*.

Retirement Information Forum

Sponsored by Big Bank and Global Investors' Services

Monday, June 3

7:30–9:00 PM

Yalta Hotel, Roosevelt Room

Hear speakers on these issues:

❖ Asset Allocation Funds
❖ IRA, SEP, and Keogh Plans
❖ Ginnie Mae Certificates
❖ U.S. Treasury Bills and Treasury Bonds
❖ Variable Annuities

Talk with financial planners.
Learn what you need to know for your future.

Remember: The Rich Are Made, Not Born!

Planning a Brochure

Like flyers, brochures employ a type of persuasive writing that relies on design as much as text to move a reader to action or belief. Because brochures are longer than flyers, however, you have more room to get your message across, and more choices to make. In addition to content, your choices involve three other factors: number of folds, paper size, and whether it will be a self-mailer or mailed in an envelope.

For example, your folder can be a three-panel self-mailer or a three-panel handout. As always, the choice depends on your audience and purpose. Here are some considerations:

❖ The cover can make or break a brochure's success, so spend the time designing an effective and attractive cover. Give readers a summary of *who, what, when, where, why,* and *how* while sparking their interest. You can do this with a catchy title or head, crisp copy, and effective art, type size, and color.

❖ The text must be clear and concise. Remember that a brochure is designed to pique interest, not to explain every last detail of the program, service, or product. A well-designed brochure will make readers want to investigate what you're selling or promoting.

❖ Use bullets, white space, and chunks of text to make your brochure visually appealing and easy to read.

❖ Visualize how the panels will work when the brochure is folded. Make sure the text flows logically, from front to back. I strongly suggest that you make a mock-up brochure by pasting the panels in the correct position. This will help you determine whether the layout makes logical sense and conveys your message as persuasively as possible.

❖ If you decide to include a tear-off card or reply form, remember that whatever is printed on the back of the card will be lost when the reader mails it off. Be sure you list crucial information somewhere other than the card. Otherwise the organization's name, address, and phone number might be mailed right back to you.

Press Releases

How do you get the word out when you've got a hot new product, service, or event? Whether you work for a large corporation, a small community group, or a mid-sized nonprofit organization, or head your own firm, it's important to keep the public up to speed. Not only do you want to publicize your company's doings, but you also want to trumpet your personal triumphs. The classic public relations method of publicizing a product, service, or event involves writing a *press release* and circulating it to the media.

A *press release* is a clear, engaging account of the event you wish to publicize. A press release follows this format:

Heading	The organization's logo or letterhead.
	The release time ("For Immediate Release" or the date of release).
	The name and address of the contact person. This can also be placed at the end of the press release.
Title	As with a newspaper headline, the title of a press release highlights the most newsworthy part of the article. Keyboard the title in all uppercase or boldface letters or both, and center it on the top of the document directly under the heading.
Lead	A summary of the contents, answering the questions, *Who? What? When? Where? Why?* and *How?*
Body	Arrange the information you wish to convey from most to least important. This allows busy readers to get the most important information first, and makes it easier for newspaper editors to cut the story, if need be, by simply lopping paragraphs from the end.
	In general, paragraphs should be short, from one to three sentences long, to create a crisp, fast-moving style.
Conclusion	Write a concise summary, preferably something memorable and quotable.

Here are some additional guidelines:

- ❖ Double-space the press release.
- ❖ If the press release is more than one page long, end each page with the word *more* and a dash, like this: —more—.
- ❖ The last page ends with —30—. This indicates that the story is over.

You'd be surprised how few press releases are revised by editors; the vast majority are picked up and published just as written, especially in smaller markets. Local newspapers, radio stations, and cable television stations often have small staffs. As a result, they just don't have the resources to revise a press release. They're grateful for well-written articles of general community interest. The conclusion is clear: The better written your press release, the better your chance of having it used in the media. If an editor has to rework your writing, the odds are good that your news isn't going to make the cut.

Larger outlets, in contrast, are more likely to assign your story to a reporter than to print or broadcast your press release. In this case, your press release serves as a persuasive document to convince the editor or news director to cover your story. Nonetheless, your press release might very well serve as background information for the reporter's article. This happened to me when I wrote a press release for a Boy Scout Eagle Scout Court of Honor. The press release convinced *Newsday*, one of the ten largest newspapers in America, to cover the story. *Newsday* used about half of my press release verbatim as background for the story.

A successful press release focuses on the same elements as any effective persuasive document: *audience* and *purpose*. To zero in on your audience, focus on specific outlets. Connect your press releases to the key issues each newspaper covers; learn what each editor likes and dislikes. For example, while most outlets favor enthusiastic but elegant prose, a handful of publications thrive on inflated, hyped-up writing.

Read several issues of a publication, listen to a radio station, and watch a TV station's shows to see what tone their press releases have. Audacious writing will please some editors but destroy your credibility with others. When in doubt, always err on the side of caution.

Press the Flesh

Here's a sample press release:

THE UNITED STATES MISSION TO THE UNITED NATIONS

799 United Nations Plaza
New York, NY 10017
USUN Press Release #103-(99)

Contact: Leslye Howard (212) 555-5555

PRESS RELEASE For release on Thursday 11 June 1999

U.S. GOVERNMENT AND UNITED NATIONS JOIN IN LANDMINE AWARENESS CAMPAIGN

NEW YORK, 11 June—Ambassador Bill Richardson, U.S. Representative to the United Nations, and Secretary General Kofi Annan today praised the latest effort of the Department of Defense and UNICEF to promote land mine awareness among children of mine-affected countries. The DOD and UNICEF have joined their considerable forces to alert children in Nicaragua, Honduras, and Costa Rica to the dangers of antipersonnel land mines. A new Spanish-language poster, the first step in the campaign, was unveiled this morning in a ceremony at UNICEF House.

> Shared problem

"We are here to celebrate the beginning of this important new campaign," said UN Secretary General Kofi Annan in his opening remarks. "Coordination and cooperation among private and public institutions at every level are key if we're to end the danger to civilians posed by antipersonnel land mines. This partnership is one of the central tenets of the U.S. Government's Demining 2010 Initiative, which seeks to eliminate by the end of the next decade land mines that threaten civilians."

> Eliminate other solutions

> Your solution

Ambassador Richardson expressed his hope that the goal of land mine awareness and demining would be "zero victims in a matter of years, not decades." Calling demining "one of the most important humanitarian missions in the post-Cold War era," Ambassador Richardson expressed the hope that the collaboration would lead to initiatives between public and private entities.

> Your request

"Children in the affected countries know they are in very real danger from land mines," said the Secretary General. "We hope to make the world safe from such tragic dangers."

The Whole Kit and Caboodle: A Press Kit

To keep your press release concise and compelling, include further details and information in attachments. The complete package is called a *press kit*. A press kit can include some or all of the following materials:

- ❖ The company's annual report.
- ❖ Biographies of people mentioned in the press release.
- ❖ A timetable for activities described in the press release.
- ❖ The company's policy statement.
- ❖ A calendar of upcoming events.
- ❖ Relevant photographs.
- ❖ Copies of relevant articles, such as newspaper clippings.
- ❖ Informational brochures and flyers issued by the company.
- ❖ Fact sheets (used to support your claims).
- ❖ Background articles.

Present the material in a folder, usually emblazoned with the company's colors and logo. Place the two most important documents—usually the press release and the fact sheet—at the front. Arrange everything else from most to least important, so the more important documents are closer to the front. Include a cover letter to explain the main purpose of the event you're publicizing. Also list the contents of the press kit.

Summary

❖ Build logic, trust, and credibility into all your persuasive appeals.

❖ Flyers and brochures rely on visuals, page layout, and design as well as on text.

❖ A *press release* is a clear, engaging account of the event you wish to publicize.

Chapter 13

The Art of the Memorable Memo

Memos go to people inside your organization; letters go to people outside your organization. As a result, most people think of the memo as an informal document, a chance to jot down a few ideas. You know better, though.

You realize that memos are at the heart of a company's internal communication and so belong to a particularly important genre of business writing. In a busy or highly stratified workplace, that seemingly minor memo may be the only chance you get to make your case, conduct vital business, or document a key point. In this chapter, you'll learn how to write a memorable memo.

Memo Madness

A *memo* is a written document sent within an organization to specific people or departments. Memos are fast, efficient, and economical ways to relay news. Stress the word *economical*—memos are concise business communications.

Memos form a vital link among members of a company, but before you add to the pile of paper on the desk of another overworked executive like yourself, define your purpose, audience, and style by asking yourself these questions:

- ❖ Why am I writing this memo?
- ❖ Is this memo really necessary?
- ❖ What do I expect from my reader?
- ❖ Who will read the memo?
- ❖ What words and attitude will help me accomplish my purpose?

The word *memorandum* comes from a Latin word that means "it is to be remembered." This etymology suggests one of the memo's functions: It reminds someone of an event, idea, policy, or procedure.

Here are some other reasons to write a memo:

❖ to inform

❖ to summarize

❖ to remind

❖ to announce new policies, changes, or improvements

❖ to suggest a solution

❖ to document a situation

❖ to record information

❖ to call to action

Memos rarely persuade. Within businesses, executives usually settle small issues on the telephone and larger problems face to face, at meetings and conferences.

How to Write an Effective Memo

Follow these 12 steps to write a memo:

1. Begin with a rough draft.

2. Jot your ideas on paper, recording your thoughts in any order. At this stage, don't worry about grammar and usage, style, or structure.

3. List questions your reader will ask. Here are some possibilities:

    ❖ Why are you calling another meeting on this issue?

    ❖ What is the purpose of getting a consultant?

    ❖ Why do you need more time for this project?

    ❖ How much more will it cost? Who is going to foot the bill?

4. Go though your ideas and underline or circle the key points.

5. Organize the points into categories and put a heading on each.

6. Start writing the memo. Remember that you don't always have to begin writing at the beginning. Sometimes it's best to start with your purpose and immediately follow with your conclusion.

7. Get right to the point. You can do this with the *subject line*, the memo's title. An effective subject line serves two purposes:

    ❖ It grabs your reader's attention.

    ❖ It summarizes the content of the memo.

    It does this by being short, specific, and adapted to the message (positive, negative, neutral).

8. Strive for vivid, concise language. "New Medical Deduction Policy," for example, is more effective than "Human Resources Department Makes Changes in Medical Deduction Policies."

9. Always assume that your readers are pressed for time, and get right to the point. Place the most important facts first. Busy readers will appreciate your consideration, and you'll get better results. In the worst-case scenario, someone could read the opening line, skip the middle section, and still get the point of the memo. Try to keep the total reading time to 15 seconds or less. Here's a sample:

    No Go: We have noticed that your department's productivity has declined in recent weeks and is now very low.

    Way to Go: Because productivity has decreased in recent weeks, I suggest the following actions:

                   1. ....

                   2. ....

                   3. ....

    Never bury important points in the middle of a memo.

10. As with a business letter, be very clear about the memo's purpose. Do you want the reader to make a decision? Expect a telephone call? Authorize a payment? Take an action? Don't be shy about expressing your purpose for writing.

    Give your readers the facts they need to take action. Don't start a memo war, whereby the memos fly thick and fast as people try to get clarification on key points. For example:

    No Go: I've studied the cost of a new scanner and decided it would be a good idea.

    Way to Go: A high-speed flatbed scanner would cost the company $2,000. We currently spend $9,000 per year to have documents scanned by an outside firm. Therefore, buying a scanner would save the company $7,000 per year.

11. Watch your *tone*. A memo is a less formal means of communication than a letter because it is circulated informally, within the company. That's no excuse for forgetting the importance of being professional, however. Don't use negative words, threats, or a brusque tone. Here are some models:

    No Go: Should you wish to remain an employee of this company, you must immediately straighten out the problem in your department. The productivity level in your department had better improve immediately.

    Way to Go: I feel confident that you will raise the productivity level of your department and so maintain your good standing in the company.

12. How the memo looks is almost as crucial as what you have to say. Keep the margins wide and insert at least one line of space between paragraphs. Use boldface type to highlight subheads and main points.

A lot can happen because of a memo, so it's always a good idea to let your writing sit a day or two and then make any necessary revisions. You might also ask for a colleague's opinion of your memo. If you don't think a memo through, you might really get burned.

Form and Function

A memo's *form* varies within different organizations. Some companies have preprinted forms for memos; others are less specific. Here's a standard format to use when your company does not have its own format:

Heading	The sender's full name and title.
	The recipients' full names and titles (or "All employees").
	The date.
	The subject.
Subject line	One- or two-line statement of purpose; a summary.
Body	Short, focused paragraphs; bullets or numbers to identify main points.
Ending	A conclusion.
	If applicable, ask for immediate action and give a date and time.

Here's a sample memo concerning a policy change:

Date: May 26, 1999   **Heading**

To: All unit employees

From: Matt Yu, Manager, Human Resources

Subject: Benefits Changes   **Subject line**

The following improvements to your benefits package were approved at the Board of Director's annual meeting: **Body**

Investment Plan

❖ Effective June 1, you can borrow from the contributions you have made to your retirement fund. The amount you can borrow is 75% of your total fund balance.

❖ Loans are issued with a five-year repayment schedule.

❖ The annual interest rate is 5%.

❖ There is a $30 service charge.

❖ A life insurance premium is charged an at annual rate of .10% and loans are fully insured after 30 days.

Health Care

Effective June 1, your health benefits now include:

❖ one pair of single-vision eyeglasses per employee and employee dependent every 24 months;

❖ a reduction in deductible for generic prescription medication, from $12 per prescription to $8 per prescription;

❖ an increase in the number of covered counseling sessions, from 8 per year to 12 per year.

For More Information

The attached booklet explains these benefits in greater detail. For additional information, visit the Employee Benefits Office at your convenience.

> Ending

Here's a memo concerning a new stock fund:

Date: December 7, 1999

To: Marketing Staff

From: Phil Fink, VP, Legal

Subject: Captain's Fund

> Heading
>
> Subject line

Please attend the meeting on December 10 at 10 AM in the main conference room to discuss fee and expense information for the *Captain's Fund.*

> Body

On January 1, the *Captain's Fund* will be open to investors. The fund seeks to achieve its objective through investment primarily in the equity securities of seasoned, financially strong, U.S. growth companies. The fund will invest primarily in common stocks of larger companies that have the following attributes:

❖ a record of above-average growth relative to the overall market (as defined by the Standard & Poor's 500 Composite Price Index) with prospects for above-average growth in earnings, cash flow, or assets in the future;

❖ important business franchises, leading products, or dominant marketing and distribution systems;

❖ attractive price relative to potential growth in earnings, cash flow, or assets;

❖ sound finances, high credit standings, and profitability;

❖ experienced, motivated management.

Political Considerations

As you decide to whom to address your memo, consider that a memo carries some heavy political weight. For example, how a memo is routed through the ranks is at least as important as what it says, if not more so. Study this chart to see what I mean:

Memo Addressed to ...	Suggests That ...
Your immediate supervisor and the CEO	You have access to the very top levels of power.
The CEO alone	You may be withholding information from your supervisor or consider that your "real" boss is the CEO.
Your supervisor alone	You're a team player and willing to share credit.

Summary

❖ A *memo* is a written document sent to specific people or departments within an organization.

❖ Memos are fast, efficient, and economical ways to relay news. Keep your memos brief.

❖ Get right to the point and be very clear about the memo's purpose.

❖ Keep your tone professional.

❖ Include a heading, subject line, body, and ending.

❖ Consider that a memo can be used as a political tool.

Chapter 14

E-Mail and Business Letters

Who *hasn't* had to write a letter on the job? No one, that's for sure! That's because letters represent *the* most common form of business writing. Increasingly, E-mail has added to our flow of correspondence. In this chapter, you'll learn how to write effective E-mail messages and letters. Let's start with E-mail.

The Wave of the Future

"E-mail doesn't apply to me," you might be thinking. "After all, I work for a traditional, conservative company." Even if it is available to you, you might not yet be comfortable with E-mail. It's tempting to skip over something that's unfamiliar and maybe a little frightening. E-mail is a lot easier to use than you might think, however, and even the most conventional firms will soon find themselves jumping on the Information Superhighway. Here's why:

❖ According to the International Data Corporation, 90 million American workers send 1.1 billion business E-mail messages per day. By the year 2000, IDC predicts that 130 million workers will be sending upward of 2.8 billion E-mail business messages a day.

❖ According to a recent article in *U.S. News and World Report*, Americans now send 2.2 billion E-mail messages a day, compared with 292 million pieces of first-class mail. At least a third of the nation sends messages over the Internet.

❖ In a recent article in *Time* magazine, Bill Gates asserted that all companies should insist that communication flow through E-mail. He argued persuasively that E-mail enables large companies to be as nimble as smaller ones.

What can you conclude from this information? Executives who plan to advance in their careers must be comfortable navigating the Internet, especially when it comes to sending and receiving E-mail. Here's how you can become an ace at business E-mail.

Writing E-Mail

E-mail, or electronic mail, lets you exchange messages with others via the Internet. You can attach formatted text files as well as files containing audio and graphics to your ASCII messages. Here are some guidelines for using E-mail:

❖   When you send E-mail, remember that its contents are harder to keep private than conventional mail (often called "snail mail"). You can make an on-line communication secure by encryption (coding), but once your recipients decode the document, they might forward it to anyone else on the Internet. This can happen accidentally as well as intentionally. Therefore, consider every E-mail message—even a private one—as a potentially public document.

❖   All E-mail includes a *subject line,* or space for a brief description of the message. The subject line appears in the recipient's E-mail directory. When you're in a hurry, it's tempting to type something quick, like "Re," in the box. Instead, take the time to provide a brief description of the contents of your message or the main point you wish to convey. Here are some samples:

Subj: Shipment of 3″ widgets.

Subj: Budget for spring sales conference.

Subj: Meeting to create virtual teams.

As an added courtesy, if your message doesn't require a reply, type FYI (For Your Information) at the beginning of the subject line. Busy executives will appreciate your consideration. For example:

Subj: FYI: Study on Sales Data.

❖   Change the subject line when you reply, if necessary. Any change in topic requires a change in the subject line. This helps your reader identify your purpose and topic at a glance.

❖   Never assume that your recipient knows your identity from your screen name. Many people, even business executives, have playful screen names. While they are fun to use, they can make it impossible for your recipient to figure out your identity. As a result, always sign your E-mail messages with a formal signature and, if necessary, your job title.

❖   Write concise messages. Get to the point quickly. In general, make your sentences and paragraphs shorter than you would in a letter, memo, or other off-line communication.

❖   Use underscores or asterisks to indicate emphasis. Because most E-mail is sent in ASCII unformatted text, you can't use italics or boldface to show emphasis. To show that a text should be read as *italicized*, surround the key text with underscore marks or asterisks. For example:

The conference was _extremely_ useful. It was money *very* well spent.

❖ Delete E-mail headers. If you respond to an E-mail message, delete the first message's header (all the routing information) so your correspondent doesn't have to scroll through it.

❖ Be considerate about sending attachments. Many systems let you send attachments with your E-mail messages. As you'll read later in this chapter, I'm a fan of attachments when you want to let a message "cool off" before you send it. However, your recipient must have specific software to be able to open the attached message. Before sending any attached file, ask your correspondents if they can accept it. If they can't, you can copy the attachment and paste it into your E-mail message, provided it isn't too long.

❖ Format carefully. Skip lines between paragraphs rather than indenting messages to make your E-mail easier to read.

❖ Edit and proofread thoroughly. E-mail can become a legal document, as can any written business communication. Therefore, before you send your message, review it carefully to make sure it conveys your precise meaning and is free of errors in grammar, spelling, punctuation, and usage.

Now that you know how to compose business E-mail, it's time to explore the culture of cyberspace and the system of manners that governs it.

Mind Your Manners: Netiquette

E-mail has its own system of manners that has come to be called netiquette, short for *network etiquette*. Simply put, netiquette is the code of appropriate on-line conduct that *netizens* (Internet citizens) observe in virtual communities. Knowing netiquette can help you conduct business on the Internet courteously and effectively. Don't assume that all the rules of conventional letter writing apply to E-mail. Some do, but others do not.

When you learn any new way of corresponding, the form is unfamiliar. As a result, you might misunderstand what your correspondent is saying and take offense at something that wasn't intended to insult. Or, you might inadvertently insult someone on-line by the way you send E-mail. Most dangerous of all, E-mail encourages a level of informality that makes it difficult to remember that you're still conducting business. It's also easy to forget that you're interacting with other real people, not just characters on a screen.

Follow these simple guidelines to become skilled in *netiquette.*

1. *Consider the forum.* Not all Internet forums follow the same forms of neti-quette; therefore, your audience's expectations determine what is—and what is not—acceptable. For example, when you're using E-mail or real-time communication (instant messages), you may sometimes be tempted to write informally, overlooking some of the accepted conventions of grammar, usage, spelling, and punctuation, because the E-mail you're reading is highly informal.

   Documents published on the Web, in contrast, are perceived as more public and permanent than E-mail or listserv postings. As a result, writers of these documents tend to pay closer attention to the conventions of standard written English.

   When you communicate through cyberspace, via E-mail or in discussion groups, your words are written and, chances are, they're stored in places where you have no control over them. As a result, there's a good chance they can come back to haunt you. You don't have to be engaged in criminal activity to want to be careful; any message you send could be saved or forwarded by its recipient. You have no control over where it goes.

   Because we're concerned with business communication, *always* assume that anything you send over the Internet is a public document that can be accessed by anyone. Always make sure your writing exhibits the diction and style appropriate for a business setting, no matter how informal the forum. This leads to the next guideline …

2. *Know where you are in cyberspace.* Because netiquette varies from domain to domain, it's important to know where you are in cyberspace. When you send E-mail, you have a specific audience in mind. But if you're spending a few minutes roaming around cyberspace, you're likely to stumble into a domain that's new to you. Before you enter any on-line conversations, pause and take a look around. Spend a while listening to the chat or reading the archives. Get a sense for how the people who are already there act. Then go ahead and participate.

3. *Remember that you're conducting business in the office.* When you send E-mail, you're typing words on a screen. You don't have the chance to use your voice and body to help communicate your meaning. When you're communicating through the World Wide Web, it's easy to misunderstand your fellow writer's meaning because you're constructing meaning from words only. It's also easy to lose sight of the fact that your correspondent is human.

   The impersonality of E-mail encourages business professionals, even executives, to lose control of their emotions. The interposition of the machine seems to make it acceptable for people to say things they don't mean. Some people even curse, make rude comments, and generally behave unprofessionally in their E-mail messages. They would never act this way in a business memo, a letter, or a face-to-face meeting. Here's a recent example:

"Old bald-headed goat." "Idiot." "Useless control freak pseudo figurehead numskull." Ben Gunn and Alec Meyers never thought that these E-mailed references to their boss would land them in court for more than two years of litigation. But that's just what happened.

In 1994, Gunn and Meyers were working at Opta Food Ingredients, a Massachusetts science company. Because the two were well-known for their sense of humor, someone played a practical joke on them. It went haywire, and Gunn and Meyers found themselves under investigation. Their E-mail became part of the evidence in the case. "We assumed that since we had passwords, no one would look at our E-mail," Gunn said. His assumption was wrong. Gunn and Meyers were fired for misconduct.

The lesson here is important: E-mail isn't as private as employees often assume it is. While nearly all of us agree that E-mail has benefited the workplace by making communication faster and eliminating the need for some tedious and time-consuming meetings, E-mail also has some far-reaching downsides.

The law regarding E-mail is still evolving, but so far the courts have held that employers can read their employees' E-mail at will. More and more supervisors are reading their managers' E-mail. The number of supervisors at major American companies who say they monitor their employees' E-mail has doubled over the past two years, to 27 percent.

"I can just delete my E-mail at the office," you might say. You can indeed "delete" it, but it won't really be gone. Even if you delete the folder that held the deleted messages, computer specialists known as forensic analysts can often retrieve deleted messages. *Always assume that whatever you write in your E-mail could be retrieved and used against you, now or in the future.*

Try this standard: If you wouldn't say something to a person's face, don't say it via E-mail. Rewrite and reread your E-mail messages until you're certain that you'd feel as comfortable saying these words to the live person as you do sending them through cyberspace. I strongly suggest that you send important messages as attached documents rather than as E-mail. That way, you've had a chance to revise the attached document and let it "cool off" before you send it.

If you disagree with someone publicly on-line, do so with tact. If you must disagree with someone strongly, consider doing so in private correspondence, through a traditional letter.

4. *Respect your audience.* People from all over the world send E-mail. As you conduct international business via the Internet, consider the needs and reactions of your global audience. It's vital that you explain your ideas fully and provide context to help others follow and understand your points.

In a quest to make E-mail correspondence even faster, a crop of *e-bbreviations*, some already common IRL (in real life), have sprung up. How many of these have you seen?

E-Mail Abbreviation	Meaning
afaik	as far as I know
afk	away from keyboard
atm	at the moment
b	be
b4	before
bbiaf	be back in a few minutes
bcnu	be seeing you
brb	be right back
btw	by the way
c	see
cul	see you later
f2f	face to face
focl	falling off the chair laughing
fwd	forwarded
fwiw	for what it's worth
gg	got to go
hhoj	Ha! Ha! Only joking!
imho	in my humble opinion
imnsho	in my not-so-humble opinion
j/k	just kidding
oic	Oh, I see!
r	are
rotfl	rolling on the floor with laughter
ttyl	talk to you later
ttfn	ta-ta for now
u	you
y	why

Never assume that the Internet slang, jargon, and abbreviations you might use are understood by everyone. I suggest that you clearly explain any unfamiliar expressions that you must use and avoid any that are too informal for your audience and subject.

5. *Don't use smileys.* Smileys (also known as emoticons) are cute little symbols that have become common in E-mail communication. Here are some of the best-known ones. Read them sideways, left-to-right.

:-)	happy face	;-)	winky face
:-(	sad face	:-D	laughing face
:-X	lips are sealed	%-)	bleary-eyed

Smileys are fun to use in personal E-mail, but they are inappropriate for business use.

6. *Don't flame.* A *flame* is a personal attack on someone. Flaming involves using capital letters as well as invectives. Using all capital letters, LIKE THIS, is considered the web equivalent of shouting. It's rude.

7. *Don't send spam.* Spam is unsolicited E-mail, the junk mail of the Internet. Spamming is sending the same message to hundreds or thousands of E-mail addresses in the hope of hitting a few interested people. Just as junk postal mail is annoying and wasteful, so is junk E-mail. You can throw away junk mail unread, but you often have to read spam to find out that it's junk. Spam clutters mailboxes, wastes time, and annoys the very consumers you want as customers. Don't send it.

8. *Respect others' time.* Remember that your readers value their time. When you send E-mail or post a message to a discussion group, you're taking up other people's time (or hoping to). It's your responsibility to ensure that the time they spend reading your posting isn't wasted.

Whenever you communicate via the Internet, do all you can to help others and yourself save time when reading, responding, or downloading. When you send E-mail, make your document easy to read and answer. For Web audiences, design your documents so they can be downloaded quickly.

Finally, think before you send copies. In the past, people made copies with carbon paper. Because you could only make about five legible copies, you thought long and hard about who you wanted to send them to. Today, it's easy to copy practically anyone on your E-mail, so we sometimes find ourselves copying people almost out of habit. Try to avoid sending unnecessary E-mail. People have less time than ever today, precisely because they have so much information to absorb. Before you copy people on your messages, ask yourself whether they really need to know. If the answer is no, don't waste their time. If the answer is maybe, think twice before you hit the "send" key.

9. *Double-check addresses.* Many E-mail users on the job dash off notes to colleagues without stopping to think about what they're writing and to whom they're writing. Misdirected messages and mix-ups abound. Further, E-mail addresses are sometimes difficult to type exactly. For instance, the letter O is often confused with the number 0.

   As a result, always check and double-check the address before you push the "send" key. I strongly suggest that you enter frequently-used addresses in your address book to prevent missed keystrokes. You can copy and paste an address from a previous message into your address book, or, if you're replying to a message, use the Reply function.

10. *Share expert knowledge.* The Internet is powerful because so many people use it. You can get answers to many questions because a lot of knowledgeable people are reading the questions. The Internet itself was founded and grew because scientists wanted to share information. Gradually, the rest of us got in on the act.

    It's considered good form to share the results of your questions with others in any discussion groups you have joined. Write up a summary and post it to the discussion group so everyone benefits from the answers of the experts who took the time to write to you.

    If you're an expert yourself, there's even more you can do. Many experts post resource lists and bibliographies, for example. If you're a leading participant in a discussion group that lacks a FAQ (frequently asked questions) area, consider writing one. If you've researched a topic that you think would be of interest to others, write it up and post it..

Now, let's take a look at business letters.

Writing Business Letters

There are two basic formats for business letters:

❖ *Traditional format*, in which the address and closing are indented.

❖ *Block format*, in which all parts of the letter are aligned at the left margin.

Which format should you use for letters you write on the job? The block format is becoming more popular for business communication, while the traditional format is more commonly used for personal letters or letters that do not carry a company letterhead.

General Format Guidelines

Include the following material, in the order stated:

- ❖ *Date.* Write the month, day, and year. For example:

  July 4, 1999   August 5, 1999

- ❖ *Inside address.* This is the recipient's address, the same address that appears on the envelope. Position the inside address two lines after the date. For example:

  May 4, 2000

  Ms. Kathryn Brown, President
  Acme Industries
  Industry Way, Suite 51A
  Baltimore, Maryland 21218

- ❖ *Salutation.* This is followed by a colon. For example:

  Dear Ms. Brown: Dear Mr. DesRault:

  If you don't know the gender of the person you're addressing, use the person's full name and omit the title. Avoid "Gentlemen" and "Dear Sir"; they are examples of biased writing. For example:

  Dear T.J. Ripley: Dear District Manager:

- ❖ *Body.* In the first paragraph, state the letter's purpose. In the second paragraph, describe the action or situation. Conclude with any specific request.

- ❖ *Close.* The close is placed two lines below the body. Capitalize only the first word and conclude with a comma. For example:

  Very truly yours,   Yours truly,

- ❖ *Signature.* Leave three lines for your signature. After your signature, type your name and title.

- ❖ *Typist's initials.* If someone other than the writer keyboards the letter, the typist's initials should be inserted below the signatory's typed name. Use lowercase letters for the typist's initials and uppercase for the writer's initials. Separate the initials with a slash (/) or colon. Place the writer's initials first. For example:

  WK/rm   WK:rm

- ❖ *Enclosures.* This word (also written *Encl.*) indicates that additional materials are included in the letter.

- ❖ *Copies.* If the letter is being sent to other people, list them alphabetically or by rank, from the highest ranking down. Preface the list with the abbreviation *cc:* (which stands for "carbon copies," a holdover from the old days) or simply *c:*. For example:

cc: Jillan Dorans
        Amy Galino
        Christopher Sieford

❖   *Letterhead.* Use $8\frac{1}{2} \times 11$-inch letterhead, with $1\frac{1}{2}$-inch margins all around. In nearly all cases, the side margins will be preset on your word processing program. For very brief letters, center the text vertically by increasing the top margin.

General Content Guidelines

No two business letters are the same, of course, but all business letters share some similarities, aside from format. All letters are:

❖   clear

❖   concise

❖   specific

❖   formal and businesslike in tone

❖   polite

Sample Business Letters

Two sample business letters are shown. The first letter is a bad-news letter explaining a delay in service. The second letter announces a change in policy.

Krell Computers
1000 Industry Way
Dallas, Texas 56221

February 5, 1999	Date
Ms. Susan Powder 89 Ferry Way Grand Rapids, Michigan 66703	Inside address
Dear Ms. Powder:	Salutation
We're delighted to hear that you're interested in the Krell Precision XPS T450 notebook computer. Thanks to the 300mhz processor, 13.3 XGA Active Matrix Display, MediaWizard 256AV AGP Video, and 32 GB Ultra ATA Hard Drive, this is truly the best notebook available for the price. As a result, interest in the product has been great. It's been so great, in fact, that we've sold our entire stock of this item in one week's time. As far as I know, that's a new record for Krell Computers.	Body

As soon as we realized how quickly our stock of the Precision XPS T450 was being sold, we began building more. Because each Krell computer is custom configured to meet your specific needs, we anticipate a delay of at least three weeks before your computer can be shipped.

In the meantime, we do have available the Krell Precision 35000 C3000XT. Like the XPS T450, it has a 32 GB Hard Drive and 32 MB SDRAM, and comes loaded with the same software. However, this machine also includes a 3-year limited warranty, 3D Surround-Sound, and a 17" rather than a 15" monitor. As a result, this model retails for $200 more. We would be happy to ship this model in place of the Precision XPS T450 at *no extra cost* to show our appreciation for your patience and patronage. If you prefer to wait for us to restock the Precision XPS T450, we will contact you as soon as it is available. Please return the enclosed reply card indicating your choice.

Very truly yours,

Leroy Jones

Leroy Jones
Executive Sales Manager

LJ:bt

Enclosures: Reply card

cc: Henry Davidson
     Nanci Fafley

Close

Signature

Typist's
initials

Enclosures

Copies

Very Big Publisher, Inc.
Business, Technical, and Professional Publishing
316 101 Street
Indianapolis, IN 46290

April 4, 1999

Mr. Nick Harris
3 Pollyanna Terrace
Paramus, New Jersey 07984

Dear Mr. Harris:

I am writing to inform you that we have recently changed the royalty accounting functions for the enclosed titles. The transition for this change will be made as follows:

Date

Inside
address

Salutation

Body

1. Enclosed is a royalty statement reporting activity through June 1999. This statement has been prepared by our current royalty department. Any questions you may have about this statement should be directed to your current contracts manager in the Indianapolis office, Ann St. Jacques.

2. Your next statement will report royalty activity from July 1999 through the normal statement period end, as specified by your contract.

3. Future statements will continue with the revised reporting period.

4. Your new Royalty Department contacts, from the period July 1999 on, will be:

    Mallory Jane Lilly   (317) 555-5555
    Adam Phillips   (317) 555-5555

We appreciate your patience during the transition process.

Sincerely,

Kathy Shoob

Kathy Shoob
Director of Accounting

KS/wp

cc: Henry Davidson
      Nanci Fafley

| Close |
| Signature |
| Typist's initials |
| Copies |

Summary

❖ Consider every E-mail document as potentially public, and don't write anything you wouldn't want everyone to read.

❖ When you send E-mail, provide a subject line and a formal signature. Write concisely and correctly, using underscores or asterisks to indicate emphasis. Don't flame, send spam, or use smileys.

❖ Delete E-mail headers in replies; be considerate with attachments, and format, edit, and proofread carefully.

❖ Follow the rules of *netiquette*, including considering the forum, knowing where you are in cyberspace, being businesslike, respecting your reader, and sharing expert knowledge.

❖ Whether written in the traditional format or the block format, business letters include the date, inside address, salutation, body, close, and signature. They may also include the typist's initials and indicate enclosures, and copies.

❖ Business letters should be clear, concise, specific, formal in tone, and polite.

Chapter 15

Business Reports

Business reports are action documents, designed to accomplish specific goals. People who request reports need to make decisions about operations, practices, or personnel; to decide whether to carry out specific projects; or to keep themselves informed. In this chapter, you'll learn how to write reports with a minimum of trauma.

What Is a Report?

Many different kinds of business documents are called *reports*. Here are the three main qualities to consider.

Length: There's a misconception that all business reports are as long as a Friday afternoon meeting. Not so. A report you write on the job can be a two-paragraph letter describing a recent inspection visit, or a thousand-page document that probes the misappropriation of funds.

Topic: Most business reports cover mundane topics, such as progress on a new branch opening, an update on sales, or a comparison of two products. But some reports you write on the job can have national and even international impact. A case in point is the *Warren Report* on the Kennedy assassination.

Research: Where do the facts in your reports come from? All reports are based on *research*. The research may be done by making a site visit, pulling up some data from the Internet, or making some telephone calls. On the other hand, it might involve organizing focus groups, conducting experiments, or taking surveys.

No matter what their length or topic, all business reports involve five steps:

1.   Defining the problem.
2.   Conducting research.

3.   Interpreting the data.

4.   Organizing the information.

5.   Writing the report.

Let's look at each step in detail.

Define the Problem

When you write a report on the job, the *problem* (or *topic*) is usually given to you—it's the reason that you're writing the report in the first place. The problem has to meet some criteria. It must be ...

❖ real

❖ important

❖ worth your time and effort

❖ something you can research

❖ something you understand

If the problem doesn't meet all five criteria, it is vital that you get clarification before you start any actual research or writing.

Write a Thesis Statement

Once you've defined and narrowed the problem, you can write a *thesis statement* (or *purpose statement*). The thesis statement should clarify three aspects of the report:

1.   The problem you'll be trying to solve through research.

2.   The materials you must gather.

3.   The purpose you have for writing the report. The purpose will include one or more of four goals: to explain, to recommend, to request, or to propose.

Plan a Proposal

If your report is persuasive, you must also consider how you can convince your audience that you can deliver the goods. When you write a persuasive report, a.k.a. a proposal, you'll also consider the following issues:

❖ *What problem will your proposal help solve?* Show that you understand the company's needs as well as the problem's varied factors.

❖ *How will you solve the problem you identify?* Demonstrate that your methods are logical and likely to be successful. Explain your plan and methodology.

❖ *What purpose will your work serve?* Show that you can build a better mousetrap or that you've already got one to sell.

❖ *What makes you trustworthy?* Demonstrate that you have the people and power to make it happen. You can do this by describing your previous success in the field as well as the qualifications of your staff.

❖ *What schedule have you laid out?* Include a specific timeline to reassure clients, colleagues, or superiors that everything has been planned carefully.

❖ *What's the budget?* Money is always a factor, so be sure to detail the bottom line.

If you're writing a proposal for a government agency, don't be creative. Instead, follow the *Request for Proposals* (RFP) exactly. This is especially crucial when the project is being sent out for bid, because all proposals are evaluated against each other. If you've selected a maverick method of organization or one that deviates even slightly from what's expected, your proposal will automatically be disqualified. This also applies to proposals written for some companies.

Conduct Research

Once you've planned the proposal, it's time to find the facts you need to present the issues or make your point. There are two kinds of research: *primary research* and *secondary research.*

❖ *Primary research* involves gathering new information. This is done through observations, surveys, experiments, and interviews.

❖ *Secondary research* involves finding information that someone else has compiled. This is done through library research or database searches.

Primary sources are not necessarily better (or worse) than secondary sources. Here are the pros and cons:

Primary sources ...

❖ provide facts and viewpoints that may not be available from other sources;

❖ often have an immediacy and freshness that secondary sources lack.

Secondary sources ...

❖ may offer a broader perspective than primary sources;

❖ tend to be less immediate than primary sources.

Many business reports use a mix of both primary and secondary sources.

Basic Search Strategy

The following suggestions can make researching faster, easier, and less frustrating.

1. *Use key words.* Search with key words. For example, key words for a report on the effects of salary and employment in the food service industry include *wages, restaurants,* and *employment rate.*

2. *Use Boolean search methods.* To narrow your search, use the words *and* and *or.* Here's how they're used:

    and   =   all the key words you include.

    or   =   one topic or the other.

    For example, typing *employment rate and wages* would result in a list of articles that includes both topics. Typing *employment rate or wages* would result in a list of articles that includes either topic.

3. *Include related words.* As you list your key words, think of synonyms that will expand or narrow your search. For example, if your report topic is "overcrowding in national parks," you might include some of these synonyms:

    environmentalism   wilderness

    national monuments   conservation

    federal lands   government lands

    Can't think of any synonyms or related terms for your research topic? Check the *Library of Congress Guide to Subject Headings.* This set of reference books identifies the subject headings used by the Library of Congress. It can help you find key words as well as related terms.

4. *Learn the lingo.* Nearly every research tool has an abbreviation—or two. You can learn the abbreviations for print sources by checking the introduction or index. For on-line sources, check the Help screen.

5. *Know your library.* All libraries offer some special services. Many libraries will get books, newspapers, and magazines for you through interlibrary loans. While there is rarely a charge for this service, it does take time, often as long as two to four weeks. Talk with a reference librarian when you start researching to find out what special services are available, the cost (if any), and the time involved.

6. *Get help.* When you have a research question that you can't answer on your own, turn to a reference librarian. They're the experts on research methods and their job is to help you find what you need.

Checklist of Sources

The following list summarizes the different sources available for research. Skim it now. As you plan your research, return to the list to help you consider different sources.

_____ Almanacs

_____ Archival materials (rare books, charts, maps, etc.)

_____ Atlases

_____ Audiovisual materials

_____ Books

_____ Encyclopedias

_____ Essays

_____ Government documents

_____ Indexes

_____ Magazines

_____ Newspapers

_____ On-line sources

_____ Pamphlets

_____ Primary sources (letters, diaries, etc.)

_____ Surveys

_____ Yearbooks

Computerized Databases

Increasingly, libraries are using *computerized databases* in place of print indexes. A computerized database is a bibliographic computer file of reference sources. Some databases include only periodicals; others include books, media, and even telephone numbers. No matter what information is indexed, each entry provides the title, author, and, sometimes, a summary.

The computer program will often print a citation for you. In some cases, you can even download the entire article. This is called full-text service.

Every library has different periodical databases. Here are some of the ones you're likely to find useful in the world of work:

❖ *Business Database Plus* combines selected newspapers and journals with data about businesses.

❖ *CompuServe* is an excellent business reference.

❖ *DataTimes* is an on-line index to local newspapers.

❖ *DIALOG* is an extensive, well-regarded database. *Dialog Business Connection* is an excellent business resource.

❖ *Dow Jones News/Dow Jones Free-Text Search* provides information about stocks and other investments.

❖ *InfoTrak* lists more than 1,000 business, technological, and general interest periodicals, as well as the *New York Times* and the *Wall Street Journal*, many as full-text.

❖ *LEXIS/NEXUS* affords access to thousands of full-text articles. It includes the *Congressional Record* and SEC reports as well as documents from newspapers and magazines.

❖ *MILCS* is a database of all the holdings of academic and public libraries in specific regions.

❖ *OCLC First Search* lists all the periodicals, media, and books in the U.S. and Canada. It has many indexes.

❖ *Valueline* has information about companies and investments.

❖ *VU/TEXT* is a newspaper database.

❖ *WILSONSEARCH* is an on-line information system containing the Wilson databases not on CD-ROM. For example, it contains the *Education Index* and the *Index to Legal Periodicals*.

Use the same search strategy with on-line and CD-ROM databases as you would with a print index: Use key words, title, author, or any combination of these.

Government Documents

The government publishes a wealth of pamphlets, reports, catalogs, and newsletters on most issues of national concern. Government documents are often excellent research sources because they tend to be factual and unbiased. To find government documents, try these CD-ROM and on-line indexes:

❖ *Monthly Catalogue of the United States Government Publications*

❖ *United States Government Publications Index*

Surveys

Surveys are useful when you want to measure the behavior or attitudes of a fairly large group. On the basis of the responses, you can draw some conclusions. Such generalizations are usually made in quantitative terms, for example: "Fewer than one-third of the respondents favored advertisements on public school Internet accounts."

If you decide to create a survey, follow these guidelines:

❖ Be sure to get a large enough sampling to make your results fair and unbiased.

❖   Don't ask loaded questions that lead people toward a specific response.

❖   To get honest answers to your questions, it is essential to guarantee your respondents' anonymity. Written surveys are best for this purpose.

❖   Make the form simple and easy. Few people are willing to take the time to fill out a long, complex form.

❖   Carefully tabulate your results. Check your math.

Interpret the Data

Data is meaningless unless it is logical, valid, and understandable. As you analyze your findings, look for answers to the questions you posed in your proposal. Here are some ideas to consider as you read and interpret the articles, Web sites, and other data you've found:

❖   Look for patterns. What does the data suggest? What trends can you discern? You may wish to create charts and other visuals to find patterns.

❖   Compare findings from different sources to check their accuracy. Be sure to verify each source to make sure that it's valid. You can do this by looking for the same results in more than one resource.

❖   Consider whether the source is biased or objective. Who commissioned the study? What do they have to gain from specific findings?

❖   Consider alternate explanations. It's tempting to embrace the material that supports your thesis, but that might not always be the correct explanation. Weigh other conclusions to help you determine whether your theory holds water.

Organize the Information

You can organize your business report in several different ways. Here are the most useful patterns:

❖   *Advantages and disadvantages.* List all the advantages and then all the disadvantages, or take each topic and consider its advantages and disadvantages in turn. Whichever method you select, give arguments for and against the issues under each heading. Remember that the information you present first will seem stronger than what you present later, simply by virtue of its position.

❖   *Chronological.* This method of report organization arranges all the information in time order, from beginning to end. It's well-suited to projects that focus on a strict timetable of events, and to projects for which time is a key factor (or *the* key factor).

❖ *Comparison and contrast.* Present all of one side and then all of the other side, or alternate points. Present all one side when one alternative is clearly better and the criteria are difficult to tease apart. Use the alternate pattern when the choices depend on what criteria are selected and the issues are easy to separate.

❖ *Functional.* Discuss the problem and solution for each aspect of the topic. For example, if the topic is the feasibility of opening a new plant in a foreign country, discuss each aspect in turn: the country's political stability, the country's economic stability, the availability of a skilled labor force, the availability of supplies, shipping costs, and so on.

❖ *General to specific (or specific to general).* In *general to specific* organization, you open with the problem in general and then discuss each aspect of the problem and possible solutions. In *specific to general* report organization, in contrast, you open with the problem as the audience perceives it and then move to larger issues of which the problem is a part. Use either method when you want to focus on the problem.

❖ *Problems and solutions.* This method can be approached in either of two ways: 1) Identify the problem, explain its background, analyze the pros and cons of each solution, and present your recommendations. 2) Open with your recommendations, and then identify the problem, trace the background, and analyze each side of the issue. Deciding which approach to use requires audience analysis: Which method would better suit your readers?

Write the Report

The method of organization you select depends, of course, on the type of report you're writing. Because writing an effective report depends on meeting the reader's needs, many companies prescribe a specific format for all standard reports. This is especially true for everyday issues, such as accident reports, real estate reports, or bids. No doubt these strict formats limit a writer's creativity, but the trade-off is sweet: The fixed format provides security.

In many instances, however, you won't have a specific format to follow for your reports. When the choice of a format is left in your capable hands, here are some standard formats you can use:

Feasibility Reports

Report Part	Contents
Introduction	Solution or suggestions, alternative choices, criteria.
Body	Evaluation of each alternative in turn.
Conclusion	Recommendation, if not given in the opening. Place your recommendation here if it is hard to accept.

Informative Reports

Report Part	Contents
Introduction	Summarize the problem. The solution can also be placed up front, depending on the audience and company's traditions.
Body	Purpose, scope, account of findings.
Conclusion	Solution or suggestions.

Justification Reports

Report Part	Contents
Introduction	The request you're making and background on the issue.
Body	Explanation of each possible solution. Summary of what it will take to effect the solution.
Conclusion	Ask readers to approve your request.

Report Style

Unlike E-mail and other relatively informal methods of business communication, reports tend to be formal, for the stakes are usually high. This is true whether the report is short or long, but as a general rule, the longer the report, the more formal its style. The following guidelines can help you strike the right note:

❖ *Be clear.* Include sufficient background to make your point; explain all unfamiliar terms.

❖ *Be concise.* Especially in long reports, avoid unnecessary words, circumlocution, and a windy style. Review Chapter 6.

❖ *Be considerate.* Use headings and visuals to highlight key points.

❖ *Be formal.* Use the company's name rather than the second-person *you*.

❖ *Be a company representative.* The style you use in your reports should always represent the company, never you personally. This is not permission to be dull, however. Avoid passive verbs, clichés, and jargon.

❖ *Be careful of tone.* You need to determine what tone will best suit your topic, audience, and position within the company. Also take into account the company's traditions. If you're in a position of authority, you can use a strong and forceful tone. If you're framing the report for people higher up the line from you, using too forceful a tone will make you sound presumptuous and undercut your effectiveness.

Report Presentation

Formal reports are longer and more complete than informal reports. The stakes are higher so the presentation is much more elaborate. A formal report may include some or all of the following components:

❖   *Cover.* Often the entire report is bound in a carefully designed folder. It may be paper or leather, depending on the audience and purpose, but it is usually emblazoned with the company's logo.

❖   *Title page.* Include the title of the report, for whom the report was written, writers, and release date. The information should be clear and straightforward.

❖   *Letter of transmittal.* This letter or memo serves to introduce the report and build goodwill for the writer and the company. The letter of transmittal tells who authorized the report and why it was written, summarizes the conclusions, points out key issues, and thanks the readers for their attention.

❖   *Table of contents.* List the headings as they appear in your report. In a short report, include all the headings; in a long report, list only the main headings.

❖   *List of figures.* This includes illustrations, charts, graphs, tables, and so on.

❖   *Body of the report.* This section includes the introduction, history of the problem, body, conclusions, recommendations, works cited, and appendices.

❖   *Conclusions and recommendations.* Depending on your audience, this section may appear earlier, right before the body. *Conclusions* include the points you've made in your report; *recommendations* are your suggestions for solving the problem or improving the situation. This is the most widely read part of your report. Your audience might skim the body of the report and the illustrations, but they'll zero in on your conclusions.

Model Report
Here's a brief informative report:

PROBLEM AND RECOMMENDATION:

On June 5, I was asked to check on the warehouse in Lindenhurst. Two complaints of theft had occurred in the preceding three months.

After a careful inspection, I can report that $5,000 worth of inventory was indeed stolen and resold at a flea market for a fraction of its worth. I recommend that we terminate the employment of the two guards, provide additional rotation of guard assignments, install a video camera in the factory, and inspect all duffel bags.

INVESTIGATION:

On June 6, I visited the Lindenhurst warehouse and inspected the stock with the head of security, Mr. Frank Madonna. An all-day meeting revealed that two guards had worked together to remove the merchandise, T-shirts. Over a period of one week during their rounds, the two guards stuffed the T-shirts into their duffel bags and made numerous trips to their cars during the day with the merchandise, under the guise of taking smoking breaks. We determined that both guards had to be involved because neither reported the missing inventory, and only one guard smokes. When confronted with the facts, they confessed.

SOLUTION:

I recommend that we terminate the employment of the two guards, provide additional rotation of guard assignments, install a video camera in the factory, and inspect all duffel bags. The video camera will cost $300 and can be installed in two days.

Summary
* Business reports are action documents, designed to accomplish specific goals.
* All business reports involve defining the problem, doing research, interpreting the data, organizing the information, and writing the report.
* The information can be organized according to advantages and disadvantages, chronological order, comparison and contrast, function, general to specific (or specific to general issues), or problems and solutions.
* Be clear, concise, considerate, and formal in tone.

Part 4

GRAMMAR.COM

Chapter 16

Common Usage Issues

When most managers complain that their employees can't write, they are most often referring to errors people make in grammar and usage.

More than ever before, good writing is essential for success in business. Simple, straightforward, and correct writing saves time, creates good faith, and prevents misunderstandings. In this chapter, we'll concentrate on the *correct* part of this equation so your writing will be "letter perfect." I'll also bring you up to speed on how grammar and usage have adapted to changing times.

Follow the Rules

You wouldn't leave the house with a spot on your suit jacket. In the same way, you wouldn't send out a letter, E-mail message, report, or other written communication that contained a grammar or usage error. Reviewing the grammar rules can help you prevent "spots" on your writing.

Read the following grammar and usage guidelines and identify the error in each one. (*Hint:* The errors are mentioned in the rules.) Then correct each sentence. You've already had a hard day at work, so I've done the first one for you.

1. Remember to never split an infinitive.

    Error: Split infinitive

    Correction: Remember never to split an infinitive.

2. This is the sort of thing I will not put up with.

3. The passive voice should never be used.

4. Avoid run-on sentences, they are hard to understand.

5. Please don't use no double negatives.

6. Use the semicolon correctly, always use it where it is appropriate; and never where it is not suitable.

7. Save the apostrophe for its' proper use and omit it where its not needed.

8. Verbs has to agree with their subjects.

9. Any sentence fragments, if you want to be clearly understood.

10. Proofread carefully to see if you have any words out.

11. Avoid commas, that are not required.

12. If you reread your work, you will find upon serious reconsideration that a great deal of repetition can be avoided by careful proofreading, attentive reevaluating, and scrupulous editing.

13. In business writing, never overuse exclamation marks!!!!

14. Place pronouns as closely as possible, especially in long sentences, as of ten or more words, to their antecedents to avoid confusion.

15. Write all adverbs correct.

16. Writing carefully, dangling participles must be avoided.

17. Take the bull by the toe and avoid mixed metaphors.

18. Everyone should be careful to use a singular pronoun in their writing.

19. Always pick in the correct idiom.

20. Last but not least, avoid clichés like the plague; seek viable alternatives.

Walk This Way

Here are explanations of the 20 rules. See how many of these usage guidelines you know.

1. *Error:* Split infinitive

   Correction: An infinitive is the base form of the verb, before it has been changed (conjugated) to show time. Infinitives often have *to* before them, as in *to hire, to fire,* and *to reallocate.* To determine whether a verb is in the infinitive form, add the *to* if it is not there and see if the sentence still makes sense.

   Traditionally, it was considered a serious error in grammar to put a word between *to* and the verb in an infinitive, thus "splitting" the infinitive. The *Star Trek* motto, "To boldly go where no man has gone before," contains a split infinitive; to be considered grammatically correct, the motto should read, "To go boldly ..."

   Fortunately, this distinction is vanishing faster than the concept of a lifelong career at one company. Now it's actually considered cool to split. Feel free to say "to boldly go" if it sounds smoother than "to go boldly."

2. *Error:* Ending with a preposition

   Correction: None.

   Along with split infinitives, ending a sentence with a preposition is a longstanding sticking point with traditionalists. Whatever the merit of the rule—that prepositions should appear before their objects—there's a considerable body of opinion against end-of-sentence prepositions. To play it safe, try to avoid ending sentences with prepositions, such as *to, with, from, at, on,* and *in.*

For example, instead of writing, "The topics we want to write on," consider, "The topics on which we want to write."

On the other hand, you should never let usage guidelines make your writing clumsy or obscure. If a sentence is more logical and elegant with a final preposition, let it stand. Remember that a sentence becomes unnecessarily obscure when it's cluttered with "from whoms" and "with whiches."

According to a famous story, when reprimanded by his assistant for ending a sentence with a preposition, Winston Churchill said, "This is the sort of thing up with which I will not put." Obviously, Churchill's original end-with-a-preposition version—"This is the sort of thing which I will not put up with"—was far better, because it was less stilted.

3.   *Error:* Passive voice

   Correction: Carefully consider when to use the passive voice.

   As you learned in Chapter 6, English has two voices, *active* and *passive.* A verb is *active* when the subject performs the action. A verb is *passive* when its action is performed upon the subject. The active voice is clearer and more concise than the passive voice. For example:

   Passive voice: The meeting was attended by the executive.

   Active voice: The executive attended the meeting.

   In business writing, however, political considerations sometimes take precedence over grammar rules. Even though the active voice is stronger than the passive voice, you should use the passive voice in two situations:

   ❖ to avoid placing blame ("A mistake was made" rather than "You made a mistake"); and

   ❖ to avoid identifying the doer of the action ("The letter was sent" rather than "Nicole sent the letter").

   Since these two considerations often intersect in business, you may wish to use the passive voice to avoid naming the speaker and thus assigning blame.

4.   *Error:* Run-on sentence

   Correction: Avoid run-on sentences; they are hard to understand. Or: Avoid run-on sentences because they are hard to understand.

   A run-on sentence occurs when two complete sentences (independent clauses) are incorrectly joined. Sentences can only be joined with a coordinating conjunction or semicolon; a comma doesn't cut the mustard. See Chapter 19 for a complete discussion of sentences.

5. *Error:* Double negative

   Correction: Please don't use any double negatives.

   A *double negative* is two negative words. They effectively cancel each other out. Along the way, they confuse the reader. To avoid this error, remember to use only one of the following negative words per sentence:

no	never
none	nothing
scarcely	barely
not or n't (couldn't, didn't ...)	hardly

6. *Error:* Misused semicolon

   Correction: Use the semicolon correctly; always use it where it is appropriate, and never where it is not suitable.

   As discussed in Chapter 21, a semicolon has two primary uses: to separate two complete sentences (independent clauses) whose ideas are closely related or to separate clauses that contain commas.

7. *Error:* Apostrophe error

   Correction: Save the apostrophe for its proper use and omit it where it's not needed.

   As discussed in Chapter 21, the apostrophe (') is used three ways: to show possession (ownership), to show plural forms, and to show contractions (where a letter or number has been omitted). The following chart shows how *its, it's,* and *its'* are used:

Word	Part of Speech	Meaning
it's	contraction	it is
its	possessive pronoun	belonging to it
its'	is not a word	none

8. *Error:* Agreement between subject and verb

   Correction: Verbs have to agree with their subjects.

   Agreement means that sentence parts match, singular to singular and plural to plural. Because the subject, *verbs,* is plural, it takes a plural verb, *agree.*

   This is confusing because we add -*s* or -*es* to make the third person *singular* form of most verbs but add -*s* or -*es* to make the *plural* form of most nouns. For example, *he start*s is singular but *six papers* is plural. Both end in *s.*

9. *Error:* Incomplete sentence

   Correction: You should not write any sentence fragments if you want to be clearly understood.

   Every sentence must have a subject and a verb. In this example, both the subject, *you,* and the verb, *write,* were missing.

10. *Error:* Missing words

    Correction: Proofread carefully to see if you have *left* any words out.

    This is a simple rule, but many executives often don't leave enough time to proofread a document. *Always* make the time to proofread your writing. Also, try to let your writing sit and "cool off" for a few hours. The errors will become much more obvious and easier to isolate then.

11. *Error:* Unnecessary commas

    Correction: Avoid commas that are not necessary.

    Have you ever been advised to "Add commas where you would take a breath"? Sometimes this advice works, but sometimes it doesn't. It's especially dangerous when you've gone over and over your writing. At that point, *nothing* looks correct. To avoid confusion and frustration, don't wing it. Instead, review the comma rules covered in Chapter 21 and use the rules as you write to help you correctly punctuate your documents.

12. *Error:* Redundancy; unnecessary words

    Correction: If you reread your work, you will find that a great deal of repetition can be avoided by careful editing.

    Long-winded writing may sound official, but it's just a time waster. Say what you need to say concisely. Your writing will be more intelligible, and it will be more likely to be read.

13. *Error:* Unnecessary exclamation marks

    Correction: In business writing, never overuse exclamation marks.

    Instead of using exclamation marks, convey emphasis through careful, vivid word choice. Exclamation marks create an overwrought tone that has no place in formal business documents.

14. *Error:* The pronouns are placed too far from their *antecedents,* the words to which they refer. This makes sentences difficult to follow and may also result in confusion or misunderstanding.

    Correction: Place pronouns as close as possible to their antecedents, especially in long sentences, of ten or more words.

    The revision corrects the error, but it is still not an effective sentence because it is hard to follow. To convey your meaning clearly and force-fully, break the long sentence into smaller sentences, as in the following example:

Place pronouns as close as possible to their antecedents. This is especially important in sentences that have ten or more words.

15. *Error:* Incorrect adverb use

   Correction: Write all adverbs correctly.

   Adverbs are words that describe verbs, adjectives, or other adverbs. Adverbs answer the questions: *How? When? Where?* or *To what extent?* For example:

Question	Examples	
How?	worked *slowly*	slept *badly*
When?	hired *yesterday*	quit *later*
Where?	fell *below*	walked *up*
To what extent?	*partly* completed	*fully* done

   Most adverbs are formed by adding *-ly* to an adjective. A very common error involves using an adjective (such as *correct*) in place of an adverb (*correctly*). This isn't acceptable usage in standard written English.

   The matter is complicated because a great many adverbs don't end in *-ly*. Here are a few of the most common ones you'll likely use in your writing:

Adverbs

afterward	already	hard	never
today	low	rather	tomorrow
then	yesterday	late	often
almost	back	long	soon
when	here	next	still
where	far	too	near

16. *Error:* Dangling modifier

   Correction: When you write carefully, you must avoid dangling participles.

   A *modifier* is a word or phrase that describes a subject, verb, or object. (To modify is to describe). The modifier is said to "dangle" when the word it modifies has been left out of the sentence. Dangling modifiers confuse your readers and obscure your meaning because the sentence doesn't make sense.

   Correct a dangling modifier by adding the word or words that have been left out of the sentence. Here, I added the subject ("When *you* write carefully …") and changed *writing* to *write* so the sentence makes sense.

   While we're dangling, let's look at another mangled construction, *dangling participles*. A *participle* is a verb ending in *-ing*. It is called *dangling* when the subject of the *-ing* verb and the subject of the sentence don't agree. For example:

Incorrect: Rushing to finish the paper, Bob's printer broke.

The subject is Bob's printer, but the printer isn't doing the rushing.

Correct: While Bob was rushing to finish the paper, his printer broke.

One way to tell whether the participle is dangling is to put the clause with the participle right after the subject of the sentence: "Bob's printer, rushing to finish the paper, broke" doesn't sound right.

Warning: Not all words that end in *-ing* are participles. In the sentence, "Completing the task by Tuesday is your next assignment," the word *completing* functions as a noun, not a verb. (Nouns ending in *-ing* are called *gerunds.* They are discussed in Chapter 18.)

17.   *Error:* A mixed metaphor

Correction: Take the bull by the horns and avoid mixed metaphors.

Metaphors are figures of speech that compare two unlike things to explain the less familiar object. When used correctly, metaphors make your writing more descriptive and precise. In most instances, metaphors express more than a literal meaning. Here, for example, we're not talking about literally grabbing a bull by the horns; rather, we're talking figuratively about seizing an opportunity.

For a metaphor to be effective, it must compare images or objects that go together. Here, for instance, a bull goes with horns, not toes. When two clashing images are combined in one comparison, we get a *mixed metaphor,* a real mishmash!

18.   *Error:* Pronoun agreement

Correction: Everyone should be careful to use a singular pronoun in his or her writing.

In rule 8, you learned that subjects and verbs must *agree* or match by having the same number (singular or plural). Therefore, a singular subject takes a singular verb, a plural subject takes a plural verb, and a singular indefinite pronoun takes a singular verb. Because *everyone* is a singular antecedent, it takes a singular pronoun, *his or her.*

Singular Indefinite Pronouns

one	everybody	anything	each
anyone	nobody	everything	much
everyone	somebody	nothing	other

someone   something   either

no one   neither

Indefinite pronouns that end in -*one* are always singular. Increasingly, however, these pronouns are paired with plural pronouns, as the following examples show:

Past: Everyone will do *his or her* work.

Present: Everyone will do *their* work.

This question also brings up the issue of gender-free language and awkward constructions. Rather than grappling with the clumsy construction *his or her,* you can make the whole sentence plural, like this:

People should be careful to use a singular pronoun in *their* writing.

This also helps you sidestep the issue of agreement.

19. *Error:* Incorrect idiom

    Correction: If you decide to use idioms, always use the correct one.

    Idioms are expressions that mean something beyond the sum of their parts. The idiom "kick the bucket," for example, means "to die," not to go around kicking buckets. Here are some common idioms and their meanings:

Idiom	Meaning
buy the farm	die
be under the weather	be sick
live high on the hog	live beyond your means
the old college try	try hard
fresh as a daisy	fresh and new
be in the driver's seat	be in control

If you decide to use idioms in your writing, be sure to use the correct phrase. For instance, it's idiomatic to say, "She talked *down* to him." It's not idiomatic to say, "She talked *under* to him."

In general, avoid idioms in any writing aimed for a multicultural audience, because idioms are difficult to decipher.

Idiomatic prepositions are much more common and just as hard to use. Here's a list of the most useful ones:

Idioms

Incorrect	Correct
according *with* the plan	according *to* the plan
accuse *with* perjury	accuse *of* perjury

apologize *about*	apologize *for*
board *of*	bored *with*
capable *to*	capable *of*
comply *to* the rules	comply *with* the rules
concerned *to*	concerned *about, over, with*
conform *in* standards	conform *to, with* standards
in search *for*	in search *of*
in accordance *to* policy	in accordance *with* policy
independent *from*	independent *of*
inferior *than* ours	inferior *to* ours
interested *about*	interested *in*
jealous *for* others	jealous *of* others
outlook *of* life	outlook *on* life
puzzled *on*	puzzled *at, by*
similar *with*	similar *to*

20.   *Error:* Clichés (shopworn phrases that have lost their punch)

Correction: Write sentences that use fresh, new comparisons and expressions. Make your writing forceful with vivid new phrases.

Shape Up!

How can you use the previous 20 guidelines to improve your writing on the job? Try these ideas:

1.   Keep track of the writing errors you make by checking your own work against the guidelines in Part 4. Review Chapters 16 to 20 every time you write an important document.

2.   Notice what points your coworkers and supervisors mention repeatedly when they discuss your written communication.

3.   Concentrate on the errors you make most often.

4.   Don't try to master all the rules of grammar and usage at once; that's both futile and frustrating. Learning the rules takes time and effort.

5.   Remember that using standard grammar with confidence will help you build the credible image you want—and need.

Use a Checklist

You make lists to help you remember key events. The same technique can help you isolate and correct the key problems in your writing. To get you started, I've prepared a checklist of the most common and damaging writing errors.

Keep this checklist handy when you edit your work.

25 TOP WRITING ERRORS

Grammar and Usage

1. Lack of clarity
2. Redundancy (unnecessary words)
3. Errors in pronouns, such as *who* or *whom*
4. Problems with subject–verb agreement
5. Lack of parallel structure
6. Wrong verb tense
7. Double negatives
8. Dangling participles
9. Misplaced modifiers
10. Misused adjectives and adverbs
11. Biased language
12. Incorrect voice (active vs. passive voice)

Sentences

13. Fragments (incomplete sentences)
14. Run-ons (two sentences that run together)

Spelling

15. Missing letters
16. Extra letters
17. Transposed letters
18. Incorrect plurals
19. Errors in homonyms (such as *their, there,* and *they're*)

Punctuation

20. Missing commas or extra commas
21. Missing or misused apostrophes
22. Missing quotation marks in dialogue
23. Misused semicolons and colons

Capitalization

24. Proper nouns and adjectives not capitalized
25. Errors in titles

Summary

- ❖ Mastering correct grammar and usage is a must in business writing.

- ❖ Learn the rules of standard written English, but never let usage guidelines make your writing clumsy or obscure.

- ❖ Track your writing errors and concentrate on correcting the ones you make most often.

- ❖ Use a checklist to isolate and correct the key problems in your writing.

Chapter 17

Grammar, Usage, and Mechanics Glossary

Here are all the elements of standard written English, arranged in alphabetical order. Use this chapter as a reference for all your writing questions.

1. Action Verbs

Action verbs tell what action someone or something is performing; *linking verbs* connect a noun or pronoun with other words. *Toil, drudge,* and *work* are action verbs; forms of *to be* (*am, are, is, was, were,* etc.) are linking verbs.

While both action verbs and linking verbs are necessary in writing, action verbs make your writing forceful while linking verbs tend to make it wordy and weak. As a result, try to use action verbs rather than linking verbs whenever possible.

2. Active Voice

(See *Voice.*)

3. Adjectives

Adjectives describe nouns and pronouns. Adjectives answer the questions *What kind? How much? Which one?* or *How many?*

There are four kinds of adjectives: articles, common adjectives, compound adjectives, and proper adjectives.

❖   *Articles:* A, *an,* and *the* are articles. *The* is the definite article because it refers to a specific thing. A and *an* are indefinite articles because they refer to general things. Use *an* in place of *a* when it precedes a vowel sound, not just a vowel. Write *an honor* (the *h* is silent), but *a UFO.* The use of definite and indefinite articles is one of the hardest things for speakers of other languages to master, because it's often entirely arbitrary; why are you *in town* but *in the city*?

178

❖ *Common adjectives:* They describe nouns or pronouns, as in *big companies* and *municipal bonds.*

❖ *Compound adjectives:* These adjectives are comprised of more than one word. They can be closed compounds, as in *whiplash injury.* They can be hyphenated compounds, as in *fixed-income investments.* Finally, they can be two-word compounds, as in *heart attack victim.*

❖ *Proper adjectives:* These adjectives are formed from proper nouns, as in *California oranges.*

Follow these rules to use adjectives correctly:

❖ Use an adjective to describe a noun or a pronoun.

❖ In business writing, use adjectives sparingly. While modifiers are necessary in any sort of writing, make sure your nouns and verbs are clear and are doing most of the work. As the great grammar gurus Strunk and White put it, "The adjective hasn't been built that can pull a weak or inaccurate noun out of a tight place."

4. Adverbs

Adverbs describe verbs, adjectives, or other adverbs. Adverbs answer the questions: *When? Where? How?* or *To What Extent?*

Most adverbs are formed by adding *-ly* to an adjective. Here is a list of the most common adverbs that do not end in *-ly:*

Adverbs That Don't End in *-ly*

afterward	almost	already	also
back	even	far	fast
hard	here	how	late
long	low	more	near
never	next	now	often
quick	rather	slow	so
soon	still	then	there
today	too	tomorrow	when
where	yesterday		

Follow these rules to use adverbs correctly:

❖ Use an adverb to describe a verb, an adjective, or another adverb.

❖ In business writing, use adverbs sparingly.

5. Agreement of Pronoun and Antecedent

Pronouns and their antecedents (the words to which they refer) must *agree* or match. Follow these rules:

❖ A pronoun replaces a noun. To make sure that your writing is clear, always use the noun before using the pronoun.

❖ Be sure that the pronoun refers directly to the noun.

❖ Use a singular personal pronoun with a singular indefinite pronoun: If *anyone* questions the policy, refer *him or her* to Human Resources. If you find this construction awkward, make the pronoun and antecedent plural: If *people* question the policy, refer *them* to Human Resources.

6. Agreement of Subject and Verb

Follow these rules to match sentence parts:

❖ A singular subject takes a singular verb. For example: *I avoid* investing in a company whose earnings don't match its sales.

❖ A plural subject takes a plural verb. For example: *They avoid* investing in a company whose earnings don't match its sales.

❖ Ignore prepositional phrases that intervene between the subject and the verb. For example: Too many *cooks in the kitchen* often *create* havoc. The plural subject *cooks* requires the plural verb *create*. Ignore the intervening prepositional phrase, *in the kitchen.*

❖ Subjects that are singular in meaning but plural in form require a singular verb. These subjects include words such as *measles, news, economics,* and *mathematics.* For example: The *news was* distressing.

❖ Singular subjects connected by *either/or, neither/nor,* and *not only/but also* require a singular verb. For example: Either the boss *or* the employee *was* not being truthful.

❖ If the subject is made up of two or more nouns or pronouns connected by *or, nor, not only,* or *but also,* the verb agrees with the noun closest to the pronoun. For example: Neither the consultant nor the area *representatives are* arriving by Tuesday. Neither the area representatives nor the *consultant is* arriving by Tuesday.

7. Apostrophes

(See *Possessive.*)

8. Biased Language

Avoid *biased language,* words and phrases that assign qualities to people on the basis of their gender, race, religion, or physical ability. Here are some guidelines:

❖   Avoid using *he* to refer to both men and women.

❖   Avoid using *man* to refer to both men and women.

❖   Avoid language that denigrates people.

9. Capitalization

❖   Capitalize the first word of a sentence, the greeting of a letter, the complimentary close of a letter, and each item in an outline.

❖   Capitalize abbreviations that appear after a person's name, geographical places and sections of the country, and the names of historical events, eras, and documents.

❖   Capitalize the names of languages, nationalities, and races.

❖   Capitalize proper nouns, proper adjectives, and brand names.

❖   Capitalize the names of organizations, institutions, courses, and famous buildings.

❖   Capitalize days, months, and holidays.

❖   Capitalize abbreviations for time.

10. Case

Case is the form of a noun or pronoun that shows how it is used in a sentence. English has three cases: *nominative, objective,* and *possessive.*

❖   Use the nominative case to show the subject of a verb. For example: *We* met with the clients.

❖   Use the objective case to show the noun or pronoun that receives the action. For example: The client was willing to speak to *us.*

❖   Use the possessive case to show ownership. For example: The clients gave us *their* account.

11. Clauses

Clauses are groups of words that have a subject and a verb.

❖   *Independent clauses* are complete sentences.

❖ *Dependent clauses* are sentence parts. As incomplete sentences, they can only be part of a sentence.

12. Commas
(See *Punctuation.*)

13. Comparative Adjectives and Adverbs
Follow these rules to make correct comparisons with adjectives and adverbs.

❖ Use the *comparative degree* (*-er* or *more* form) to compare two things.

❖ Use the *superlative form* (*-est* or *most* form) to compare more than two things.

❖ Never use *-er* and *more* or *-est* and *most* together.

Here are some examples:

Part of Speech	Positive	Comparative	Superlative
adjective	slow	slower	slowest
adverb	slowly	more slowly	most slowly

Good and *bad* do not follow these guidelines. They have irregular forms.

Part of Speech	Positive	Comparative	Superlative
adjective	good	better	best
adverb	well	better	best
adjective	bad	worse	worst
adverb	badly	worse	worst

14. Colons
(See *Punctuation.*)

15. Conjunctions
Conjunctions connect words or groups of words. Conjunctions include:

Conjunctions		
after	although	and
as	as if	because
before	both ... and	but

either ... or	even though	for
if	neither ... nor or	not only ... but also
nor	since	so
so that	than	though
unless	until	when
where	wherever	whether ... or
while	yet	

16. Clichés

Clichés are descriptive phrases that have lost their effectiveness through overuse. For example: *Let's do lunch; My people will call your people; Tried and true.* Replace clichés with fresh, new descriptions.

17. Contractions

Contractions are two words combined into one. When you contract words, add an apostrophe in the space where the letters have been taken out. For example:

I	+	am	=	I'm
you	+	are	=	you're
he	+	is	=	he's

Don't confuse *contractions* with *possessive pronouns*. Study this chart to compare the two:

Contraction	Possessive Pronoun
it's (it is)	its
you're (you are)	your
they're (they are)	their
who's (who is)	whose

18. Dangling Modifiers

A *dangling modifier* is a word or phrase that describes something that has been left out of the sentence. The following headline illustrates a dangling modifier:

| *Dangling:* | Miners Refuse to Work after Death |
| *Correct:* | Miners Refuse to Work after *Coworker's* Death |

19. Diction

Diction is a writer's choice of words. Select words that are suitable to your audience, purpose, and tone.

20. Double Negatives

Use only one negative word to express a negative idea. Here are the most frequently used negative words:

Negative Words

-n't (don't, etc.)	no	nobody
not	no one	nothing
nowhere	never	neither
scarcely	only	

21. Exclamation Marks

(See *Punctuation.*)

22. Fragments

A *sentence fragment* is a group of words that does not express a complete thought. The fragment may be missing a subject, a verb, or both, or may not express a complete thought. The following fragment is missing a complete verb:

Fragment: Big companies increasing their returns on equity faster than small companies.

Sentence: Big companies *are* increasing their returns on equity faster than small companies.

23. Interjections

Interjections are words that show strong emotion. Often, interjections are set off with an exclamation mark, for example: *Watch out!*, *Oh!*, or *Wow!* Interjections are almost never used in business writing.

24. Misplaced Modifiers

A *misplaced modifier* is a descriptive word or phrase that is placed too far away from the noun or the pronoun that it is describing. As a result, the sentence does not convey precise meaning. It may also produce confusion or amusement in the reader.

To correct the error, move the modifier as close as possible to the word or phrase it is describing. For example:

Misplaced: The executive read the memo wearing reading glasses.

Correct: The executive wearing reading glasses read the memo.

25. Nonstandard English

Nonstandard English consists of words and phrases that are not considered correct usage in writing, especially in a professional setting. Here is a list of words and phrases to avoid:

Nonstandard English	Standard Written English
being that	because
had ought	ought
hisself	himself
irregardless	regardless
kind of a	kind of
like I told you	as I told you
off of	off
that there	that
the reason is because	the reason is that
this here	this

26. Nouns

A *noun* is a word that names a person, place, or thing.

❖   *Common nouns* name a type of person, place, or thing, such as *computer, city,* or *resort.*

❖   *Proper nouns* name a specific person, place, or thing, such as *Pentium, Des Moines,* or *Club Med.*

27. Parts of Speech

English words are divided into eight different parts of speech according to their function in a sentence. See *Adjectives, Adverbs, Conjunctions, Interjections, Nouns, Prepositions, Pronouns,* and *Verbs* for a description of each kind.

28. Periods
(See *Punctuation.*)

29. Phrases
Phrases are groups of words that function in a sentence as one part of speech. Phrases do not have subjects or verbs, for example: *in a company, near the exit.*

30. Plural Nouns
Plural nouns name more than one person, place, or thing. Follow these guidelines to form the plural of nouns:

Add *s* to form the plural of most nouns. For example:

| office | offices |
| executive | executives |

Add *es* if the noun ends in *s, sh, ch,* or *x.* For example:

| inch | inches |
| box | boxes |

If the noun ends in *y* preceded by a *consonant,* change the *y* to *i* and add *es.* For example:

| city | cities |

If the noun ends in *y* preceded by a *vowel,* add *s.* For example:

| key | keys |

If the noun ends in *o* preceded by a *vowel,* add *s.* For example:

| ratio | ratios |

If the noun ends in *o* preceded by a *consonant,* the noun can take *es,* or *s.* For example:

potato	potatoes
solo	solos
zeros	zeroes

Add *s* to most nouns ending in *f.* For example:

chief   chiefs

Exceptions: Change the *f* or *fe* to *v* and add *es* with the following words:

| self | leaf | life |
| wife | half | thief |

In compound words, make the main word plural. For example:

    attorney-at-law   attorneys-at-law

Some nouns change their spelling when they become plural. For example:

    child   children

    man   men

Some nouns have the same form whether they are singular or plural. For example:

    swine   series

    deer   species

31. Possession

Possession shows ownership. Follow these rules to create possessive nouns.

With singular nouns, add an apostrophe and *s*. For example:

    employee   employee's responsibilities

With plural nouns ending in *s*, add an apostrophe after the *s*. For example:

    employees   employees' responsibilities

With plural nouns not ending in *s*, add an apostrophe and an *s*. For example:

    women   women's room

32. Predicate Adjectives

Predicate adjectives are adjectives separated from the noun or pronoun by a linking verb. Predicate adjectives describe the subject of the sentence, for example: The weather was *cold* all week.

33. Prepositions

Prepositions are words that link a noun or a pronoun to another word in the sentence.

Common Prepositions

about	above	across	after
against	along	amid	around
as	at	before	behind
below	beneath	beside	between

beyond	but	by	despite
down	during	for	except
from	inside	near	of
off	on	onto	opposite
out	outside	over	in
into	like	since	to
through	under	underneath	until
up	upon	with	within

34. Prepositional Phrase

A *prepositional phrase* is a preposition and its object, for example: *on the table, in the meeting.*

35. Pronouns

Pronouns are words used in place of a noun or another pronoun. Here are four main types of pronouns that you'll use in business writing: *personal pronouns, possessive pronouns, interrogative pronouns,* and *indefinite pronouns.*

Personal pronouns refer to a specific person, place, object, or thing.

	Singular	Plural
first-person	I, me, mine, my	we, us, our, ours
second-person	you, your, yours	you, your, yours
third-person	he, him, his	they, them, their
	she, her, hers, it	theirs, its

Possessive pronouns show ownership, for example: *yours, his, hers, its, ours, theirs,* and *whose.*

Interrogative pronouns begin a question, for example: *who, what, which, whom,* and *whose.*

Indefinite pronouns refer to people, places, objects, or things without pointing to a specific one. The following chart lists the most common indefinite pronouns:

Indefinite Pronouns

all	another	any	anybody
anyone	anything	both	either

each	everybody	everyone	everything
few	little	many	more
most	much	neither	nobody
none	no one	others	one
nothing	several	some	someone
somebody	something		

36. Pronoun and Antecedent Agreement
(See *Agreement of pronoun and antecedent.*)

37. Punctuation

Apostrophes: Use an apostrophe (') to show possession (ownership), plural forms, and contractions (where a letter or number has been omitted).

Colons: Use a colon before a list.

Commas: Use a comma after introductory words and expressions, to separate items in a series, to set off interrupting words and expressions, to separate parts of a compound sentence, and after the close of any letter.

Exclamation marks: Avoid using exclamation marks in business writing.

Hyphens: Use a hyphen to show a word break at the end of a line, in certain compound nouns, in fractions, and in compound numbers from twenty-one to ninety-nine.

Parentheses: Use parentheses to enclose additional information.

Periods: Use a period after a complete sentence, after most abbreviations, and after initials.

Question marks: Use a question mark after a question.

Quotation marks: Use quotation marks to set off a speaker's exact words.

Semicolons: Use a semicolon between main clauses when the conjunction (*and, but, for, or*) has been left out, and to separate items in a series when the items contain commas.

38. Question Marks
(See *Punctuation.*)

39. Quotation Marks
(See *Punctuation.*)

40. Run-On Sentences
A *run-on sentence* consists of two incorrectly joined sentences. Example: You don't think you're cut out to be an officer in a trade group volunteer for a position writing or editing its newsletter.

> Correct a run-on sentence by separating the run-on into two sentences:
>> You don't think you're cut out to be an officer in a trade group. Volunteer for a position writing or editing its newsletter.
>
> Add a coordinating conjunction (*and, but, or, for, yet, so*):
>> You don't think you're cut out to be an officer in a trade group, *so* volunteer for a position writing or editing its newsletter.
>
> Add a subordinating conjunction:
>> *If* you don't think you're cut out to be an officer in a trade group, volunteer for a position writing or editing its newsletter.
>
> Add a semicolon: You don't think you're cut out to be an officer in a trade group; volunteer for a position writing or editing its newsletter.

41. Semicolons
(See *Punctuation.*)

42. Sentences
A *sentence* is a group of words that express a complete thought. A sentence has two parts: a *subject* and a *predicate*. The subject includes the noun or pronoun that tells what the subject is about. The predicate contains the verb that describes what the subject is doing.

43. Subordinating Conjunctions
Subordinating conjunctions are words that connect dependent and independent clauses. Use subordinating conjunctions to show the relationship between ideas. The following chart lists some subordinating conjunctions and the relationships they create.

Subordinating Conjunctions

Relationship	Subordinating	Conjunctions
Choice	rather than whether	than if
Condition	if provided that	even if unless
Contrast	although	even though though
Location	where	wherever
Reason or Cause	as	because since
Result or Effect	in order that so that	so that
Time	after once until whenever	before since when while

44. Tense

Verbs can show time, called *tense*. Avoid shifting tenses in the middle of a sentence or paragraph.

45. Transitions

Transitions—words and expressions that signal connections between ideas—can help you achieve coherence in your writing. Each transition signals the reader as to how one idea is connected to the next. This chart lists the most useful transitions for business writing.

Transitions

Relationship	Transition Words	
Addition	also besides in addition to	and too further
Example	for example thus	for instance namely

Time	next	then
	finally	first
	second	third
	fourth	afterward
	before	during
	soon	later
	meanwhile	subsequently
Contrast	but	nevertheless
	yet	in contrast
	however	still
	if	
Comparison	likewise	in comparison
	similarly	
Location	in the front	here
	in the back	there
	nearby	
Result	therefore	thus
	consequently	accordingly
	as a result	due to this
	if	
Summary	as a result	in brief
	in conclusion	hence
	in short	finally

46. Verbs

Verbs are words that name an action or describe a state of being. There are three types of verbs: action verbs, linking verbs, helping verbs.

Action verbs tell what the subject does.

Linking verbs join the subject and the predicate and describe the subject. For example: *be, feel, grow, seem, smell, remain, appear, sound, stay, look, taste, turn, become.*

Helping verbs are added to another verb to make the meaning clearer. For example: *am, does, had, shall, can, did, may, should, could, have, might, will, do, has, must, would.*

47. Verb Tense

The *tense* of a verb shows its time. Every verb has three tenses: present tense, past tense, and past participle.

48. Voice

In addition to indicating time through tense, most verbs also indicate whether the subject is performing an action or having an action performed on it. English uses the *active voice* and the *passive voice*.

❖   In *active voice*, the subject performs the action.

❖   In *passive voice*, the action is performed upon the subject.

The active voice is usually preferable to the passive voice because it is more vigorous and concise. Use the passive voice when you wish to avoid placing blame, for example: *An error has occurred.*

49. Word Choice

(See *Diction.*)

50. Wordiness

Write simply and directly. Omit unnecessary details or ideas that you have already stated. Use a lot of important detail, but no unnecessary words.

Chapter 18

Phrases and Clauses

Now that we've covered individual words, it's time to put them together into logical units of expression: *phrases* and *clauses*. In the first half of this chapter, you'll review all the different phrases, including prepositional phrases, verbal phrases, and appositives. In the second half, you'll study the two types of clauses: *independent* and *dependent* clauses, including adverb, adjective, and noun clauses.

It's not enough just to identify phrases and clauses; you also have to know how to use these sentence parts to state your meaning clearly in all your business writing. In this chapter, you'll also learn how to use phrases and clauses to communicate clearly and build goodwill.

What's a Phrase?

A *phrase* is a group of words, without a subject or verb, that functions in a sentence as a single part of speech. As a result, a phrase cannot stand alone as an independent unit. You use phrases in your writing to make your meaning more exact.

There are eight different types of phrases: prepositional phrases, adjective phrases, adverbial phrases, verbal phrases, gerund phrases, infinitive phrases, participle phrases, and appositive phrases. The following chart explains each type of phrase:

Type of Phrase	Definition	Example
Prepositional	Begins with a preposition and ends with a noun or pronoun.	Her desk is *near the water cooler*
Adjective	Prepositional phrase that functions as an adjective.	We had a binder *with a red cover.*
Adverb	Prepositional phrase that functions as an adverb.	The executive worked *at the XYZ division.*
Verbal	Verb form used as another part of speech.	Seeing is believing.

Gerund	Verbal phrase that functions as a noun.	*Waiting for the airplane* exhausted their patience.
Infinitive	Verbal phrase that functions as a noun, adjective, or adverb.	*To sleep late on Sunday* is a treat.
Participle	Verbal phrase that functions as an adjective.	*Speaking slowly*, the boss was clear.
Appositive	Noun or pronoun that renames another noun or pronoun.	Nick, *a corporate raider*, is ruthless.

Prepositional Phrases

A *prepositional phrase* is a group of words that begins with a preposition and ends with a noun or a pronoun. The noun or pronoun is called the object of the preposition.

The preposition is highlighted in each of the following prepositional phrases:

by the window   *near* the desk
in the conference room   *with* the staff
over the shelf   *under* the desk

Adjective Phrases

When a prepositional phrase serves as an adjective, it is called an *adjective phrase*. Like an adjective, an adjective phrase modifies a noun or a pronoun. A prepositional phrase is functioning as an adjective phrase when it answers the questions, "Which one?" or, "What kind?" For example:

The supervisor with the layoff notices terrorized the staff.
    The adjective phrase *with the layoff notices* describes the noun *supervisor*.
The price of the promotion was much too steep. The adjective phrase *of the promotion* describes the noun *price*.

Adverb Phrases

Depending on how it is used in a sentence, a prepositional phrase can also serve as an *adverb phrase* by describing a verb, an adjective, or an adverb. A prepositional phrase is functioning as an adverb phrase when it answers one of these questions: "Where?" "When?" "In what manner?" "To what extent?" For example:

The boss is always tougher on newcomers.

> The adverb phrase *on newcomers* describes the adjective *tougher*.

The shipment arrived late at night.

> The adverb phrase *at night* describes the adverb *late*.

Verbal Phrases

A *verbal phrase* includes a verb form used as another part of speech. There are three kinds of verbals: gerunds, infinitives, and participles. Each type has a different function in a sentence:

1. *Gerunds* function as nouns.
2. *Infinitives* function as nouns, adjectives, or adverbs.
3. *Participles* function as adjectives.

Gerund Phrases

A *gerund* functions as a noun. Gerunds always end in *-ing* and can function as subjects, direct objects, indirect objects, objects of a preposition, predicate nominatives, and appositives. For example:

> Meditating can help a stressed executive relax.
>
> > The gerund *meditating* is the subject of the sentence.
>
> Clever people expand their 401K plans by investing.
>
> > The gerund *investing* is the object of the preposition *by*.

Infinitive Phrases

Infinitives are verb forms that come after the word *to* and act as nouns, adjectives, or adverbs. Like gerunds, infinitives can fill different grammatical functions within a sentence, as the following examples show:

> To get ahead in business takes nerve, intelligence, and luck.
>
> > The infinitive *to get ahead* functions as the subject of the sentence.
>
> All she wanted was to avoid taking the blame for the project's failure.
>
> > The infinitive *to avoid* functions as the direct object.

Participle Phrases

A *participle* is a form of a verb that functions as an adjective. There are two kinds of participles: present participles and past participles.

> Present participles end in *-ing* (*training, burning, eating*).

Past participles usually end in *-ed, -t,* or *-en (trained, burnt, eaten).*

Here are some examples of participles:

Smiling, the boss shook my hand.

> The present participle *smiling* describes the noun *boss.*

The disappointed team vowed to do better on the next campaign.

> The past participle *disappointed* describes the noun *team.*

Participle phrases contain a participle modified by an adverb or an adverbial phrase. The entire phrase functions as an adjective, as these examples show:

Walking quickly, Jack didn't notice the paper stuck to his heel.

> The participle phrase *walking quickly* describes the noun *Jack.*

The assistant, unjamming the copier, looked angry.

> The participle phrase *unjamming the copier* describes the noun *assistant.*

Appositive Phrases

An *appositive phrase* provides additional information and description. As such, it renames another noun or pronoun. Appositives are placed directly after the noun or pronoun they identify. For example:

Michelle Tullier, an adjunct professor of career counseling at New York University, is the author of *Connecting with People for Career and Job Success.*

> The appositive *adjunct professor of career counseling at New York University* renames the noun *Michelle Tullier.*

Using Phrases to Improve Your Writing

Phrases add detail to your writing, which allows you to make your meaning more precise. Participles and participle phrases are especially useful in business writing because they help you combine sentences to create crisp, concise writing. Notice how the weak sentences below are improved when they are combined with a participle:

Weak: We skimmed the annual report. We could see it was not yet complete.

Better: *Skimming* the annual report, we could see it was not yet complete.

Weak: The CEO shook hands with shareholders at the annual meeting. He could barely make his way through the crowd.

Better:	*Shaking* hands with the shareholders at the annual meeting, the CEO could barely make his way through the crowd.
Weak:	Jessica placed her shot carefully. She hit the ball to her opponent's backhand.
Better:	*Placing* her shot carefully, Jessica hit the ball to her opponent's backhand.

Here are two sentences combined with appositives:

Weak:	Dr. William Teish is a rheumatologist in Reno, Nevada. He is the leader of a study of 500 patients with carpal tunnel syndrome.
Better:	Dr. William Teish, *a rheumatologist in Reno, Nevada*, is the leader of a study of 500 patients with carpal tunnel syndrome.
Weak:	Kent Clark is an optometrist in Alabama. He asserts that eyeglasses designed just for computer use can be a good choice for people who suffer headaches when using computer screens.
Better:	Kent Clark, *an optometrist in Alabama*, asserts that eyeglasses designed just for computer use can be a good choice for people who suffer headaches when using computer screens.

What's a Clause?

A *clause* is a group of words with its own subject and verb.

Like phrases, clauses enrich your writing by adding details and helping to make your meaning more exact. Clauses allow you to combine ideas to show their relationship, adding logic and cohesion to help you communicate your meaning more precisely.

There are two types of clauses: *dependent* clauses and *independent* clauses.

❖ A *dependent (subordinate) clause* is part of a sentence; it cannot stand alone.

❖ An *independent clause* is a complete sentence; it can stand alone.

As you read the three examples of each type of clause, notice that you can't decide whether a word group is a clause by its length, because both dependent and independent clauses can be short or long.

Dependent Clauses	Independent Clauses
If you're asked to write a reference letter,	be sure to answer truthfully.
While making at least the minimum payment on all other debts,	pay off your smallest debts as quickly as possible.

When the smallest debt is paid,	take the money you were putting toward that debt and add it to the minimum payment on the next smallest debt.

Let's look at each type of clause in greater detail, starting with dependent clauses.

Dependent Clauses

Dependent clauses add additional information to a main clause, but they don't express a complete thought. As a result, a dependent clause "depends" on its connection to an independent clause to make sense.

A dependent clause often contains a *subordinating conjunction* that makes it a fragment. Look back at the three dependent clauses on the first chart. Each one starts with a subordinating conjunction: *if*, *while*, and *when*.

As you learned in Chapter 17, subordinating conjunctions link dependent clauses to independent clauses. Each subordinating conjunction expresses a relationship between the dependent clause and the independent clause. For example, some conjunctions show time order; others, result or effect. This is explained in detail in Chapter 17.

There are three different kinds of dependent clauses: *adverb clauses*, *adjective clauses*, and *noun clauses*. Let's review each one to see how you can use them to create more logical and economical sentences.

Adverb Clauses

An *adverb clause* is a dependent clause that modifies a verb, adjective, or other adverb. Adverb clauses answer one of these questions: Where? Why? When? To what extent? Under what condition? In what manner?

You can place an adverb clause in the beginning, middle, or end of a sentence. For example:

They leave their business cards behind wherever they travel.

> The adverb clause *wherever they travel* modifies the verb *leave*.

If it is rainy, we will hold the seminar inside.

> The adverb clause *if it is rainy* modifies the verb *hold*.

As with other phrases and clauses, adverb clauses can help you create more concise sentences. Notice how the following sentences improve when they are combined into one with an adverb clause.

Weak: We were in the conference room. The courier arrived with the package.

Better: While we were in the conference room, the courier
                            arrived with the package.

Adjective Clauses

Adjective clauses describe nouns and pronouns. Like an adjective, an adjective
clause answers the questions *Which one?* or *What kind?* Most adjective clauses
start with the pronouns *who, whom, whose, which, that, when,* or *where.* They can
also start with *whoever, whichever, whatever, what, whomever,* and *why.*

Here are some examples:

The television station that uses radar for tracking the weather is popular with
business travelers.

> The adjective clause *that uses radar for tracking the weather* describes the
> noun *television station.*

The sun never shines on days when I can enjoy it.

> The adjective clause *when I can enjoy it* describes the noun *days.*

Relative Clauses

Adjective clauses that begin with one of the relative pronouns are also called *relative clauses.* The relative pronouns are *who, whom, whose, which,* or *that.*

Relative pronouns connect (or relate) an adjective clause to the word the
clause describes. In addition, relative pronouns function within the clause as a
subject, direct object, object of a preposition, or adjective. For example:

The boat that we chartered for the marketing meeting is beautifully furnished.

> The relative clause *that we chartered for the marketing meeting* functions
> as a subject.

The software that you recommended is very good.

> The relative clause *that you recommended* is the direct object of the sub-
> ject *you.*

The person of whom you spoke is my boss.

> The relative clause *whom you spoke* is the object of the preposition *of.*

The assistant whose manual I borrowed is well-versed in PowerPoint.

> The relative clause *whose manual I borrowed* describes the noun *assis-
> tant.*

As with adverb clauses, you can use adjective clauses to link ideas, combine
information, and create more effective sentences. In addition to adding description to sentences, adjective clauses allow you to convey relationships between
ideas. For example:

Weak:	We borrowed a van to transport the late shipment. It was too small for our needs.
Better:	The van *that we borrowed to transport the late shipment* was too small for our needs.

Noun Clauses

A *noun clause* is a dependent clause that functions as a noun. A noun clause can be a subject, direct object, indirect object, object of a preposition, or appositive. For example:

Whomever you bring to the holiday party will be welcome.

> The noun clause *Whomever you bring to the holiday party* functions as a subject.

Louis does whatever the boss asks him to do.

> The noun clause *whatever the boss asks him to do* functions as a direct object.

The boss gave whomever worked overtime a comp day.

> The noun clause *whomever worked overtime* functions as an indirect object.

Hand your ticket to whoever is standing at the door.

> The noun clause *whoever is standing at the door* functions as the object of the preposition *to*.

The manager did not accept my excuse that the train was late.

> The noun clause *that the train was late* functions as an appositive because it adds extra information to the sentence.

Independent Clauses

An *independent clause* contains a subject and a predicate. It can stand alone as a sentence because it expresses a complete thought. The following chart shows some independent clauses divided into their subjects and predicates.

Independent Clauses

Subject	Predicate
Internet news groups	can function like trade association meetings.
You	join when your schedule permits.
A list of your accomplishments	can be a useful self-promotion tool.
A portfolio	eases the awkwardness of having to sing your own praises.

Summary

❖ A *phrase* is a group of words, without a subject or a verb, that functions as a single part of speech. Phrases cannot stand alone as independent units.

❖ *Prepositional phrases* begin with a preposition and end with a noun or pronoun; they can function as *adjective phrases* or *adverb phrases*.

❖ *Verbals* are verb forms used as another part of speech. *Participles* function as adjectives; *gerunds* function as nouns; *infinitives* function as nouns, adjectives, or adverbs.

❖ *Appositives* rename another noun or pronoun; *appositive phrases* include modifiers.

❖ A *dependent clause* is a fragment, not a complete sentence.

❖ Dependent clauses include *adverb clauses*, *adjective clauses*, and *noun clauses*.

❖ An *independent (main) clause* is a complete sentence.

Chapter 19

Sentences

Which of the following four word groups is a sentence?

❖ A natural setbacks process of success are part of the.

❖ The of process of success setbacks are a natural part.

❖ Success process of setbacks are part a natural of the.

❖ Setbacks are a natural part of the process of success.

Each word group contains exactly the same words, but only the last one is a sentence. How were you able to pick it out? You recognized the sentence from the word groups because you know how English works.

But maybe you're a little rusty when it comes to the different kinds of sentences and how they're used. Perhaps you're not sure how to vary your sentences to make your business writing clear. Overall, you want to feel more self-assured about your business writing. That's what this chapter is all about.

The chapter opens with a discussion of the two elements in every sentence: the *subject* and the *predicate.* Next you'll learn about the four different types of sentences: *simple, compound, complex,* and *compound-complex.* Then you'll find a discussion of the four different sentence functions. Last but certainly not least, I'll show you how to make your writing correct by eliminating incomplete sentences.

What Is a Sentence?

Sentence: Halt!

Sentence: You halt!

Sentence: You halt right now or I'll call the authorities!

Each of these word groups is a sentence because each one meets the three requirements for a sentence. To be a sentence, a group of words must ...

❖ have a *subject* (noun or pronoun),

❖ have a *predicate* (verb or verb phrase), and

❖ express a *complete thought.*

Every *sentence* has two parts: a *subject* and a *predicate*. The subject includes the noun or pronoun that tells what the subject is about. The predicate includes the predicate that describes what the subject is doing. Here are some examples of complete sentences:

Subject	Predicate
[understood subject *You*]	Halt!
You	halt!
You	halt right now or I'll call the authorities.

Finding Subjects and Predicates

Being able to recognize the subject and the predicate in a sentence will help you write complete, clear sentences. In most sentences, the subject comes before the predicate. In a question, however, the subject comes after the predicate. To check that you've included the subject and predicate in your sentences, follow these steps:

❖ To find the subject, ask yourself, "What word does the sentence describe?"

❖ To find an action verb, ask yourself, "What is the subject doing?" (or, "What did the subject do?").

❖ If you can't find an action verb, look for a linking verb.

Sentences That Start with *Here* or *There*

It can be tricky finding the subject in sentences that start with *here* or *there*. Neither *here* nor *there* can ever be the subject of a sentence. To find the subject in a sentence that starts with *here* or *there*, rewrite the sentence to place the subject first. For example:

Here is my projected annual budget.

> The subject of the sentence is *budget*. Rewrite the sentence this way: *My projected budget is here.*

There goes my projected annual budget, shot down from on high.

> The subject of the sentence is still *budget*. Rewrite the sentence this way: *My projected annual budget has been shot down from on high.*

Sentence Structure

In Chapter 18, you learned about *independent* and *dependent* clauses. Remember that *independent clauses* are complete sentences because they have a subject and predicate and express a complete thought. *Dependent clauses,* in contrast, cannot stand alone because they do not express a complete thought, even though they contain a subject and a predicate. Independent and dependent clauses can be used in a number of ways to form the four basic types of sentences: simple, compound, complex, and compound-complex.

Knowing the four sentence types and how to use them can help you express your ideas more clearly in print.

Simple Sentences

A *simple sentence* has one independent clause. As a result, a simple sentence has one subject and one predicate, although either or both can be compound. In addition, a simple sentence can have adjectives and adverbs. What a simple sentence *can't* have is another independent clause or any subordinate clauses. For example:

Many workers *one subject*	feel like cogs in a machine. *one predicate*
My assistant *one subject*	photocopies and collates the document. *compound predicate*
Early to bed and early to rise *compound subject*	is first in the bathroom. *one predicate*

Don't be misled by the name; the simple sentence may be simple but it is not for simpletons. When it comes to business writing, the simple sentence is a winner because it allows you to create short, clear, and punchy sentences. Busy executives want the information they need fast. They don't have the time—or desire—to grapple with long and windy sentences. The simple sentence allows you to make your point and build goodwill.

This sample paragraph is written exclusively in simple sentences. Notice the clear and direct style. Isn't this the kind of writing you wish crossed your desk everyday?

> Internet trading is not for bonds. There is no exchange on which most bonds trade. Further, the Internet does not have an accurate way to check the current prices of most bonds. Therefore, there is no way to compare prices. In addition, the cost of Internet bond trading is about the same as trading through a dealer. Here's the good news. On-line bond trading is evolving rapidly. In the near future, it could become a good alternative to using a bond dealer.

Now, I'm not advocating that you reduce all your writing to a series of simple sentences. Not only would you start to feel as if you were filling out a puzzle, but you'd also have difficulty linking ideas. What I *am* suggesting, however, is that you *always* take your audience's needs into account when you decide which sentence form to use. With that in mind, let's look at the next type of sentence, the *compound sentence*.

Compound Sentences

A *compound sentence* consists of two or more independent clauses. The independent clauses can be joined in one of two ways:

❖   with a coordinating conjunction: *for, and, nor, but, or, yet, so*

❖   with a semicolon (;)

Like a simple sentence, a compound sentence can't have any subordinate clauses. For example:

Everyone has a photographic memory	but	some people don't have film.
independent clause	*conjunction*	*independent clause*
Tell some people a bench has wet paint	and	they have to touch it.
independent clause	*conjunction*	*independent clause*
Some people play golf	so	they can wear clothes they would not be caught dead in otherwise.
independent clause	*conjunction*	*independent clause*
Don't count your chickens	;	it takes too long.
independent clause	*semicolon*	*independent clause*

You may also add a conjunctive adverb to a compound sentence, as in this example:

We put suits in a garment bag; *however*, we put garments in a suitcase.

Here's how our bond paragraph looks when some of the simple sentences are changed to compound ones. The coordinating conjunctions serve to connect ideas and create greater logic.

Internet trading is not for bonds; there is no exchange on which most bonds trade. Further, the Internet does not have an accurate way to check the current prices of most bonds *so* there is no way to compare prices. In addition, the cost of Internet bond trading is about the same as trading through a dealer. Here's the good news. On-line bond trading is evolving rapidly, *so* in the near future it could become a good alternative to using a bond dealer.

Complex Sentences

A *complex sentence* contains one independent clause and at least one dependent clause. The independent clause is called the main clause. These sentences use *subordinating conjunctions* to link ideas.

Here's a quick refresher on subordinating conjunctions:

Subordinating Conjunctions

Relationship	Transition Words	
Choice	rather than	than
	whether	if
Condition	if	even if
	provided that	unless
Contrast	although	even though
	though	
Location	where	wherever
Reason or Cause	as	because
	since	
Result or Effect	in order that	so
	so that	that
Time	after	before
	once	since
	until	when
	whenever	while

Study these examples of complex sentences:

If	I want your opinion	I'll ask you to fill out the necessary forms.
conjunction	*dependent clause*	*independent clause*

Many people quit looking for work	when	they find a job.
independent clause	*conjunction*	*dependent clause*

Since	everything seems to be going well	you have obviously overlooked something.
conjunction	*dependent clause*	*independent clause*

Here's how the same bond paragraph looks when some of the simple and compound sentences are revised as complex sentences. You'll notice that this sentence form allows writers to create more sophisticated connections among ideas.

Internet trading is not for bonds; there is no exchange on which most bonds trade. Further, the Internet does not have an accurate way to check the current prices of most bonds *unless they develop* a way to compare prices. In addition, the cost of Internet bond trading is about the same as trading through a dealer. Here's the good news. On-line bond trading is evolving rapidly, *so that* in the near future it could become a good alternative to using a bond dealer.

Compound-Complex Sentences

A *compound-complex sentence* has at least two independent clauses and at least one dependent clause. The dependent clause can be part of the independent clause. For instance:

When	layoffs take place,	we worry a lot,
conjunction	*dependent clause*	*independent clause*

and	we prepare for the worst.
conjunction	*independent clause*

I planned to take the train to Boston,	but
independent clause	*conjunction*

I couldn't	until	the strike ended.
independent clause	*conjunction*	*dependent clause*

Crafting Your Style

Now that you know you have four different sentence types at your disposal, which ones should you use? Successful business writing requires not only that you write complete sentences, but also that you write sentences that say exactly what you mean and build goodwill. The following guidelines can help you decide which sentence types to use and when:

❖   Your choice of sentence type always depends on your *audience* and *purpose*.

❖   Most business writing sent outside the company or organization relies on simple and compound sentences, because they help your readers grasp your message quickly. Documents distributed inside the company often include complex sentences. It is rare to have compound-complex sentences in a business document, because these sentences tend to be long and thus more difficult to read. This isn't to say that you can't include complex or compound-complex sentences in external documents; it is to say, however, that you must carefully consider your readers and their needs when you select sentence types.

❖ Stress the main point or the most important detail at the beginning of every sentence. Don't make your readers hunt for the information. This creates ill will and blocks communication.

❖ Write clearly, concisely, and completely. Make sure that each sentence says exactly what you mean in a way that your audience can clearly understand.

Sentence Functions

In addition to classifying sentences by the number of clauses they contain, we can categorize sentences according to their function. There are four sentence functions in English: declarative, exclamatory, interrogative, and imperative.

Let's look at each type in detail:

1. *Declarative sentences* state an idea. They end with a period. For example:

   The average person is about a quarter of an inch taller at night.

   Because they are on opposite sides of the San Andreas fault, Los Angeles and San Francisco become 2.5 inches closer together each year.

   All office-seekers in the Roman Empire were obliged to wear a certain white toga for a period of one year before the election.

2. *Exclamatory sentences* show strong emotions. They end with an exclamation mark. For example:

   Put that pen down!

   Don't sit in my chair!

   Get out of my office—it's my private space!

   As mentioned earlier in this guide, exclamatory sentences are rarely used in business writing because they convey the wrong tone. You don't want your everyday communication to be hyped up. Instead, use precise predicates and nouns to make your writing vivid and exact.

3. *Interrogative sentences* ask a question. As you would expect, they end with a question mark. For example:

   Is it better to invest in tax-free or taxable bonds?

   What effect do digital tools have on organizational structure?

   How can you motivate people to take responsibility for the product?

4.   *Imperative sentences* give orders or directions, and so end with a period or an exclamation mark. For example:

Take one uncoated aspirin when you think you might be having a heart attack.

Exercise your brain by learning at least one new fact a day.

Fasten your seatbelts when the sign is illuminated.

Sentence Errors

You know that your sentences have to be clear and concise so they create good-will. But they also have to be *correct*.

There are two basic types of sentence errors: *fragments* and *run-ons*. Each type of sentence error causes confusion that results in rereading and ill will. Let's review each of these sentence errors so you'll be able to fix them with ease.

Fragments

As its name suggests, a *sentence fragment* is a group of words that does not express a complete thought. Sometimes a fragment results from a word group that is missing a subject, a predicate, or both. At other times, a fragment results from a word group that has a subject and a predicate but still doesn't express a complete thought.

1.   A fragment occurs when a sentence is missing a subject or predicate. For example:

Fragment: Two credit cards for every person in the United States.

Sentence: *There are* two credit cards for every person in the United States.

Fragment: In the mid to late 1980s, an IBM-compatible computer one hundred percent compatible unless it could run Microsoft's Flight Simulator.

Sentence: In the mid to late 1980s, an IBM-compatible computer *wasn't considered* one hundred percent compatible unless it could run Microsoft's Flight Simulator.

2.   A fragment occurs when a word group has a subject and a predicate but doesn't express a complete thought. For example:

Fragment: Because nothing in the known universe travels faster than a bad check.

Sentence: Nothing in the known universe travels faster than a bad check.

Fragment:	Although silence is sometimes the best answer.
Sentence:	Silence is sometimes the best answer.

3.   Fragments also result from word groups that use the wrong form of a predicate. For example:

Fragment:	Remembering that your character is your destiny.
Sentence:	Remember that your character is your destiny.
Fragment:	To judge your success by what you had to give up in order to get it.
Sentence:	Judge your success by what you had to give up in order to get it.

As these examples show, you can correct a fragment in two ways:

1.   Add the missing part to the sentence.

Fragment:	If you make a lot of money.
Sentence:	If you make a lot of money, put it to use helping others while you are living.

2.   Omit the subordinating conjunction or connect it to another sentence.

Fragment:	Since vital papers will demonstrate their vitality by moving from where you left them to where you can't find them.
Sentence:	Vital papers will demonstrate their vitality by moving from where you left them to where you can't find them.

Run-Ons and Comma Splices

A *run-on sentence* is two incorrectly joined independent clauses. A *comma splice* is a run-on with a comma where the two independent clauses run together. When your sentences run together, your ideas are not clear. For instance:

Run-on:	To be more productive, get one last thing done before leaving the office make one phone call, write one letter, or do one small task.
Sentence:	To be more productive, get one last thing done before leaving the office. Make one phone call, write one letter, or do one small task.
Run-on:	To revisit and reactivate your dreams without giving up what you have achieved so far, remove the pressures of youth, imagine that you no longer need to win approval for being successful.

Sentence: To revisit and reactivate your dreams without giving up what you have achieved so far, remove the pressures of youth *and* imagine that you no longer need to win approval for being successful.

Even though these sentences are long, run-ons can be short. For example:
He worked we rested.

Stocks soar bonds bomb.

You can correct a run-on sentence in several different ways:

1. Separate the run-on into two sentences by adding end punctuation such as periods and question marks.

    Run-on: Avoid double taxation of retirement on assets by using them during your retirement save your capital gains assets for bequests since they are not subject to income tax at death.

    Sentence: Avoid double taxation of retirement on assets by using them during your retirement. Save your capital gains assets for bequests since they are not subject to income tax at death.

2. Add a coordinating conjunction (*and, nor, but, or, for, yet, so*) to create a compound sentence. Be sure to use a comma before the coordinating conjunction in a compound sentence. For example:

    Run-on: Our eyes are always the same size from birth, our noses and ears never stop growing.

    Sentence: Our eyes are always the same size from birth, *but* our noses and ears never stop growing.

3. Add a subordinating conjunction to create a complex sentence.

    Run-on: Your earliest career decisions were driven by the need to make money to start your family the second half of your life can be driven by the dreams you set aside in your youth.

    Sentence: *Although* your earliest career decisions were driven by the need to make money to start your family, the second half of your life can be driven by the dreams you set aside in your youth.

4. Use a semicolon to create a compound sentence.

    Run-on :   Nondairy creamer is flammable milk is not.

    Sentence: Nondairy creamer is flammable; milk is not.

Summary

❖ A *sentence* has a subject and a predicate and expresses a complete thought.

❖ There are four types of sentences: *simple, compound, complex,* and *compound-complex.*

❖ There are four sentence functions: *declarative, exclamatory, interrogative,* and *imperative.*

❖ *Fragments and run-ons* are sentence errors.

Part 5

TOOLS OF THE TRADE

Chapter 20

The Power of Punctuation

Did you know ...

> The total weight of all insects on Earth is twelve times greater than the weight of all people.

Little things *do* matter a lot, especially when it comes to the signposts of our language—punctuation. Just as all those little buggies add up, so do all those little marks of punctuation.

Punctuation *is* a crucial aspect of all good writing, especially in the business world. In fact, the best writers know that they can have wonderful ideas and well-phrased sentences, but poor or inaccurate punctuation can ruin their writing. Unfortunately, many business executives are confused about punctuation. People often ask me, "Do all the punctuation rules I learned in school apply on the job?" The answer is yes, they do.

Another business executive once told me, "I like to use a lot of different marks of punctuation, just so my readers will think I'm more intelligent." The executive added, "I'm not even sure that the marks I use are correct, but I figure that the more semicolons, question marks, colons, and exclamation points people find in my writing, the more intelligent they'll believe I am." See what I mean about confusion?

In this chapter, you'll review punctuation in business writing and banish the confusion all those little marks can cause. By the end of this chapter, you'll be more confident in your ability to use the signposts of written discourse correctly.

The Period

The period is the workhorse of punctuation. Like a generous pension, it's always welcome at the end. In general, business writing demands short, crisp sentences. As a result, effective business writing uses more periods than any other form of punctuation.

Here's a case in point. The second passage is better business writing because it breaks up a long and windy sentence into two succinct sentences. As a result, that passage is more readable than the first one.

Weak: Your analysis of the brochure we are considering publishing this quarter was a good starting point but I still would like some more concise explanations because a number of your examples can be more specific.

Better: Your analysis of the brochure we are considering publishing this quarter was a good starting point, but I still would like some more concise explanations. A number of your examples can be more specific.

Here's how to use periods.

Use a period after a complete sentence (one complete thought).

Example: I am writing to let you know that your March 31, 1999 paycheck will contain the 3.5 percent on-base salary increase negotiated in the last contract.

Use a period after a command.

Example: Please submit the report by Friday.

Use a period after most abbreviations. If an abbreviation comes at the end of a sentence, don't add another period.

Examples: Dr.   Ms.   Jr.

Don't use periods after acronyms.

Examples: CNN   NATO   CBS

Use a period after an initial.

Example: Franklin D. Roosevelt

Use a period after each Roman numeral, letter, or number in an outline.

Example: I.

              A.
              B.

                  1.
                  2.

Always place a period inside a quotation mark that ends a sentence.

Example: The sign read, "The IRS—Be audit you can be."

The Question Mark

Use a question mark after a question.

Example: Don't you want the best product at the best price?

Place the question mark inside closing quotation marks if it *is* part of the quotation.

Example: "Are negotiations a political process?" he asked.

Place the question mark outside the closing quotation marks if it *is not* part of the quotation.

Example: Was it your boss who said, "Generally, dividends from net investment income are taxable to shareholders as ordinary income"?

The Exclamation Mark

In speech, exclamations are used freely, especially in moments of passion (like when your vacation is canceled because of an office crisis). In business writing, however, it is far more convincing to create emphasis with the force of your words rather than the force of your punctuation. It's likely that you'll write on the job for many years without ever using an exclamation mark.

If by some odd chance you do have to use an exclamation mark, use it after an exclamatory sentence. *Don't* combine an exclamation mark with a period, comma, or question mark, as in !? or !.

The Comma

Punctuation helps readers identify clusters of words between and within sentences. *Between* sentences, the most common mark of punctuation is the period; *within* sentences, the most common mark of punctuation is the comma. Always remember that a comma cannot be used to separate two complete sentences. Using a comma that way creates a type of sentence error called a comma splice.

Too many business documents suffer from a kind of comma fever—pages are littered with unnecessary commas. Although the comma is a very important punctuation mark, it can be overdone. Because you don't want to break up the flow of a sentence unnecessarily, delete any extraneous commas. If necessary, cut and paste to achieve a less choppy style. For example:

Weak: Please, analyze, prepare, and evaluate, then, print out a new, complete brochure, so that James, the editor, can reread your work.

Better: Please analyze, prepare, and evaluate the document. Then print out a new copy so that James, the editor, can reread your work.

Commas tell us how to read and understand sentences because they tell us where to pause. A correctly placed comma helps move readers from the beginning of a sentence to the end. Here are the guidelines that govern comma use:

At the beginning of a sentence ...

Use a comma after introductory expressions or any group of words that opens a sentence. Possibilities include introductory prepositional phrases, introductory participial phrases, and introductory subordinate clauses.

Examples: For temporary defensive purposes, the fund may invest without limit in cash or cash equivalents.

In such a case, the fund may not achieve its investment objective.

When this occurs, the use of derivatives could magnify losses.

As a business manager, you need to take a hard look at your core competencies.

In the middle of a sentence ...

Use a comma before a coordinating conjunction in a compound sentence. Remember that the coordinating conjunctions are *and, but, for, nor, or, so, yet.*

Examples: Give your workers more sophisticated jobs along with better tools, and you'll discover that your employees will become more responsible.

Explain that this isn't an adversarial position, but a way to reduce the stress that comes with misunderstandings and disappointed expectations.

Use a comma after interrupting words and expressions. (The interrupting words and expressions in these examples are in italics.)

Examples: *Yes,* I know the report is due on Tuesday.

Windows, *did you know,* is the best $89 solitaire game you can buy.

Use a comma to set off *appositives* (words that give additional information by renaming a noun or pronoun). Appositives can be moved around, as the following examples show. (The words in apposition are in italics in the examples.)

Examples: Egghead.com, *a major retail software chain,* closed all its physical stores nationwide in 1998 and set up shop exclusively on the Internet.

A *major retail software chain,* Egghead.com closed all its physical stores nationwide in 1998 and set up shop exclusively on the Internet.

Never use commas to set off an *essential clause,* a clause that cannot be omitted, as these examples show:

Nonessential: The Web workstyle, *in which each contributor or company organizes itself optimally,* enables companies to extend their electronic partnerships.

Essential: The Web workstyle lets each contributor or company organize itself optimally.

Use a comma to separate items in a series. The comma before *and* in a series of items is optional.

Examples: You need to plan, delegate, and categorize.

Some people are overwhelmed at work because they spend too much time talking to friends, tracking the stock market, or giving subordinates more guidance than they should.

Use a comma to clarify any potentially confusing sentences. Of course, you are usually much better off just revising the sentences so there is no possibility of misunderstanding.

Confusing: To get through a tunnel must be dug.

Clear: To get through, a tunnel must be dug.

At the end of a sentence ...

Use a comma after ending expressions that show contrast.

Example: The district supervisor likes to assign long reports, often right before sales conferences.

Other comma uses ...

Use a comma to set off a direct quotation.

Examples: He said, "Most business travel is a waste of time."

"Most business travel," he said, "is a waste of time."

Use a comma to separate the parts of an address. Do not use a comma before the zip code in an address.

Example: The new office is located at 17 Federal Way, Orlando, Florida 72893.

Use a comma to separate names and titles.
Examples: Luis Ramon, Ph.D.
              Alfonse Franco, M.D.

Use a comma after the greeting in an informal letter.
Examples: Dear Freda,   Dear Leon,

Use a comma at the close of any letter.
Examples: Yours truly,   Sincerely,

Use a comma between the day of the month and the year.
Examples: December 7, 1941   July 20, 1969

Use commas to show thousands, millions, and so on.
Examples: 1,000   10,000   100,000   1,000,000

Note on Numbering
Numbering systems throughout the world differ in their use of punctuation. Some numbering systems use a period to mark a division of thousands, so *ten thousand* would be written 10.000. In the United States, commas are used to mark divisions of thousands.

The Semicolon
What about the semicolon? Many people are confused, even frightened, about using the semicolon. The semicolon is actually an easy mark of punctuation to use, and a surprisingly useful one.

A semicolon has two primary uses: to separate two complete sentences (independent clauses) whose ideas are closely related and to separate clauses that contain a comma. Let's look at each use more closely.

Use a semicolon between closely related independent clauses.
Example: The original materials came from our Charleston plant; the product was made in Toledo.

Use a semicolon between main clauses when the coordinating conjunction has been left out.
Example: Don't be so obsessed with setting things right that you can't let go of an assignment; never feel guilty about backing off and using resources to reach your goals at work.

Use a semicolon to join independent clauses when one or both clauses contain a comma.

Example: Compared to other classes of financial assets, such as bonds or cash equivalents, common stocks have historically offered the greatest potential for gain on your investment; but the market value of common stocks can fluctuate significantly, reflecting such things as the business performance of the issuing company, investors' perceptions of the company, or the general economic or financial market.

Use a semicolon between main clauses connected by conjunctive adverbs such as *however, nevertheless, moreover, for example,* and *consequently.*

Example: Tackle your toughest or least pleasant projects when you feel most productive; however, your hardest tasks should be slotted for the early hours.

The Colon

The semicolon and the colon are often confused and so misused. They're not interchangeable. Here's how to use the colon.

Use a colon before a list. Often, the word *following* will be used to introduce the list.

Example: The new contract contains the following provisions: cost of living increases, guarantees of no outsourcing, and no loss of jobs in the bargaining unit.

Use a colon before a part of a sentence that explains what has just been stated.

Example: Life is a series of rude awakenings: It is what happens to you while you are making other plans.

Use a colon before a long quotation, especially a formal one.

Example: Bill Gates said: "A company's middle managers and line employees, not just its high-level executives, need to see business data. They're the people who need precise, actionable data because they're the ones who need to act. They need an immediate, constant flow and rich views of the right information."

Use a colon after the salutation in a business letter.

Examples: Dear Ms. Smyth:

To Whom It May Concern:

Use a colon to distinguish hours from minutes, and titles from subtitles.

Examples: 11:30 AM

Invest Wisely: How to Bulletproof Your Portfolio

Note on Punctuation and Spacing

Typists and word processors normally put one space after a comma or semicolon, two spaces after a period or question mark, and one or two spaces after colons, but there's no firm rule on this. Typesetters put only one space after all punctuation.

Quotation Marks

Use quotation marks to set off a speaker's exact words.

Example: "We and our fellow members of the Company's Annual Giving Committee came together to help improve the lives of others," the chairman said.

Use quotation marks to set off a definition.

Example: The expression *minutes* means "the record of events at a meeting."

The Hyphen, the Dash, and Ellipses

A *hyphen* is one click of the button (-), while a *dash* is two clicks of the button (—). Ellipses are three spaced periods (...). Here's how each mark of punctuation is used.

A hyphen is used in certain compound nouns and adjectives.

Examples: half-price   well-known

Hyphenate compound adjectives when they are used together before the noun they modify, as in *the well-known project.* Don't hyphenate compound adjectives if they follow the noun: *The project was well known.*

A hyphen is used in fractions and in compound numbers from twenty-one to ninety-nine.

Examples: one-third   forty-five

A dash is used to show emphasis, such as a sudden change of thought.

Examples: Perfectionists may mean well, but they can drive you crazy—if you give them half a chance.

We all signed the contract—finally.

Use ellipses to show that you have deleted words or sentences from a passage you are quoting. Don't use ellipses to show that words have been omitted from the beginning of a sentence. Just omit the words and keep right on going.

Example: Generally, dividends from net investments are taxable to share-holders as ordinary income. Long-term capital gains distributions, if any, are taxable to shareholders as long-term capital gains ... short-term capital gains and other taxable income distributions are taxed as ordinary income.

Parentheses and Brackets

These are *parentheses:* ( ). These are *brackets:* [ ].

Use parentheses to set off nonessential information. Consider the information in the parentheses as an appositive, because it gives the reader additional information that can be deleted from the sentence.

Example: Net asset value per share is calculated by dividing the value of total fund assets, less all liabilities, by the total number of shares outstanding. (See Figure 1, page 12.)

Use parentheses if you give the full name of a company or document, followed by the abbreviated form or acronym. The parentheses should enclose the acronym when it first appears. You can then refer to the acronym only, without parentheses, throughout the rest of the letter. This lets your reader know the meaning of any acronyms you're using.

Example: Employees Assistance Program (EAP).

Use parentheses to enclose numbers or letters.

Examples: E-mail has many uses: (1) It helps turn middle managers into doers; (2) it flattens an organization's hierarchical structure; and (3) it encourages people to speak up.

The general manager called the meeting for two reasons: (a) to identify the problem; and (b) to determine a feasible resolution to the problem.

Use brackets for editorial clarification. It's highly unlikely that you'll be using brackets in business writing.

The Apostrophe

The apostrophe (') is used in three ways: to show possession (ownership), to show plural forms, and to show contractions (where a letter or number has been omitted).

1. Use an apostrophe to show possession.

    With singular nouns *not* ending in s, add an apostrophe and an s.

Examples:	manager	manager's office
	computer	computer's hard drive

    With singular nouns ending in s, add an apostrophe and an s.

Examples:	Charles	Charles's book
	hostess	hostess's menu

    If the new word is hard to say, leave off the s, as in *Charles' book* and *hostess' menu*. Remember the cardinal rule for using grammar and punctuation in business: Logic and common sense rule.

    With plural nouns ending in s, add an apostrophe after the s.

Examples:	companies	companies' headquarters
	directors	directors' mandates

    With plural nouns *not* ending in s, add an apostrophe and an s.

Examples:	women	women's room

2. Use an apostrophe to show plural forms.

    Use an apostrophe and s to show the plural of a letter.

Example:	Mind your p's and q's.

    Use an apostrophe and s to show the plural of a word referred to as a word.

Example:	There are too many distracting like's and huh's in his speech.

3. Use an apostrophe to show contractions. *Contractions* are two words combined. When you contract words, add an apostrophe in the space where the letters have been taken out, as in *does + not = doesn't.*

    Don't confuse contractions with possessive pronouns. Study this chart:

Contraction	**Possessive Pronoun**
it's (it is)	its
you're (you are)	your

they're (they are)   their
who's (who is)   whose

Use an apostrophe to show numbers have been left out of a date.
Examples: the '70s   '90s

Remember: Using the correct punctuation is more than following the grammar rules. Correct punctuation enables your audience to understand your ideas more clearly. Like traffic signals, punctuation marks keep your ideas flowing in the right direction.

Summary

* ❖ Punctuation helps readers identify clusters of words between and within sentences.

* ❖ *Between* sentences, the most common mark of punctuation is the period; *within* sentences, the most common mark is the comma.

* ❖ Semicolons separate complete sentences; colons show lists.

* ❖ Hyphens separate word parts; dashes separate sentence parts or sentences.

* ❖ Use quotation marks to set off a speaker's exact words or a definition.

* ❖ A hyphen (-) shows a break in words, a dash (—) shows emphasis, and ellipses (…) show a deletion from a direct quotation.

* ❖ Use parentheses (   ) to set off nonessential information and brackets [   ] for editorial clarification.

* ❖ The apostrophe (') shows possession (ownership), plural forms, and contractions (where a letter or number has been omitted).

Chapter 21

Abbreviations, Capitalization, and Numbers

Abbreviations have been found on the most ancient monuments, tombs, and coins. It made a lot of sense to shorten words and phrases in the dawn of time, when people were writing everything by hand. It still makes sense to use abbreviations, even though today's movers and shakers rarely carve their letters into stone tablets. Abbreviations allow writers to save time and space, so they're handy for modern busy professionals.

Our system of capital and lowercase letters also serves a useful purpose: It allows writers to point out specific words within a sentence and to signal the start of a new sentence. In this chapter, you'll learn how to use abbreviations and capital letters in your business documents. In addition, I'll show you how to use numbers in writing.

Abbreviations

An *abbreviation* is an *existing* shortened form of a word or phrase. Note the word *existing*; it means that you can't make up your own abbreviations. If you do, you'll only confuse your readers. Remember that most abbreviations start with a capital letter and end with a period. Here's how to use abbreviations correctly.

Abbreviate Names and Titles

1. Abbreviate social titles.

    Examples: Mr.   Mrs.

                   Ms.   Dr.

    Always match your abbreviation style to the house style, the way abbreviations (as well as capitalization, etc.) are used in the company for which you work.

2. Abbreviate titles of rank. When only the surname is given, the title is usually written out.

    Examples: Col. Hawkeye   Maj. Hot Lips

                   Colonel Pierce   Major Hoolihan

The following chart lists some of the most common titles of rank and their abbreviations.

Note: People work hard to earn titles of rank and often feel very strongly about them. Doing good business means getting the title right; an entire deal may hinge on it.

Title	Abbreviation	Title	Abbreviation
Superintendent	Supt.	Lieutenant	Lt.
Representative	Rep.	Captain	Capt.
Senator	Sen.	Lieutenant Colonel	Lt. Col.
Governor	Gov.	Colonel	Col.
Treasurer	Treas.	Major	Maj.
Secretary	Sec.	General	Gen.
Ambassador	Amb.	Lieutenant General	Lt. Gen.
President	Pres.	Professor	Prof.
Sergeant	Sgt.	Honorable	Hon.

3.   Abbreviate earned degrees.

Examples: J.B. Lung, M.D.   Herman Mudslinger, Ph.D.

Never combine the abbreviations *Mr., Mrs.,* or *Ms.* with an abbreviation for a professional or academic title. For example: Louise Carman, Ph.D., *not* Ms. Louise Carman, Ph.D.

Because of their Latin roots, abbreviations for many degrees can be written in either direction: M.A. or A.M. for Masters of Arts, for instance. The following chart lists some of the most common abbreviations for earned degrees:

Degree	Abbreviation
Bachelor of Science	B.S.
Bachelor of Business Administration	B.B.A.
Masters of Arts	M.A. or A.M.
Masters of Science	M.S. or S.M.
Masters of Business Administration	M.B.A.
Medical Doctor	M.D.
Doctor of Philosophy	Ph.D.
Doctor of Divinity	D.D.
Doctor of Dental Surgery	D.D.S.
Registered Nurse	R.N.

4.   Abbreviate the titles of some organizations and things. Notice that these abbreviations are not followed by a period, whether or not they're acronyms (abbreviations formed from the first letter of each word in the title).

Examples: GM   General Motors

IRS   Internal Revenue Service

Abbreviate Time and Dates

5.   Abbreviate times of day. Traditionally, either capital letters followed by periods or small letters followed by periods are acceptable.

Examples: A.M. or a.m. (before noon; *ante meridian*)

P.M. or p.m. (afternoon; *post meridian*)

6.   Abbreviate some historical periods. In most instances, the abbreviation is placed after the date; in other instances, it comes before it.

Examples: *Ancient times (before the Julian calendar began)*

B.C. (before the birth of Christ)
B.C.E. (before the common era)
These abbreviations always follow the number, as in 233 B.C. (or B.C.E.)

Modern times (since the Julian calendar began)

C.E. (common era)
A.D. (*anno Domini*)
C.E. comes after the number. A.D. may come before or after the number, as in A.D. *14* (or C.E. *14*). If the century is spelled out, A.D. must come after it, as in the *sixth century* A.D.

Abbreviate Geographical Terms

7.   Abbreviate terms that refer to geography.

Examples: The building site is at the intersection of Craft Ave. and Fifth St., near Bengels Blvd.

The following chart lists some of the most common abbreviations for geographical terms. Never use these abbreviations if there is the slightest chance of a misdelivery or misunderstanding. In that case, write out the full place name.

Place	Abbreviation	Place	Abbreviation
Avenue	Ave.	National	Natl.
Building	Bldg.	Peninsula	Pen.
Boulevard	Blvd.	Point	Pt.
County	Co.	Province	Prov.
District	Dist.	Road	Rd.
Drive	Dr.	Route	Rte.
Fort	Ft.	Square	Sq.
Highway	Hwy.	Street	St.
Island	Is.	Territory	Terr.
Mountain	Mt.		

8. Abbreviate states. Use the official U.S. Postal Service zip code abbreviations, not the traditional abbreviations for states (N. Mex. vs. NM for New Mexico, for example). Notice that the zip code abbreviations for states aren't followed by periods.

Examples: NY (New York)   CA (California)

Here's the complete list:

State Abbreviations

Alabama	AL	Louisiana	LA	Ohio	OH
Alaska	AK	Maine	ME	Oklahoma	OK
Arizona	AZ	Maryland	MD	Oregon	OR
Arkansas	AR	Massachusetts	MA	Pennsylvania	PA
California	CA	Michigan	MI	Rhode Island	RI
Colorado	CO	Minnesota	MN	South Carolina	SC
Connecticut	CT	Mississippi	MS	South Dakota	SD
Delaware	DE	Missouri	MO	Tennessee	TN
Florida	FL	Montana	MT	Texas	TX
Georgia	GA	Nebraska	NE	Utah	UT
Hawaii	HI	Nevada	NV	Vermont	VT
Idaho	ID	New Hampshire	NH	Virginia	VA
Illinois	IL	New Jersey	NJ	Washington	WA
Indiana	IN	New Mexico	NM	West Virginia	WV
Iowa	IA	New York	NY	Wisconsin	WI
Kansas	KS	North Carolina	NC	Wyoming	WY
Kentucky	KY	North Dakota	ND		

Abbreviate Measurements

9.   Abbreviate measurements.
Examples: in. (inches)   ft. (feet)

Here are some of the most common abbreviations for measurements. Notice that temperature and metric abbreviations aren't followed by a period.

Item	Abbreviation	Item	Abbreviation
yards	yd.	Celsius	C
miles	mi.	grams	g
teaspoon	tsp.	kilograms	kg
tablespoon	tbs.	millimeters	mm
ounce	oz.	liters	l
pound	lb.	centimeters	cm
pint	pt.	meters	m
quart	qt.	kilometers	km
Fahrenheit	F		

Capitalization

Capital letters provide important visual clues to readers, showing where sentences begin and pointing out proper nouns within sentences. As a result, capital letters help determine meaning. Here are the guidelines for capitalizing correctly.

Capitalize Names and Titles

1.   Capitalize each part of a person's name.
Examples: Hillary Rodham Clinton   Bill Gates
If a last name begins with *Mc, O', or St.,* capitalize the next letter as well: *McMannus, O'Connor, St. Smithens.*

If the name begins with *la, le, Mac, van, von, de,* or *D',* the capitalization varies: *le Blanc* and *Le Blanc* are both correct, for example. Ask the person for clarification.

Capitalize President when you refer to the President of the United States, but don't capitalize if you refer to all the presidents of the U.S. The presidents of corporations don't warrant caps unless you're using president as a title.

2.   Capitalize titles before a person's name.
Examples: Dr. Feelgood   Ms. Clinton
                      President Branco   Mr. Iacocco

3. Capitalize titles used in direct address.
   Example: "Really, Doctor, I have a headache."

4. Capitalize abbreviations that appear after a person's name.
   Examples: Martin Luther King, Jr.
   Michael Carvo, D.O.

5. Capitalize the titles of books, plays, newspapers, and magazines.
   Example: *The Literate Executive*

6. Capitalize the names of specific historical events, eras, and documents.
   Examples: World War II   the Bill of Rights

7. Capitalize the names of languages, nationalities, countries, and races.
   Examples: Languages   Spanish, Japanese
   Nationalities   American, Swiss
   Countries   Russia, England
   Races   Chinese, Greek

8. Capitalize proper nouns and proper adjectives.
   Examples: Shakespeare   Asia
   Shakespearean   Asian

   In a hyphenated proper adjective, capitalize only the adjective.
   Example: French-speaking residents

   Don't capitalize the prefix attached to a proper adjective unless the prefix refers to a nationality.
   Example: all-American

9. Capitalize brand names and trademarks.
   Examples: Dell computers   Rolodex file
   Microsoft Word   Hewlett-Packard
   PepsiCola   Canon

10. Capitalize the names of organizations, institutions, courses, businesses, and famous buildings.
    Examples: United Nations
    Red Cross
    the Republican Party, the Democrats
    General Business 101 (but business class)
    General Motors
    the World Trade Center

11. Capitalize the names of awards.
    Examples: the Nobel Peace Prize   the Pulitzer Prize

12. Capitalize trademarks.
    Examples: HP LaserJet   Coca-Cola

Capitalize Sentences

13. Capitalize the first word of a sentence.
    Example: Study sales data on line to share insights easily.

14. Capitalize a complete sentence after a colon.
    Example: The company officers all had the same reaction: How were they going to deal with the Asian monetary crisis?

15. Capitalize a quotation, if it is a complete sentence.
    Examples: Dr. Schwartz said, "Social ties boost your immune system."
    "Social ties," Dr. Schwartz said, "boost your immune system."
    When you quote a fragment of dialogue, don't capitalize it, as in this example: *The investment counselor told us the stock fund performed "like wildfire."*

Capitalize Geographical Places

16. Capitalize places and sections of the country.
    Examples: America   Europe
    Africa   Lake Michigan
    Venus   the South

17. Capitalize a compass point when it identifies a specific area of the country.
    Example: The new office is in the East.

    Don't capitalize a compass point when it refers to direction.
    Example: The shipment came from the west.

Miscellaneous

18. Capitalize days, months, and holidays.
    Examples: Monday   March
    Fourth of July Thanksgiving

19. Capitalize the first word of the greeting and the complimentary close of a letter.

    Example: Dear Ms. Lopez: Yours very truly,

20. Capitalize each item in an outline.

    Example: I. Starting your own business
                      A. Buying into a franchise
                      B. Doing freelance work
                      C. Selling a product

Numbers

A great deal of the writing you do on the job will involve numbers. Unfortunately, the rules for using numbers in writing vary according to the company and the discipline. Here's the run-down:

1. In scientific and technical writing, most numbers are written in figures. This is especially true for statistics and measurements.

    Examples: The pressure increased by 4 kilometers per square centimeter.

                     Fewer than 1/10 of those polled responded.

2. In nontechnical writing, fractions and the numbers one hundred and below are usually written out.

    Examples: thirty employees

                     three-fourths of the eligible employees

    For numbers over one hundred, write out round numbers if they can be expressed in two words. Otherwise, use figures.

    Examples: five hundred strikers   471 strikers

                     more than fifty thousand   53,201

    If in doubt, use the most logical method.

    Example: The Census Bureau calculates that the U.S. population exceeds 250 million.

3. Use numbers consistently.

    Poor: Last year, eighty-five managers and 74 salespeople were hired.

    Better: Last year, eighty-five managers and seventy-four salespeople were hired.

    Best: Last year, 85 managers and 74 salespeople were hired.

4.   Use figures in dates and addresses and with abbreviations and symbols.

Examples: April 15, 1999

7663 Greene Street, Apt. 34B

74%   53¢ $65.21

5.   Numbers used with *o'clock, past, to, till,* and *until* are generally written out as words.

Examples: at seven o'clock   twenty past one

Summary

❖   Abbreviate social titles, titles of rank, earned degrees, and titles of some organizations and things.

❖   Abbreviate times, dates, some historical periods, geographical terms, states, and measurements.

❖   Capitalize names, titles, and languages; proper nouns and proper adjectives; brand names and trademarks; the names of organizations, institutions, courses, businesses, and famous buildings; awards and trademarks.

❖   Capitalize the first word of a sentence.

❖   Capitalize geographical places, days, months, and holidays; abbreviations for time; the greeting and the complimentary close of a letter; and each item in an outline.

❖   The rules for writing out numbers vary. In scientific and technical writing, most numbers are written in figures. In nontechnical writing, fractions and the numbers one hundred and below are written out.

❖   Always follow the style used in your company or organization, even if it violates these guidelines.

Chapter 22

Spelling Matters

Even though there is little evidence to suggest that spelling aptitude has anything to do with intelligence, people are nonetheless judged on their ability to spell. This is especially true in business, because spelling an important word incorrectly can have serious ramifications, even changing the meaning of a document.

But even misspelling a relatively unimportant word makes a writer look careless and poorly educated. This creates a negative impression among colleagues and clients. Therefore, it's well worth the time spent to learn to spell correctly.

"What about computerized spell checkers?" you ask. A computerized spell checker is a useful tool, but it can't help you distinguish between words with the same pronunciation but different spellings, such as *all together or altogether, stationary or stationery,* and *led or lead.* In addition, you might not always have a computer or even a print dictionary at your disposal.

Learning a few simple spelling rules, contractions, possessives, plurals, and easily confused words can help you create polished and professional business documents—and prevent potentially embarrassing and expensive errors in spelling.

Let's start with the spelling rules that are likely to prove most useful to busy executives, people like *you.*

Spelling Rules

i before *e* except after *c* ...
i before *e* except after *c* or when sounded as *a*, as in neighbor and weigh

Examples:

i before e	*except after c*	*sounded as a*
achieve	conceit	neighbor
believe	ceiling	weigh
siege	receive	freight

relief	conceive	reign
grief	deceit	sleigh
chief	deceive	vein
fierce	perceive	weight
fiend	receipt	beige
piece	receive	eight
shriek		feint
bier		heir
yield		surveillance
relieve		veil
piece		

The common exceptions to this rule are:

codeine	counterfeit	either	Fahrenheit
financier	foreign	glacier	height
leisure	neither	seize	

Here's a hint: In most cases, when the *c* sounds like *sh*, the order of the letters is *ie*, not *ei*. Words that fit this rule include *ancient, efficient, coefficient, conscientious*, and *prescience*.

-ceed/-cede rule
There are only three verbs in English that end in *-ceed: succeed, proceed*, and *exceed*. All the other verbs with that sound end in *-cede*. For example: *secede, recede, intercede, concede, accede, cede*, and *precede*. Only one English verb ends in *-sede: supersede*.

-ful rule
The sound *full* at the end of a word is spelled with only one *l*; for example, *careful, healthful*. When the suffix is *-ful* plus *-ly*, there are two *l*'s; for example, *thankfully*.

-ery or -ary?
Only six common words end with *-ery* as opposed to *-ary: cemetery, confectionery, millinery, monastery, distillery, stationery* (writing paper).

q is followed by u
Quarter, quality, and *equality* all fit the rule, as do many other words.

The rule doesn't fit with abbreviations or foreign words, however. For instance, the abbreviation for *quart* is *qt.* (not *qut.*) The eastern Arabia peninsula on the Persian Gulf is *Qatar*, not *Quatar*.

Contractions

Traditionally, contractions were not used in formal writing such as business reports and business letters. Dress-down days reflect a general trend toward business informality, in writing as well as dress. In keeping with that trend, you'll no doubt be using contractions in some documents you write. Contractions create a more relaxed tone, so they're espccially useful to build goodwill and establish rapport with a client or colleague.

To combine two words, insert an apostrophe in the space where the letter or letters have been omitted.

Word #1		Word #2		Contraction
does	+	not	=	doesn't
can	+	not	=	can't
could	+	not	=	couldn't
has	+	not	=	hasn't
he	+	is	=	he's
he	+	will	=	he'll
I	+	am	=	I'm
I	+	have	=	I've
it	+	is	=	it's
she	+	would	=	she'd
she	+	will	=	she'll
there	+	is	=	there's
they	+	are	=	they're
was	+	not	=	wasn't
we	+	will	=	we'll
were	+	not	=	weren't
who	+	is	=	who's
would	+	not	=	wouldn't
you	+	are	=	you're
you	+	have	=	you've

Will + *not* = *won't* (not *willn't*) is the exception to the rule.

Possessives

Possession shows ownership. Follow these rules to create possessive nouns.

With singular nouns, add an apostrophe and an *s*.

Example: employee   employee's yearly evaluation

With plural nouns ending in *s*, add an apostrophe after the s.

Example: workers   workers' ideas

With plural nouns not ending in *s*, add an apostrophe and an *s*.

Example: women   women's room

Remember that possessive pronouns do not require an apostrophe. The possessive pronouns are *yours, hers, its, ours, theirs,* and *whose.*

Example: The report was hers.

To form the possessive of a business name, joint owner, or compound noun, put an apostrophe and *s* after the last word.

Example: Ben and Jerry's ice cream.

In many languages other than English, the object possessed is named first, followed by the person or thing that possesses it, for example: *This is the office of Spencer.* The way possessives are formed in English often poses problems for nonnative speakers.

Plurals

Singular and plural refer to the number of a noun, how many are being discussed. *Singular* means "one"; *plural* means "more than one."

    Plural nouns name more than one person, place, or thing. There are regular plurals and irregular ones. The regular plurals rarely result in spelling errors, but irregular plurals are brutal. Follow these guidelines to form the plurals of nouns:

Most regular plurals are formed by adding *s* to the end of the word.

Example: office   offices

Add *es* if the noun ends in *s, sh, ch,* or *x.*

Examples: Jones   Joneses

                 inch   inches

                 tax   taxes

If the noun ends in *y* preceded by a *vowel*, add *s*.

Examples: attorney   attorneys

Words that end in *-quy* (*soliloquy, soliloquies*) are the exceptions.

If the noun ends in *o* preceded by a *vowel*, add *s*.

Example: ratio   ratios

If the noun ends in *o* preceded by a *consonant*, the noun can take *es*, *s*, or either *s* or *es*. Study the following chart:

Singular	Plural	
takes *es*	veto	vetoes
	tomato	tomatoes
takes *s*	silo	silo
	alto	altos
	dynamo	dynamos
either	zero	zeros, zeroes
	echo	echoes
es or *s*	tornado	tornados, tornadoes
	cargo	cargos, cargoes
	motto	mottos, mottoes

Most irregular plurals that end in *y* preceded by a *consonant* change the *y* to *i* and add *es*.

Examples: city   cities

            activity   activities

Words that end in *-ey*, *-ay*, or *-oy* don't have *-ies* plurals.

Examples: valley   valleys

            tray   trays

            ploy   ploys

Add *s* to most nouns ending in *f*. However, the *f* endings are so irregular as to be nearly random. If you have any doubts at all, consult a dictionary. In the case of names, just add an s: *Mr. and Ms. Wolf* becomes *the Wolfs.*

Examples:

Singular	Plural
brief	brief
belief	beliefs
chief	chiefs
proof	proofs
belief	beliefs
staff	staffs
sheriff	sheriffs

Exceptions: In some cases, change the *f* or *fe* to *v* and add *es*:

Singular	Plural
self	selves
leaf	leaves
knife	knives
life	lives
thief	thieves

In compound words, make the main word plural.

Example: attorney-at-law   attorneys-at-law

There are two exceptions. First, if there is no noun in the compound word, add an *s* to the end of the word.

Example: takeoff   takeoffs

Second, if the compound word ends in *-ful*, add an *s* to the end of the word.

Example: cupful   cupfuls

Some nouns change their spelling when they become plural.

Examples: woman   women
              man   men

Some nouns have the same form whether they are singular or plural.

Examples: series   species   Portuguese

Some words from other languages form plurals in other ways, often determined by the laws of the language of origin.

Singular	Plural
alumnus	alumni (male)
alumna	alumnae (female)
analysis	analyses
axis	axes
bacterium	bacteria
basis	bases
crisis	crises
criterion	criteria
hypothesis	hypotheses
index	index, indices
memorandum	memorandums, memoranda
parenthesis	parentheses
phenomenon	phenomena
stimulus	stimuli
thesis	theses

Pronunciation

One of the easiest and most effective ways to become a good speller is to pronounce words correctly, getting every letter right. Writers often misspell words because they mispronounce them. You may drop letters, add unnecessary letters, or simply mispronounce a word. Knowing the correct pronunciation for a word can often help you eliminate spelling errors.

Here are twenty-six terms often used in business writing that are frequently misspelled because the speaker drops a letter or syllable.

1. accidentally

   Accidentally has five syllables; drop one and it becomes *accidently*.

2. accompaniment

   The second *a* and the only *i* are the problems with *accompaniment*. To remember the *i*, you might want to use this trick: There's a lot of *animal* in *accompaniment*.

3. acreage

   The *e* presents the spelling problem because it is rarely stressed in speech. That's how people end up with *acrage*.

4. asked

   Asked gets mangled as *ast* or even *axed* and results in such curious spellings as *askd*, *askt*, and *axst*.

5. asterisk

   This word can end up spelled *aterisk*, *askterisk*, or even *acksterisk*.

6. calisthenics

   Stress the first *i* and the *e* to avoid dropping these letters when you exercise your brain to spell *calisthenics*.

7. category

   The misspelled *catagory* results from a small shift in pronunciation. Make sure you say that *e* as an *e* rather than an *a* to avoid this spelling faux pas.

8. cemetery

   Cemetary is the misspelled result when the third *e* is pronounced as an *a*.

9. characteristic

   Again, we have a five-syllable word. Losing one of the syllables results in the misspelling *charactristic* or *charcteristic*.

10. disassemble

    Dissemble results when the *as* gets dropped. *Dissemble* is also a word, but it may not be the one you want.

11. environment

    The second *n* gets dropped, resulting in the misspellings *envirment* or *enviroment*.

12. government

    An extremely common mistake is to skip the *n*, and so misspell the word as *goverment*.

13. incidentally

    Often, the *al* gets lost and so the word is misspelled as *incidently*.

14. laboratory

    Many times, the *o* is omitted, resulting in the misspelling *labratory*.

15. library

    Say that first *r* or you could end up writing *libary* or even *liberry*.

16. plaintiff

    The word is often pronounced *plainiff*, resulting in a lost *t*. To help you remember to include the *t* in *plaintiff*, try this hint: A *plaintiff* starts a *tiff*.

17. quantity

    Like *plaintiff*, the first *t* is often omitted when people mispronounce *quantity* as *quanity*.

18. representative

   This word emerges misspelled as *represenative,* with the loss of a *t.*

19. separate

   When used as an adjective, this word is often mispronounced as *seperate.*

20. temperature

   Reduced to three syllables, we get *temperture.* You can avoid this problem by saying all four syllables and slightly stressing the *a.*

21. valuable

   The second *a* gets lost unless you remember to stress it when you say the word. Say the *a* to avoid spelling *valuable* as *valuble.*

22. Wednesday

   Wensday is the most common misspelling.

23. disastrous

   When said incorrectly, *disastrous* ends up with *disaster* stuck in there: *disasterous.*

24. grievous

   Another common speech slip results in *grieveous* or *grievious.*

25. hindrance

   Hindrance falls prey to the same problem as *disastrous:* add *hinder* to *hindrance* and you get *hinderance.*

26. perseverance

   People often add an extra *r,* resulting in *perserverance.* Saying the word correctly will prevent this error.

Scrambled Letters

Mispronunciation can also result in scrambled letters. The following chart lists ten of the most commonly scrambled words.

Ten Most Commonly Scrambled Words

Word	Scrambling
allegiance	alligeance
analysis	analsyis
analyze	anylaze
anonymous	anyonmous
auxiliary	auxilairy
bureaucrat	buracueracy

entrepreneur	enterpreneur
gauge	guage
irrelevant	irrelavent
mileage	milage

Easily Confused Words

Homonyms are words with the same spelling and pronunciations but different meanings, such as *beam* and *beam*. *Homophones* are words with the same pronunciation but different spellings and meanings, such as *coarse* and *course*. In general, homophones are more commonplace than homonyms.

Distinguishing between these confusing words is crucial because it helps you write exactly what you mean and avoid making embarrassing errors.

Here is a list of the most commonly confused words. Refer to it as you write business documents.

1. *air*: atmosphere
    err: make a mistake
2. *all together*: all at one time
    altogether: completely
3. *a lot*: many
    allot: divide
4. *already*: previously
    all ready: completely prepared
5. *altar*: a platform upon which religious rites are performed
    alter: change
6. *allowed*: given permission
    aloud: out loud, verbally
7. *arc*: part of the circumference of a circle, curved line
    ark: boat
8. *are*: plural verb
    our: belonging to us
9. *ascent*: to move up
    assent: to agree
10. *bare*: not dressed, plain
    bear: carnivorous mammal
    bear (v.): carry, hold

11. *base:* the bottom part of an object, the plate in baseball, morally low
    bass: the lowest male voice, a type of fish, a musical instrument
12. *born:* native, brought forth by birth
    borne: endured (past participle of *to bear*)
13. *brake:* a device for slowing a vehicle
    break: to crack or destroy
14. *breadth:* the measure of the side-to-side dimension of an object
    breath: inhalation and exhalation
15. *beau:* sweetheart
    bow: to bend from the waist, a device used to propel arrows, loops of rib-bon, the forward end of a ship
16. *berth:* a sleeping area in a ship
    birth: being born
17. *board:* a thin piece of wood, a group of directors
    bored: not interested
18. *bread:* baked goods
    bred: to cause to be born (past participle of *to breed*)
19. *buy:* to purchase
    by: near or next to
20. *capital:* the city or town that is the official seat of government, highly important; net worth of a business
    Capitol: the building in Washington, D.C. where the U.S. Congress meets
21. *cede:* yield
    seed: kernel
22. *cite:* document
    sight: vision
    site: location, place
23. *complement:* to complete or add to
    compliment: praise
24. *conscience:* moral sense
    conscious: awake
25. *cheep:* what a bird says
    cheap: not expensive
26. *descent:* go down
    dissent: disagreement, conflict

27. *desert*: arid region
    dessert: sweet
28. *discreet*: tactful
    discrete: distinct, separate
29. *do*: act or make (verb)
    due: caused by (adjective), expected at a certain time or place
30. *draft*: breeze
    draft: sketch
31. *elicit*: draw out
    illicit: unlawful
32. *fare*: the price charged for transporting a passenger
    fair: not biased, moderately large, moderately good
33. *faze*: to stun
    phase: a stage
34. *grate*: irritate, reduce to small pieces
    great: big, wonderful
35. *it's*: contraction of *it is*
    its: possessive pronoun
36. *lay*: to put down
    lie: be flat
37. *lead*: to conduct, bluish-gray metal
    led: past tense of *to lead*
38. *lessen*: to reduce
    lesson: a lecture or other means of instruction
39. *peace*: calm
    piece: section
40. *plain*: not beautiful, obvious
    plane: airplane
41. *presence*: close proximity
    presents: gifts
42. *principal*: main, head of a school
    principle: rule
43. *site*: place
    sight: vision

44. *than*: comparison
    then: at that time
45. *their*: belonging to them
    they're: contraction of *they are*
    there: place

Summary

❖ People are judged on their ability to spell, especially in business.

❖ Learning a few simple spelling rules can help you spell many different words correctly.

❖ To form a contraction, insert an apostrophe in the space where the letter or letters have been omitted.

❖ *Possession* shows ownership. With singular nouns, add an apostrophe (') and an *s*. With plural nouns ending in *s*, add an apostrophe after the *s*. With plural nouns not ending in *s*, add an apostrophe and an *s*.

❖ Most regular plurals are formed by adding *s* to the end of the word. Add *es* if the noun ends in *s*, *sh*, *ch*, or *x*. If the noun ends in *y* preceded by a *vowel*, add *s*. If the noun ends in *o* preceded by a *vowel*, add *s*. If the noun ends in *o* preceded by a *consonant*, the noun can take *es*, *s*, or either *s* or *es*.

❖ One of the easiest and most effective ways to become a good speller is to pronounce words correctly.

❖ Distinguishing between *confusing word pairs* helps you write exactly what you mean and avoid making embarrassing errors.

Chapter 23

Building a Powerful Vocabulary

Want a more effective and powerful vocabulary to help you with all your business dealings? Well, you can memorize lists of words, and there's nothing wrong with that, except it's really *boring*. As a result, even business executives with the best intentions soon decide that they have better things to do than stare at word lists (and they do!).

To unlock the secret to a wide and useful vocabulary, you need to do more than memorize lists of words. Rather, your goal should be to develop a system that will ...

❖ help you remember the vocabulary words you'll learn; and

❖ increase your chances of correctly defining and using many other words that you've yet to encounter.

The following guidelines can help you develop just such a strategy. Whatever your level of skill, you can benefit from the following time-tested vocabulary techniques. They're easy and they work. Here they are:

1. Learn denotation and connotation.
2. Create mnemonics.
3. Learn word parts (prefixes, roots, and suffixes).
4. Pick up on context clues.
5. Learn words from other languages and professional words.
6. Use new words.

To get the greatest benefit from this section, read the suggestions through several times. Then practice them with the vocabulary words provided in this chapter. Finally, use the suggestions to help you learn the new words you hear and read on the job.

Understand a Word's Unstated Meaning: Denotation and Connotation

Every word has a *denotation*, its dictionary meaning. In addition, some words have *connotations*, their emotional overtones. For example, both *house* and *home* have the same denotation, a shelter. The word *home*, however, carries a connotation of warmth and love not present in the word *house*.

Slight differences in connotative meaning are important for precise speech and writing, especially in a business setting. For example, *thrifty* and *cheap* have the same denotation, but being *thrifty* is a virtue, while being *cheap* is a fault.

Create Mnemonics

Mnemonics are memory tricks that help you remember everything from the order of the planets to your grocery list. As a technique to help you learn new vocabulary, mnemonics are especially useful for distinguishing between easily confused words. For example, to remember that *principal* means "main" (as in principal partner), look at the last three letters: the princi**pal** is your **pal**. To remember that *principle* means "rule," remember that both words end in **le**.

Likewise, *stationary* means "standing still" (both words contain an *a*) while *stationery* is for "letters" (both words contain *er*). *Desert* and *dessert* become easier to define when you remember that *dessert* has a double *s*, like *strawberry shortcake*. Create your own mnemonics too.

Learn Prefixes

A surprisingly large number of words can be divided into parts that you can figure out easily. If you can define the parts, then you can often decode the entire word. There are three main word parts to know: *prefixes*, *suffixes*, and *roots*.

* ❖ A *prefix* is a letter or group of letters placed at the beginning of a word to change its meaning.
* ❖ A *suffix* is a letter or group of letters placed at the end of a word to change its meaning.
* ❖ A *root* is the base or stem form of many words.

Learning prefixes, suffixes, and roots can help you understand professional, technical, and academic vocabularies, in which Greek and Latin sources are common. Let's start at the very beginning, with prefixes.

Greek Prefixes

Here are 25 prefixes to get you started. (Some of these prefixes can also function as roots, depending on their placement in the word.)

Prefix	Meaning	Example	Definition
1. a	not, without	atypical	not typical
2. anthro	man	anthropology	study of man
3. anti	against	antipathy	hatred
4. aster astro	star	asteroid	starlike body
5. auto	self	automobile	self-driving
6. biblio	book	bibliophile	book lover
7. bio	life	biography	person's life story
8. chrom	color	polychromatic	many colors
9. chron	time	chronological	time order
10. cosmo	world	cosmopolitan	metropolitan
11. dem	people	epidemic	among the people
12. eu	good	eulogize	speak well of someone
13. gee, geo	earth	geography	writing about earth
14. graph	write	autograph	self-writing
15. hydra	water	hydrophobia	fear of water
16. hyper	over	hypercritical	overly critical
17. hypo	under	hypodermic	under the skin
18. micro	small	microscope	tool for looking at small objects
19. mis	hate	misanthropy	hatred of people
20. mono	one	monotone	one tone
21. pan	all	panacea	cure-all
22. peri	around	perimeter	outer measurement
23. phil	love	philanthropy	love of humanity
24. phob	fear	claustrophobia	fear of confined spaces
25. poly	many	polyphonic	many sounds

Latin Prefixes

Not to be outdone by Greek, Latin has given us some extremely useful prefixes. Here are 20 examples:

Prefix	Meaning	Examples
1. a	to, toward	ascribe
2. act, ag	do, act	action

3.	ad	to, toward	adverb
4.	ante	before	anteroom
5.	bene	good	beneficial
6.	bi	two	bicycle
7.	capt, cept	take	precept
8.	ceed, cess	go	proceeding, process
9.	clud, clus	close	exclude, inclusion
10.	co, com, con, col	with, together	coworker, commotion, conduct, collaborate
11.	contra	against, opposite	contraband
12.	cur	run	current
13.	de	down	demolish
14.	e, ex	out	elongate
15.	inter	between	intercom
16.	infra	under	infrared
17.	mal, male	bad, evil	malodor
18.	ob	toward	obedient
19.	per	through	perambulate
20.	post	after	postpone

You Can Count on It

Here are the Greek and Latin prefixes that indicate the numbers one to ten.

Number	Prefix	Example
1	uni	unicycle
2	bi	bicycle
3	tri	tripod
4	quad	quadrangle
5	penta	pentameter
6	hexa	hexagon
7	hepta	Heptateuch
8	oct	octet
9	nov	novena
10	deca	decalogue

Learn Roots

> After interviewing a particularly short-spoken job candidate, the interviewer described the person to a colleague as rather *monosyllabic*. The colleague replied, "Really? Where is Monosyllabia?"
>
> Thinking that he was just kidding, the interviewer played along and said that it was just south of Elbonia. The colleague replied, "Oh, you mean over by Croatia?"

You've just learned that knowing prefixes can help you decode many unfamiliar words. You'd never get tricked by the word *monosyllabic* because you know that *mono* means "one." In this section, you'll learn word roots. Then you'll realize that *syllable* means "a sound group." *Monosyllabic*, then, must mean "one syllable."

Whenever you come upon an unfamiliar word, first check to see if it has a recognizable root. Even if you can't define a word exactly, recognizing the root will still give you a general idea of the word's meaning. For instance, if you see *geocentric*, you might not know its exact meaning, but knowing the root *center* and the prefix *geo* would help you figure out that *geocentric* has to do with the center of the earth or earth as the center.

Let me introduce you to some common word roots that can help you figure out the meaning of many words that you'll come upon in your business speech and writing.

Root Rules

1. A word can contain more than one root.
   Example: *Matrilineal* contains the roots *matra* and *lineal*.

   Matra means "mother."
   Lineal means "line."
   Matrilineal means "determining descent through the female line."

2. Some roots form whole words by themselves.
   Example: *Pater* means "father."

   Term means "end."

3. Some roots must be combined with other word elements to form words.
   Example: *prim* (first) + *al* = *primal*

4. Prefixes and suffixes are often added to roots to alter the word's meaning.
   Example: *harmonic* means "music"

   philharmonic means "love of music"

5. Some roots can also function as prefixes, depending on their placement in a word.

> *Examples:*   *graphy* means "writing"
>
>   used as a root   *calligraphy*
>
>   used as a prefix   *graphology*

Greek Roots

Here are 15 useful Greek roots:

Root	Meaning	Example	Definition
1. andr	man	androgen	male hormone
2. acr	top	acrophobia	fear of high places
3. arch	first	archbishop	highest bishop
4. gen	race	genetic	pertaining to genes
5. ger, paleo	old	geriatric	relating to old age
6. gno	to know	cognizant	awareness
7. horo	hour	horologe	time piece
8. ichthy	fish	ichthyology	study of fish
9. macro, mega	large	megalomania	delusions of greatness
10. meter	measure	altimeter	device to measure
11. ornith	bird	ornithology	study of birds
12. ped	foot	pedometer	device for measuring steps
13. polit	citizen	cosmopolitan	sophisticated
14. pyr	fire	pyrogenic	producing heat
15. thermo	heat	thermostat	device for regulating heat

Latin Roots

If you think English has borrowed a lot of roots from the Greeks, wait until you see what we've recycled from Latin. Here are 25 good ones:

Root	Meaning	Example	Definition
1. dict	say	dictate	authoritative command
2. duct	lead	ductile	easily molded
3. fact	make	factory	place where things are made
4. fer	carry	transfer	carry to another place
5. fic	make, do	petrifaction	make into stone
6. funct	perform	functional	able to be performed

7. grad	go, step	degrade	go down, corrupt
8. ject	throw	reject	throw aside, discard
9. pel, puls	move	impel	urge
10. scrib	write	scribble	scrawl
11. alt	high	altitude	height above surface
12. ann	year	annual	yearly
13. brev	short	abbreviation	shortened form
14. centr	center	centrist	moderate viewpoint
15. dors	back	dorsal	back fin
16. fin, term	final	terminus	end
17. magni	large	magnify	grow larger
18. med	middle	medial	in the middle
19. mult	many	multiply	increase
20. nihil	nothing	annihilate	kill
21. omni	all	omnipotent	all-powerful
22. pend	weigh	pendant	hanging ornament
23. sed, sess	sit	sedate	quiet
24. ten, tin	hold	tenet	belief held as true
25. vvid, vis	see	provide	get ready before

Learn Suffixes

A *suffix* is a letter or group of letters added to the end of a word or root to change the word's meaning. Suffixes determine a word's part of speech—whether it is used as a noun, verb, adjective, or adverb. Just as knowing a small number of prefixes and roots can help you figure out many unfamiliar words, so knowing a few everyday suffixes can help you add many useful words to your vocabulary.

Here are 12 suffixes that describe a state of being.

Suffix	Example
1. -ance	appearance
2. -ant	deviant
3. -cy	infancy
4. -dom	freedom
5. -ence	independence
6. -ent	corpulent

7. -hood	neighborhood
8. -mony	matrimony
9. -ness	lightness
10. -sis	thesis
11. -tic	gigantic
12. -ty	novelty

Here are nine suffixes that indicate a person who is something, does something, or deals with something.

Suffix	Example
1. -ar	scholar
2. -ard	dullard
3. -ary	revolutionary
4. -er	worker
5. -ian	historian
6. -ier	furrier
7. -ist	psychologist
8. -ite	socialite
9. -or	bettor

Here are ten suffixes that show amount or extent. Study them and the examples to help your vocabulary grow by leaps and bounds!

Suffix	Meaning	Example
1. -aceous	having	curvaceous
2. -ed	characterized by	cultured
3. -lent	inclined to be	prevalent
4. -ose	full of	morose
5. -ous	full of	perilous
6. -ious	having	vicious
7. -less	without	guiltless
8. -ling	minor	yearling
9. -fold	increased by	tenfold
10. -ful	full	healthful

Let's finish up with 15 suffixes that crop up in many of the words and expressions you use on the job.

Suffix	Meaning	Example
1. -erly	to, directly	easterly
2. -escent	beginning	opalescent
3. -eum	place for	museum
4. -ferous	carrying, bearing	odoriferous
5. -ia	condition	anorexia
6. -fy	marked by	magnify
7. -ical	having to do with	musical
8. -id	inclined to be	florid
9. -ive	inclined to be	festive
10. -ism	practice, quality	baptism
11. -itis	inflammation	arthritis
12. -ment	result of	judgment
13. -tude	condition	rectitude
14. -ure	means, quality	rapture
15. -ward	to	sideward

Use Context Clues

You can often get clues to the meaning of an unfamiliar word by the information surrounding the word, its *context*. To figure out the meaning of an unfamiliar word, you make inferences based on what you already know and the details that you are given in the sentence or paragraph. Here's an example:

> Just before midnight on April 14, 1912, one of the most dramatic and famous of all *maritime* disasters occurred, the sinking of the Titanic. The Titanic was the most luxurious ship afloat at the time, with its beautifully decorated staterooms, glittering crystal chandeliers, and elaborate food service.

How can you figure out that *maritime* must mean "related to the sea, nautical"? Use context clues:

What you already know	*+ context clues =*	*definition*
The Titanic was an ocean liner.	"The Titanic was the most luxurious *ship afloat* …"	related to the sea; the sea; nautical

Give it a try with this example to define *gory*:

> A company trying to continue its five-year perfect safety record showed its workers a film aimed at encouraging the use of safety goggles on the job. According to *Industrial Machinery News*, the film's depiction of *gory* industrial accidents was so bloody that 25 workers suffered minor injuries in their rush to leave the screening room. Thirteen others fainted, and one man required seven stitches after he cut his head falling off a chair while watching the film.

What you already know	*+ context details =*	*definition*
Accidents inflict harm.	Twenty-five people suffered injuries as a result of the film's content.	gruesome; bloody

Add context clues to what you learned about word parts to define *forerunner* as it is used in the following passage:

> In 1862, in order to support the Civil War effort, Congress enacted the nation's first income tax law. It was a *forerunner* of our modern income tax in that it was based on the principles of graduated or progressive taxation and of withholding income at the source.

What you already know	*+ context details =*	*definition*
Fore means "before."	The *forerunner* was the "nation's first income tax law."	come before; precede

Learn Terms from Other Languages

Knowing a word's country of origin can often help you figure out what it means and how it is used. This also helps you link related words, so you can figure out the meaning and usage of many other commonplace words that have entered English from other countries. The following three suggestions can help you make these foreign-born words part of your daily vocabulary:

1. Jot down unfamiliar words that you hear or read.

2. Look the word up in the dictionary to find out its origin. Note the foreign language the word comes from.

3. Group related words. For example, put all the words from French together. This will make it easier for you to see how the words are similar.

Here are some useful words that have entered English from other languages.

English Words from French

We've imported a number of words from French. Some are adjectives like *naive*, which means "unsophisticated, simple." Others are nouns like *ingenue*, which means "a frank or artless young woman."

How many of the following ten words from French do you use regularly? How many have you heard or read and wished you understood?

Word	Meaning
1. bon mot	clever saying
2. bourgeois	middle-class
3. charlatan	faker, quack
4. faux pas	social blunder
5. gauche	socially inept
6. genteel	elegant, refined
7. nonchalance	indifference
8. rapport	harmony, accord
9. repartee	witty talk
10. raconteur	expert storyteller

English Words from Spanish

Spanish words have entered English not only from Spain, but also from the many other Spanish-speaking places in the world, including Mexico, Puerto Rico, South America, Guatemala, El Salvador, Cuba, Costa Rica, Nicaragua, and Panama.

Here are 12 English words from Spanish that describe places and people.

Word	Meaning
1. adobe	sun-dried brick
2. arroyo	gulch
3. canyon	valley with steep sides
4. hacienda	landed estate
5. patio	courtyard
6. pueblo	adobe house
7. rancho	hut that shelters travelers
8. sierra	chain of hills or mountains
9. bravado	bluster
10. desperado	bold, reckless criminal

11. hombre   man

12. renegade   deserter

English Words from Italian

Next to Latin and French, the most words that we use frequently have come into English from Italian. Many of our imported Italian words are in art, music, and literature, but other areas have been flavored by Italian as well. Knowing these words can help you with the social aspects of doing business.

Word	Meaning
1. arcade	arched passageway, shops
2. mezzanine	lowest balcony
3. cornice	molding
4. portico	porch
5. rotunda	round building
6. carat	a unit of weight in gemstones
7. mercantile	pertaining to trade
8. contraband	smuggled goods
9. impresario	a person who organizes or manages public entertainment
10. maestro	a famous conductor

English Words from Arabic, Indian, and Iranian

English has also adopted important everyday vocabulary from the Arab states, India, and Iran. Many of these words were introduced to English by traders. Here's a handful:

Word	Meaning
1. nabob	wealthy, powerful person
2. nirvana	heaven, freedom
3. guru	wise leader
4. pundit	expert, authority
5. karma	fate
6. chutney	sweet and sour sauce
7. bandanna	scarf

Created Words

Our language, like the weather, is a popular topic: Everybody's got something to say about it. Like the weather, where there's language, there is also change. A *neologism* is a newly minted word. President Thomas Jefferson created the word *belittle*; writer Lewis Carroll created the word *chortle*. The invented word *sputnik* appeared in the dictionary faster than any other word in history, says David Barnhart, editor of the *Barnhart Dictionary*. In 1957, six hours after the Russian satellite was launched, Barnhart's father stopped the presses to include the word in the newest edition of the dictionary.

Here are ten newly-coined words that may or may not make the cut to commonly accepted usage. Cast your vote early and often. Your use of these words will determine which ones eventually make it into the dictionaries and boardrooms.

1. *freeman* (noun): A unit that measures the amount of plagiarism in a text. The word was coined in 1987 during a successful copyright infringement suit.

2. *mad-dog* (verb): To stare at someone as though to spark a fight. The shift in meaning from a noun (a rabid dog) to a verb originated in Los Angeles.

3. *rug-ranking* (noun): A policy that assigns secretarial status and pay on the basis of the boss's status rather than on secretarial skills required for the job. The earliest known usage of this word occurred in 1990.

4. *urban yoga* (noun): A new form of exercise, also known as power yoga. This coinage is similar to words like *urban guerrilla, urban homesteading, urban renewal,* and *urban sprawl.*

5. *attack fax*: To aggressively fax an opponent.

6. *domo*: A downwardly-mobile professional.

7. *ghost rider*: A person who fakes an injury at the scene of an accident in which he or she wasn't involved, hoping to profit from any lawsuits. *Add-on* and *jump-on* are other new terms for the same scam.

8. *going postal*: Having a messy, violent breakdown. The term comes from several incidents involving former postal service workers.

9. *starter marriage*: A first marriage.

10. *whinner*: A person who whines even when he or she wins.

Learn Professional Words

The professions of computer technology, engineering, and law greatly affect your business life, so knowing words from these professions is essential in today's complex world.

You know that each profession has its own special words, called *jargon*. For example, we call a mistake in a computer program a *bug*. You know that a computer bug is not the same as the insect you swatted yesterday. That's because the computer term *bug,* like many specialized terms, has become part of our every-day vocabulary. Executives like you understand how important it is to know these terms to keep pace with a fast-changing world. Let's start by looking at some important computer terms that have entered everyday vocabulary.

Words from Computer Technology

Hardware is the term for the physical and mechanical components of a computer system—the electronic circuitry, chips, screens, disk drives, keyboards, and printers. *Software* refers to the computer programs. Here are some additional terms you should know:

Word	Meaning
1. disk	flexible mylar plastic wafers used to store information
2. disk drive	the drive that accepts a floppy disk; the hard disk drive
3. DOS	Disk Operating System, a program that gives instructions to the computer itself
4. laptop	a notebook computer
5. memory	term for storage of information
6. menu	collection of commands for performing actions in a program
7. modem	device that enables computers to connect and transfer data over phone lines by converting digital signals into analog signals
8. mouse	pointing device that controls the cursor movement on the screen

Words from Engineering

Here are some engineering terms that educated professionals should know.

Word	Meaning
1. benchmark	a reference point
2. conductor	a substance that transports heat, energy, etc.
3. equilibrium	balance
4. fabrication	to produce specific parts
5. kinetic	motion
6. operational	ready to be used
7. pulse	vibration
8. quality control	standards for maintaining the product's worth
9. transformer	device that transfers electrical energy
10. transitor	device that controls the flow of electrical current.

Words from Law

Here are 20 terms from the legal profession that are often used in business.

Word	Meaning
1. accuse	to charge someone with a crime
2. acquit	to free from blame
3. assault	an attempt or threat to do violence to another person
4. battery	an unlawful attack on another person
5. collusion	a secret agreement for fraudulent purposes, conspiracy
6. commute	reduce a charge or punishment
7. culpability	blame
8. defendant	person being accused or sued
9. embezzlement	misappropriation or theft of money
10. extortion	the wrongful seizure of a person's money or property with consent but by the use of violence or threat
11. hearsay	evidence based on someone else's statements
12. jurisdiction	legal power to hear and decide cases
13. larceny	robbery, theft
14. litigation	lawsuit
15. perjury	uttering false statements while under oath
16. plaintiff	person who brings a lawsuit
17. slander	false and malicious statements
18. subpoena	written order compelling a person to testify in court
19. tort	a civil wrong for which the injured party is entitled to compensation
20. writ	court order that authorizes specific actions; a *writ of habeas corpus,* for example, safeguards individuals from being unlawfully taken into custody

Use Newly Learned Words in Your Conversation and Writing

"Use it or lose it" applies to many fields, but especially to retaining the new words that you've learned. Using a word often in conversation and writing (when it fits, of course!) will help you make it part of your everyday vocabulary.

Summary

- ❖ Consider a word's *connotations* (its emotional overtones) as well as its *denotation* (dictionary meaning) to help you use each word properly.

- ❖ Create *mnemonics*, memory tricks, to help you distinguish between confusing words.

- ❖ Learn word parts (prefixes, suffixes, and roots) to help you decode unfamiliar words.

- ❖ Pick up on context clues (how a word is used in speech or writing) to figure out what a word means.

- ❖ Learn words from other languages and professional words, because they are often used in business.

- ❖ Use the new words you learn in your speech and writing, but only when they fit your audience, purpose, and tone.

Chapter 24

Further Help

Today's technology has given us some wonderful tools to make the business writer's task easier. In addition, some of the traditional, old-fashioned writer's helpers still work quite well in a modern business setting. In this chapter, you'll learn about both the latest technological marvels and the tried-and-true techniques available to people who write on the job. Then you can select the ones that work best for *you*. Let's start with dictionaries, in paper and software forms.

Print Dictionaries

We all know that looking up a word's spelling is a nuisance. So is exercise, but they both work. As you're deciding which dictionary to purchase, know that there are two main kinds of dictionaries: *unabridged* and *abridged*.

❖   An *unabridged* dictionary is complete. The *Oxford English Dictionary* is the standard unabridged dictionary. It contains more than 500,000 entries. Don't rush right out to buy one to stash in your briefcase, however, because the *Oxford English Dictionary* attempts to record the birth, history, and death of every printed word in English from about AD 1000 to the current date of publication. The *OED* now contains about 60 million words in its 20 volumes.

❖   An *abridged* dictionary is shortened, but it is fine for all business writing. In most cases, you'll want an abridged dictionary.

Here are five of the standard abridged dictionaries you may wish to consider. Compare them to see which one best suits your needs.

1.   *Webster's New World Dictionary of the American Language*
2.   *Webster's New Collegiate Dictionary*
3.   *The American Heritage Dictionary*
4.   *The Concise Oxford Dictionary of Current English*
5.   *The Random House College Dictionary*

The term *print* in the heading of this section is misleading, because many print dictionaries aren't really printed versions at all: They're available on floppy disks or CD-ROMs. Many come bundled with preinstalled software packages, so you might already have one installed on your computer. Among the most popular are *Merriam-Webster's Collegiate Dictionary*, *The Random House Dictionary*, and *Webster's Unabridged Dictionary*. These electronic versions are identical to their print relatives, so the choice is yours.

Specialized Dictionaries

If you find that your job requires you to define and use regional and foreign terms, you may wish to consult the following dictionaries:

- ❖ *Dictionary of American Regional English*
- ❖ *Dictionary of Foreign Phrases and Abbreviations*
- ❖ *Dictionary of Foreign Terms*
- ❖ *Harper's Dictionary of Foreign Terms*

Using a Dictionary

You can use a dictionary to check what a word means and how it is used, but dictionaries give you a lot more than a list of words and their meanings. Let's examine the different ways a dictionary can help you improve your writing on the job.

1. *Spelling.* If more than one spelling for a word is shown, the first is the most commonly used, and the others are acceptable. *Candlestick*, for example, has one spelling. *Theatergoer*, in contrast, has two. The first spelling is common in America, the second in England.

   can-dle-stick (kan'dəl stik'), *n.* a holder having a socket or a spike for a candle.
   [ME]
   theatergoer (thé tər go' ər) *n.* a playgoer. Also. *esp. Brit.*
   theatregoer.

   Using this part of the entry helps you suit the spelling to your audience. If you're writing for American clients, for example, you'll use the American spelling of *theatergoer*. If you're writing a document for distribution in Great Britain, Indian, or certain Caribbean islands, however, you might want to consider using the English spelling, *theatregoer*.

2. *Word division.* Dots (or bars, in some dictionaries) separate the syllables in a word. They tell you where to hyphenate a word, if necessary. *Candlewood*, for instance, has three syllables, as the following entry shows:

> **can-dle-wood** (kan'd$_e$l woŏd') *n.* 1. any resinous wood used for torches or as a substitute for candles. 2. any or various trees or shrubs yielding such wood.

3. *Pronunciation.* The symbols in parentheses show pronunciation. If more than one pronunciation is given, the first is the most common but the others are acceptable.

   As you learned in Chapter 22, knowing how to pronounce a word can make it easier for you to spell it correctly when you next use it. Look in the front of the dictionary to find the pronunciation guide. How do you pronounce *celebrate?*

   > **cel-e-brate** (səl' ə brāt')

   The accent mark after the *l* shows that the stressed syllable is *sel.* The symbol ə, called a *schwa*, is pronounced "uh," as in ago. The line over the *a* indicates the long *a* sound, as in ate.

4. *Part of speech.* This section of the entry tells you how to use the word. Knowing a word's part of speech can prevent embarrassing misuses in your documents.

   The word's part of speech is indicated by abbreviations. These are explained in the front of the dictionary. For example, *n.* is often used for *noun*, *v.* for *verb*. Remember that many words can function as more than one part of speech. As the following example shows, *candlewick* can function as a noun or an adjective:

   > **can-dle-wick** (kan'dəl wik') *n.* 1. the wick of a candle. —*adj.* 2. (of a fabric, usually unbleached muslin) having small, short bunch-es of wicking tufted to form a design.

5. *Grammatical forms.* This part of the entry describes variations in grammar for different parts of speech. For example, the entry may describe the principal parts and form variations for a verb, the plural of a noun if it is irregular, or the comparative and superlative forms of adjectives and adverbs. As a result, this section of the entry tells you how to conjugate the word. Here's a sample for the word *candy:*

   > **can-dy** (kan'dē), *n. pl.* -dies, *v.*, -died, -dying. —n. 1. any of a variety of confections made with sugar, syrup, etc. combined with other ingredients. ...

6. *History.* This part of the entry traces the history of the way the word has evolved through other languages over the years to become the word with

its meaning currently in use. The history of the word *candy*, for example, shows that it came from Middle English (ME) and Arabic (Ar) words, derived from Persian (Pers) and close to a similar word from Sanskrit (Skt).

> [ME *sugre candy* candied sugar < Ar *qandi* or sugar = *qand* sugar (< Pers; perh. orig. piece of sugar candy; if so, akin to Skt *khanda* piece)]

Knowing a word's etymology can help you link it to other related words and thus add to your vocabulary.

7. *Definitions.* If a word has more than one meaning, the definitions can be arranged from the oldest to the newest or from the newest to the oldest. The definitions are set off with numbers, as the following entry for *cane* shows.

> cane (kān) *n., v.,* **caned, can-ing.** —*n.* 1. a short staff, often having a curved handle, used as a support for walking; walking stick. 2. a long, hollow, or pithy, jointed woody stem, as that of bamboo, rattan, sugar cane, certain palms, etc. 3. a plant having such a stem. 4. split rattan, used for chair seats, wickerwork, etc. 5. any of several tall, bamboo-like grasses, esp. of the genus *Arundinaria.* 6. the stem of the raspberry or blackberry. 7. See **sugar cane.** 8. any rod used for flogging. 9. to furnish or make with cane, to *cane chairs.* [ME, MF < L *cann(a)* < Gk *kánna*]

You must know the different meanings a word may have so you will know how to use it correctly when you write.

8. *Usage labels.* This part of every dictionary entry is crucial for writers in a business setting because it explains how the word should be used. This can prevent you from selecting a word that is inappropriate to your audience. For example, you might find a word you want to use is considered colloquial or slang, which would make it inappropriate in formal writing.

The following chart describes the usage labels and their meaning:

	Usage Labels	
Label	**Definition**	**Examples**
colloquial	used in informal writing and conversation	*sis* (for *sister*)
slang	not acceptable in standard written English; used in informal conversation.	*phat, rad, groovy, cool*

obsolete	no longer being used	*greaves* (part of armor)
poetic	words found in poetry	*ne'er* (for *never*)
dialect	used in some geographical areas	*spider* (for *frying pan*)

The following entry shows that *candor* is no longer used to mean "kindliness" or "purity":

can-dor (kan' d e r), *n.* 1. the state or quality of being frank, open, and sincere in speech or expression; candidness. 2. freedom from bias; fairness; impartiality; *to consider an issue with candor.* 3. *Obs.* kindliness. 4. *Obs.* purity. Also, *esp. Brit.,* can'dour. [< L: sincerity]

9. *Related words.* Some entries include related words. This can help you select the word that captures your precise meaning. Here's an example:

can-dle-pin (kan' d e l pin') *n.* 1. a bowling pin that is almost cylindrical, used in a game resembling tenpins. 2. candlepins (*construed as sing.*), the game played with these pins.

10. *Synonyms and antonyms.* Some dictionary entries list *synonyms* (words with a similar meaning) and *antonyms* (words with the opposite meaning). The synonyms come first, followed by the antonyms. For example:

knot ... —Syn. 3. band, crew, gang, crowd.

This part of an entry can help you select the exact word you need to convey your precise shade of meaning, helping you to build goodwill by preventing misunderstandings.

Spell-Check Programs

The spelling checkers built into most word processors leave a lot to be desired, but they can be very useful for a quick proofreading check, especially when it comes to certain slips of the fingers. Whereas grammar checkers tend to give at least as much bad advice as good, spell checkers are usually right when they tell you a word is misspelled. However, a spell checker can't tell you if a word is missing or that a specific meaning is called for in a specific situation.

Only names and rare words are likely to be flagged incorrectly, but you can create your own on-line dictionary by adding words to your spell checker. I add all the proper nouns I regularly use, for example.

The problem, though, isn't false positives, but false negatives: Spell checkers often tell you something is right when it isn't. For example, if you type *to* instead of *too*, the spelling checker will let it slip right through, because both are legitimate words. The same occurs with *rest* and *wrest*, and with more word pairs than I have space to include here.

Typos are one thing, but if you have any question about the meaning or usage of a word, use a real dictionary, not a spell checker. Remember that using a computerized spell checker doesn't eliminate the need to proofread everything carefully.

Thesauruses

A built-in computer thesaurus program provides synonyms and antonyms for any word you highlight. These programs are part of any standard word-processing package, such as Microsoft Word. A print thesaurus does the same thing, but you have to use your fingers to turn the pages. I've always been a fan of print thesauruses (or their identical CD-ROM cousins) because they are far more complete than the built-in computer versions, but I'll admit that the computer versions have their advantages. Here are the biggest ones:

❖ First, computer thesaurus programs are easy to use. Press a button and you get a list of synonyms and antonyms. Anything that's easy to use gets my vote.

❖ Second, thesaurus programs are especially useful for distinguishing among homonyms. If you intended to type *whether* but instead key-boarded *weather*, the thesaurus will give you synonyms for *weather* like *atmospheric conditions, climate, meteorology,* and *the elements.* This can help you keep your homonyms straight.

However, there's one big drawback to any thesaurus, whether print, CD-ROM, or software: Unless you know the exact meaning of the synonym you're considering, as well as its part of speech, you run the risk of using the wrong word or making a grammar blunder. For example, a standard thesaurus offers the choices *low, below,* and *subterranean* for the word *deep.* If you're describing your *deep mis-givings* about a project, for example, saying you have *subterranean misgivings* doesn't cut the mustard.

What about grammar aids? Let's explore them now.

Style-Check Programs

Computer style-check programs examine your document against strict interpretations of grammar, usage, mechanics, and punctuation rules. They alert you to any writing that differs from the program's standards. Unfortunately, grammar and style checkers cannot substitute for a real understanding of grammar and mechanics.

Spell checkers often miss typos, but they rarely give advice that's downright wrong. Computerized grammar checkers, on the other hand, often give ineffective or incorrect advice. Because they have no sense of style, they can only apply rules pedantically with no sense of context. If you've got a few hours to kill, keyboard part of a great work of literature into a grammar checker to see what mincemeat the program makes of it.

The critical issue for business writers is that style-check programs don't account for the importance of bending the rules to accommodate your audience, meet the style conventions of your company, and build goodwill. As a result, these programs can do far more harm than good to your writing.

Writers with a handle on grammar and usage still do much better than the grammar programs currently available. If you're a little shaky on grammar, a grammar checker can bail you out now and again. But I find that the programs are usually not worth the effort required to use them. They call out just about everything, and leave most people utterly confused. Study Chapters 16 and 17 instead.

Summary

❖   For most business writing, you'll use an abridged dictionary rather than an unabridged one.

❖   Take advantage of all the great features in each dictionary entry, including spelling, word division, pronunciation, part of speech, grammatical form, etymology, definitions, usage labels, related words, and *synonyms* and *antonyms.*

❖   The spelling checkers and thesaurus programs built into most word processors are useful, but computer style-check programs often give ineffective or incorrect advice.

❖   *Always* proofread your documents, even if you use a spelling or style-check program.

Index